# Riding the Storm Out

*Wall Street's Demise*

*After the Subprime Economic Crisis . . .*

*What Do <u>You</u> As Investors Do Now?*

BY JOHN BOUGEAREL

Riding the Storm Out: Wall Street's Demise and Stock Market Crash, After the Subprime
Crisis...What Can You as an Investor Do Now?
© 2009 John Bougearel. All Rights Reserved.

Cover art by Jennie Heckel • www.webstudiosecrets.com

About the Book Cover:
Whether or not to include Dorothy's house from the Wizard of Oz was controversial.
Artistically, the cover is stronger as a design without the house. But as I told my designer, I
felt strongly the cover should convey a meaning that sets this Wall Street crash apart from the
dotcom bust of 2000 and the crash of 1987.

Author Frank Baum wrote *The Wizard of OZ* in the late 1890's, during a decade-long
Depression. Farmers were losing their homes due to tight money supply being controlled by
private banks producing deflation. By 1894, almost half the farms in Kansas became the
property of banks by foreclosure. Discontent and unrest was particularly acute among Kansas
farmers. Although the Wizard of Oz had scary elements, Dorothy's determined spirit and that
of her friends triumphed in the end and Dorothy's heart's desire ultimately led her back home.
Invoking Dorothy's spirit today seems appropriate for the challenges we now face.

Published By Financial Futures Analysis, Inc, IN

ISBN 978-0-615-23092-4

Library of Congress Control Number: 2008912045

Book design by Darlene Swanson of Van-garde Imagery, Inc. • www.van-garde.com

# CONTENTS

# ILLUSTRATIONS

## Chapter Six

## Chapter Seven

\*\*\* Readers who end up subscribing to: Dismal Scientist, Contrary Investor, Birinyi Associates, Inc , CQG.com, Pimco, GaveKal Research, or Economagic, please let them know that you found them through my book. Many thanks in advance!

# ACKNOWLEDGEMENTS AND FOREWORD

FIRST AND FOREMOST I would like to thank Robert Beardsley, who was one of the market makers in the S&P 500 trading pits at the CME. His career at the CME spanned 20 years, from 1985 to 2005. Robert took me under his wing in 1995 to head up the research department for the S&P 500 trading group he had established several years prior. This research opportunity allowed me the freedom to eclectically pull in and synthesize resources and research from a variety of different disciplines. My collaboration with Robert on a daily basis over these past 13 years has been an invaluable mentoring for me. This book would never have been written without Bob's support through the years.

My ability to even venture into the real-time historical details of this credit crisis would not be possible without *Bloomberg News*. Bloomberg's staff of editors and writers chronicled the unfolding events moment by moment. They are to be applauded for the diligent work they all do. Their financial reporting is outstanding. As a financial analyst myself, I avidly read *Bloomberg News* every day and take copious notes that I sprinkle into my newsletters to clients. I have even jokingly referred to myself as a "Bloomberg News Derivative." Another source I reference almost on a daily basis is Moody's

Economy.com. Economy.com provides brief summaries of the economic reports that are spewed out each day.

In the past few years I have discovered several excellent financial blogs that have been quite helpful for the composition of this book. Most notable among this group of financial sleuths are the five from which I have quoted liberally: Barry Ritholtz from *The Big Picture*, Yves Smith from *Naked Capitalism*, Paul McCulley and Bill Gross from *Pimco*, and Chris Whalen from *Institutional Risk Analyst*. To these people I owe an immense debt of gratitude! Through their publications and insights, they have proved an invaluable guide in areas where I was out of my depth. They saved me countless times from heading in the wrong direction. They are to be commended for their selfless and inexhaustible attention to this crisis. More than that, they have been voices in the wilderness, aggregating their experiences and insight to shine a light on one of the darkest chapters in our economic history. Lastly, I would like to thank my editor, Natalie Damschroder, who surprised me pleasantly several times with her ability to cross-reference and check obscure details that I thought would have been impossible to trail.

This book is intended to be historical, but it is also written almost as if in real time as the drama was unfolding. I began composing the book in April 2008, shortly after the Bear Stearns debacle, and finished in early January 2009, just after the White House and Treasury had figured out how to provide a bridge loan to the automakers. Writing so shortly after the real historical events are being recorded seems a bit like writing in retrograde. I wrote it in retrograde as well. The story begins with the collapse of the financial system and stock market crash in the second half of 2008. Then it loops back around to where it all began the summer of 2007. I close the loop with the GSE crisis in the summer of 2008 in the final chapter.

Writing history so close to real time is like painting on a canvas.

It could go on forever and always remain a "work in progress," never to be finished. Much like the radio legend Paul Harvey, too, who greeted the nation each new morning with his trademark "and now, for the rest of the story." Paul Harvey's stories just roll over one day into the next. But the climactic collapse of the financial system, the stock market and the economy in the latter half of 2008, seemed to be a fitting place to bring to a close this climactic chapter in our financial history and end this book.

I have strived throughout the book to present this epochal chapter of financial and economic crisis in American history in a lively and animated format that is educational, interesting and understandable to everyone. I have also made a point to touch on and underscore the substantive issues we will be facing over the course of the next five to ten years. Finally, I hope this work serves as an excellent resource for other historians and students of American and economic history.

I close with a thought from Max Guyll, who once said, "Eventually, everything we believe in will be revised. What we believe then is necessarily untrue. We can only believe in things that are not the truth... I think." What seems true to us today is that this epochal phase of our financial history has been full of unimaginable events and uncertainties. The twists and turns that read like fiction and stock market gyrations we experienced rival any roller coaster I have ever been on. As revisions take place and codify everything neatly, this period will probably seem like a time filled with absolute certainties. I hope historians do not make that mistake, because nothing could be further from the truth! And so the story as I tell it begins with the almost fantastical and unimaginable Nightmare on Main Street...

# NIGHTMARE ON MAIN STREET

*Things nearly always get better if you give them time. That is
particularly true with collateral and properties and people.*[1]

Jesse H. Jones, before the House
of Representatives Committee on
Appropriations,
December 18, 1939

WHEN HURRICANE KATRINA hit and breached the levees of New
Orleans in August 2005, everyone who lived in New Orleans had their
lives affected materially. Similarly, with U.S. homeownership rates at
nearly 70%, the collapsing housing market affected virtually everyone
who lives in the U.S. And if the housing depression just happened to
miss your neighborhood—and home price deflation did "pass-over"
some communities—lucky for you. Unfortunately, for anyone who
owned a portfolio of stocks, there simply was no place to hide. The
stock market crash in 2008 grabbed everyone by the jugular.

The housing crisis had already produced a severe economic
downturn even before the stock market crashed. The stock market
crash only compounded the problem by several orders of magnitude. This left both the U.S. economy and the global community
exposed to some very hard-landing scenarios. The fact that Fed
officials began acknowledging the possibility of a deep U.S. recession at the end of the first quarter of 2008 (Q1 2008) was wor-

risome enough, as the direction of their forecast revisions tend to be correct. However, the severity and rapidity of the financial and economic collapse in the second half of 2008 took even them by surprise. As 2008 draws to a close, our Fed officials are still revising down their economic forecasts and pointing out the risks that remain to the downside - cheery news to be sure. The question left is when will we bottom and when will we pull out of this? The historical record is not good. Precedents of previous severe economic downturns suggest that while we may find a bottom in 2008-2009, the economic recovery may be quite tepid and scrape along the bottom for years to come—what economists call L-shaped recoveries.

In August 2008, a year after the housing and credit crisis had begun, the brightest minds among central bankers and economists gathered for their annual meeting at the Jackson Hole Symposium. The brightest of the bright minds could shine no light on our dismal plight. A consensus could not be reached that there was any end in sight to the unfolding crisis. In fact, very disappointingly, the Bank of Israel Governor Stanley Fischer observed in his closing speech, that the symposium "did not settle a whole lot... It was clear from what was said that most people don't believe the financial crisis is necessarily over or close to being over." [2]

Two weeks later, the global financial system collapsed like a house of cards.

The housing crisis that had originated in the U.S. spread globally by virtue of linkages throughout the entire global financial system. As underscored by many economists with an eye on global events, the American housing crisis swept downstream to affect other developed countries such as: the U.K., Spain, Germany, Japan, Italy and Australia. Even emerging markets such as China and Central and South America were affected. Officials from the U.K. confirmed the darkening horizons on the global landscape. On August 28, 2008, the Chancellor of the Exchequer Alistair Darling told the *Guardian* that the U.K. is facing "arguably the worst" economic crisis in 60 years, and that "the downturn would be profound and long-lasting." The Treasury of the U.K. added that:

Darling's comments on the economy are entirely consistent with the challenging times the U.K. is currently facing. These are the same difficult economic circumstances that every other country in the world has to deal with. [3]

A non-farm payroll report showed the U.S. economy had shed 533,000 jobs in November 2008, the most since 1974. A total of 1,848,000 jobs had been lost through November 2008 according the Bureau of Labor Statistics. Moody's Chief Economist Mark Zandi commented, "Almost all businesses are in survival mode. Policymakers...are going to have to be very aggressive."[4] Dr. Zandi missed stating the obvious, namely that this crisis is going to be very difficult for millions of Americans. The irony in Dr. Zandi's statement is that our policymakers have been very aggressive to date, particularly at the Federal Reserve. And still, we are well on our way to the worst recession since the Great Depression. Fed policy during this crisis has all the earmarks of pushing on a string. For all their accommodations, by their increases in the money supply and to the adjusted monetary base, the velocity of money has been contracting all throughout 2008. This means banks aren't lending and consumers aren't borrowing. Money is just being parked for now as the risks and heightened tensions in the credit markets remain far too high.

One of the most important lessons learned in the collapse of the global financial system in September 2008 was that the linkages within the financial system were far too tight and consequently jeopardized the whole system. It only took a few missteps from our policymakers to trigger a chain reaction of collapsing financial institutions. When the global financial system is finally reconstituted, it is hoped that regulators will attempt to safeguard against these linkages from ever being so tight again in the future. This can be implemented by re-introducing or setting up several "firewalls" or "Chinese walls" as and where needed.

During the Great Depression, regulators separated banks by the different types of activities they were conducting to reduce risks to depositors and to ensure the safety and soundness of the banking system. They did this under the Glass-Steagall Act of 1933. Thus it was that Chinese walls separated investment banks and commercial banks until it was repealed under the Gramm-Leach-Bliley Act in 1999.

Commercial banks are institutions that take deposits. The repeal of Glass-Steagall in 1999 allowed lending (depository) and investing (security) institutions to merge their activities again. More to the point, the repeal of Glass-Steagall allowed commercial banks like Citigroup to underwrite and invest in mortgage-backed securities and the like. Investing in securities (shaky collateral) is generally considered to be risky; risk that can lead to enormous losses and threaten the deposits and safety and soundness of commercial lenders. After the Glass-Steagall act and up until the time of its repeal in 1999, depository institutions were supposed to be managed to limit risks to their depositors and reduce the potential for bank runs.

Unfortunately for us, policymakers have thus far only responded to the collapse of the financial system by allowing these linkages to tighten even further. They gave their blessings to a slew of mergers and acquisitions within the banking industry, beginning with Bank of America's purchase of Countrywide Financial Corp in January 2008 and JP Morgan's purchase of Bear Stearns in March 2008. The urge to merge investment and commercial banks took precedence over maintaining firewalls that protect against inherent multiple conflicts of interest. At the peak of the financial crisis in September 2008, the safety and soundness of the financial system had entirely blown up. With no ifs, ands or buts by September 2008, investment banks were either compelled to get into a commercial bank or apply to become a commercial bank. Getting into the commercial bank business or becoming a commercial bank became a mandate.

How to unravel future conflicts of interests will be a sticky problem following all this activity to get into a commercial bank or become one. But we can hope. With any luck, when we get to the other side of this financial and economic collapse, our policymakers will reduce and never again permit such tight coupling within the financial system. The systemic risks are far too great, and not as low-risk as they had claimed.

The rupturing of the global financial system in September 2008 caused the epicenter of the crisis to shift into the real economy, where it now resides and will remain for quite some time. For readers who come from Main Street and not Wall Street and are asking themselves how they can best "weather" this financial storm, I can only suggest keeping your wits about you, hunkering down and battening down the hatches. Don those protection-flotation-devices (PFDs) and be prepared to ride out a very rough financial storm. A bunker mentality may prove to be quite handy to have at your disposal.

Bizarrely, in the first half of 2008, as the financial system began crumbling in earnest, we found food and energy prices skyrocketing. In hindsight, we can see that these rising commodity prices were latent fumes from the preceding economic boom. (What we don't know is exactly when those fumes will come back to bite us in the behinds again). In particular, the biggest and most obvious inflation cost to the American consumer was the price of gasoline jumping almost 40% from $3 a gallon in 2007 to more than $4 a gallon in 2008.

All throughout 2008, jobs were lost, and at an escalating rate. Through November 2008, the unemployment rate in the U.S. had already jumped a full 2.2% to 6.7% from its trough at 4.5%. Part of the sharp rise in the unemployment rate is a direct result of the bottom falling out of the finance markets in September 2008. Literally, the world as we knew it changed in mid-September 2008. That was not hyperbole. The change was sudden. The falling dominoes slashed the entire financial landscape within a matter of weeks. Not one financial giant was left untouched. Along with that world view revision, economists began revising their unemployment forecasts upward. Before September 2008, economists expected a recession that would be accompanied by a rise in the unemployment rate that would peak around 7.5% by the end of 2009. Not so anymore: some economists are now expecting the U.S. unemployment rate to ascend into the double digits. This is even after accounting for President-elect Barack Obama's plan to create 2.5 million jobs rebuilding the country's infrastructure. This would be the worst increase in joblessness since the 1981-1982 recession. Consistent with that outlook was the Labor Department report on December 4, 2008, that 4.09 million Americans out of work are receiving government

## Unemployment Rate 1948-2008

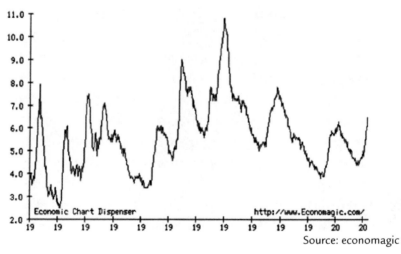

Source: economagic

unemployment checks, the most since December 1982. The horizons we face will be new to us, and we can't expect the signs along the way to be filled with white lace and promises. And yes, we have only just begun...

Another feature that makes this recessionary environment in the U.S. potentially so much worse than any other recession in the past 70 years is the high, rising, and geographically concentrated rate of home foreclosures. While spending some time on the Gulf Coast of Florida this August, I happened to visit Cape Coral, a middle-class, upscale community with an estimated population of 166,000 in 2008. Cape Coral, Florida, could very well be considered the foreclosure capital of the world.

## KICKED TO THE CURB

An insurance agent I met in Florida figured local builders had built a three-year excess supply of new homes during the boom years. Many of the jobs in the community were tied to the housing boom. When the jig was up and the boom ended in 2006, many of the construction workers and others tied to the housing industry who had bought new homes in the area suddenly found themselves out of a job. As foreclosures inevitably rose, home prices fell by as much as 60% by August 2008. Homes under construction were left abandoned by builders. Many of the foreclosed homes that I drove by had their entire insides just tossed into a heap on the curb, as if they had been kicked there.

If we flash back once again to the Great Depression, it was the real estate market that stayed frozen far longer than any other U.S. industry, according to Jesse. H. Jones, chairman of the Reconstruction Finance Corporation. We should be mindful of and sensitive to this concern going forward. Mortgage loan modification efforts are being overwhelmed by the sheer size of the problem. The re-default rates on modifications that reduced mortgage rates and extended terms in the first half of 2008 were over 50%. This is clearly not good. The foreclosure crisis is intensifying as we enter 2009. The loan modifications to date have been largely unsuccessful, and the escalating unemployment rate will only serve to exacerbate the magnitude of the foreclosure crisis.

With the collapse of the boom unfinished buildings blurred the sky line of [Chicago's] suburbs. Weeds sprouted in the streets... Between 1929 and 1934 the bonds of well-known buildings in almost every American city had sold at a fraction of their real value, simply because there was no fair market for them and no funds were available to reorganize the properties.[5]

The amount of household debt that is either delinquent or in default in the U.S. has almost quadrupled since the beginning of this decade. Worse, the debt continues to spiral higher as we enter 2009. "The erosion of household credit is evident...in nearly every corner of the country," notes Moody's Economy.com chief economist, Mark Zandi. As the first half of 2008 came to a close, 2.72 million loans were in default and "could very well hit 3 million" by year end.[6]

Given the accelerating unemployment rate and with the stock market crash and collapse of the economy in 2008, there is a clear and present danger that actual foreclosures will be well above Dr. Zandi's mortgage default forecast. Several million homeowners are threatened with foreclosures. Foreclosures will cause home values to fall significantly further in a classic debt-deflation spiral. "This will further undermine the wealth of all homeowners, resulting in significantly more credit losses for the financial system, and deepen the already severe recession," said Dr. Zandi.[7]

We are still in the eye of this hurricane, as we are only now being hit with the full brunt of homeowner foreclosures and job losses. By some analysts' estimates, we are only one-third of the way to the

## Foreclosure Estimates through 2010

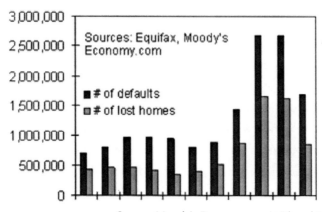

Source: Moody's Economy.com's Dismal Scientist

bottom, while other analysts believe we are roughly halfway to the bottom. There are downside risks to the more rosy forecasts, to be sure. We are only passing through the front side of this hurricane; the backside of the storm is what lies ahead for us.

## DEMORALIZATION AND GREEN PAINTED LAWNS

Another region of the country acutely affected by the housing crisis is Southern California, where escalating foreclosures have become a way of life for many young middle class families. In the second half of 2008, Val Zavala from KCET's *SOCAL Connected* TV reported that 700 homeowners a day were losing their homes. Foreclosures have also created an unusual boom opportunity for some businesses. One such enterprising company, called "You Walk Away," counsels homeowners on how to stay in their homes "payment free" for as long as possible, but also helps prepare them, from a legal stand-point, to leave their homes.

But the sad truth is that families that walk away from their homes are profoundly discouraged. The crews that are hired by the banks to clean out foreclosed homes know a little bit about the sadness of these families. These families must leave behind all their worldly belongings and leave with only the shirts on their backs. The clean up crews' load up the entire contents of the families' lives into a dumpster, which they haul out to the landfill. The family photos, children's toys, little girl dolls, closets full of clothes, computers, big screen TVs, rotting food, and literally their entire lives get tossed into the dumpster.

These families are entirely tapped out financially and are maxed out on credit. Asked why they would leave everything behind, John Plocher, the owner of these haulout crews, says, that these families don't have any money to even get a moving van. They just take what they can throw into their cars and drive away, to where he doesn't even know. Plocher feels that people who finally get to this point are depressed, are not thinking straight, and must be in great despair. This is a disaster on a grand scale. Everything that's left behind is because they want to leave it there. There is no coercion; they're not being forced out of the house immediately. They have plenty of time to take it out, so it's their decision, not the bank's, not the crew's.[8]

After the haulout crews clean out these homes, realty companies hire other companies to go in and paint the browned-out lawns green, to give the foreclosed home instant curb appeal and to make the whole neighborhood look a whole lot nicer.

The mechanism that made it possible for these young, upwardly mobile families to reach for their piece of the American dream only, to be later displaced and demoralized, was the miracle and promise of the subprime and adjustable-rate mortgage (ARM) loan.

> This housing crisis is not a result of millions
> of borrowers going wild, buying beyond
> their means, or where everyone lied to buy a

home. Nor was it caused by gangs of mortgage brokers who cruised the streets with 1003s and pens in hand recruiting straw buyers to steal homes. This crisis was caused by fraud, but not by the consumer or loan officers to any great degree.

The greatest real estate bubble of all time was only able to occur because of the unregulated investment and commercial banks' insatiable thirst for parts for their Frankenstein securities... If not for the unregulated institutions providing unlimited and irresponsible credit and leverage to every household in America, this never would have happened...

As parts ran low when housing stretched or interest rates rose to levels that made the asset class unaffordable every few months, the constant re-engineering of loan programs occurred. Focusing on low monthly payments and the elimination of income and assets as a variable [kept bringing] affordability back. This continually repeated for years until virtually anyone with a heartbeat and a hand needed to sign the loan documents were active participants in the market.

Lenders didn't worry over what would happen to the loan after a few months because the loan was sold and they lose all liability after six months or so. The 2/28 Subprime ARM was a perfect example of a loan program not designed to hold over the initial teaser period.

It was one that the lender didn't care about because most were sold and securitized. Prime 5/1 interest-only ARMs and Pay Option ARMs were also sold the same way... Therefore, who cares about creating loans that will last? Just make loans that will last at least six months... [And] regulators turning a blind eye endorsed their actions.[9]

Subverted, the American dream became a nightmare for these young, upwardly mobile families and the communities they lived in. From the foregoing, you might imagine that I am a bleeding heart liberal—far from it. The point of underscoring these realities happening on the American landscape is that this was all so unnecessary. Had the miracle of subprime never been created and made available

to anyone and everyone, these family hardships would never have had to happen. Local economies would never have had to experience these depressing setbacks. This is anything but a proud moment in our history.

Consider for a moment how tough it will be to gut out the backside of the hurricane and its reverberating aftermath. To a degree, I am less concerned about what has gone before and am far more concerned about the aftermath for the individual families, the local communities, and the broad U.S. economy. Like our financial institutions, the average American on balance carries too much toxic debt on their hands. That consumer debt has to shrink in the coming years. Overconsumption will have to be followed by years of underconsumption. You won't be seeing those big flat screen TVs and such in many middle-class homes. Skittish consumers are not going to be spending lavishly, and that will curtail businesses from investing.

The economy has three engines of growth: the consumer, businesses and the government, with the U.S. consumer being the biggest engine of growth. In recent decades, roughly 70% of economic growth in the U.S., as measured by the GDP (Gross Domestic Product), was consumer driven. It was debt that fueled the consumer spending growth, until the consumer could no longer service that debt. Now we must rely on the government's deficit spending to prop up the ailing economy. This might be reassuring if it weren't for the fact that the government is already up to its eyeballs and drowning in debt that soon become unmanageable. If the economy can't be made whole in a short period of time, then it is quite possible the U.S. government may also be unable to service its own debt growth. These are the challenges that lie before us as Americans.

And what will happen to our capitalist landscape, given the extent of the government intrusion into the markets? In the long run, will our capitalist model be forever supplanted by the socialist model just as the starving Esau's birthright was stolen away from him by his brother Jacob for a bowl of lentils? From this perch, the future we face looks like a disaster-in-waiting. It is ahead of us, not behind us. The fallout from the crisis and from this shift in the capitalist economic model for many Americans may be proportionate to this anonymous person's recounting of his experience in Hurricane Charley's aftermath:

## THOUGHTS FROM THE BACKSIDE OF HURRICANE CHARLEY WE NEVER BELIEVED WOULD COME

It is very difficult to express thoughts and feeling related to the natural disaster that has occurred in our beautiful Charlotte Harbor community. The destruction, severe conditions and emotional scars are incomprehensible. Denial moves quickly to numb reality.

Everywhere we look there are brutal reminders of the force that ravaged our homes, our businesses and environment. Charley's devastation races through our brains creating a constant buzz of tension. It sits heavy on our chests where our hearts are thumping. It rattles through our nervous system to keep us on constant high alert, until we crash each night in exhaustion only to revisit the chaos in our dreams.

I spotted a mangrove crab clinging to a Styrofoam piece of wreckage in the water. It appeared as a double metaphor for all who will hold on tight to whatever remains of normalcy while using post-storm opportunities to rebuild. Just as the plants and wildlife will rebound, so will we. The trembling will subside.

Strength and determination will arise from our
inner being and we will move along, one small,
brave step at a time. We are a naturally caring
community. [10]

Or it may be proportionate to the experience described by Fred
Schwed in the aftermath of the Great Crash of 1929, which evokes
images of Edvard Munch's "The Scream."

Shortly [after the crash] I was forced to be an
unwilling spectator and participant in the Depression. This was far more tragic, and had only
the wretched dramatic values of a drab nightmare. It seemed to the men of importance...as
impossible to cope with as is any other nightmare before the terrified dreamer can wake up. [11]

If the devastation wreaked upon our economy deteriorates into a
depression or even a deep and prolonged recession, it is almost certain to be a nightmarish experience for most everyone living in the
U.S. Some parts of the country are already in a depression, including
Detroit, the home of the Big Three automakers and one of the great
cities from the last century. Anecdotally, a friend of mine who visited
family in Detroit this past Thanksgiving and is never pre-disposed to
bouts of psychological depression, spoke of being depressed while
he was there, the living conditions were so bad. And the chaos in
the financial markets is just as frightening. In fact, market strate-
gists that had hoped the worst of the credit crisis would already be
behind them were not finding this so a year later. In response to the
heightened tensions in the financial markets, Resolution Investment
Management's Stuart Thomson stated in August 2008, that:

It's like an ongoing nightmare and no one is
sure when we're going to wake up. Things are
going to get worse before they get better. The
suspicion is that banks are still hiding losses.
The banking system relies on trust and at the
minute there quite simply isn't any.[12]

## THE U.S. GOVERNMENT'S CHAOTIC RESPONSE TO MAIN STREET IS BOTH DELAYED AND INADEQUATE

We would do well to recall the U.S. government and FEMA were
heavily criticized for their response to the storm both before and
after Hurricane Katrina hit New Orleans. Plans and provisions to
evacuate residents of the city were both delayed and inadequate.
Those who were evacuated to "**shelters of last resort**" such as the
Superdome found themselves without adequate water, food, security or sanitary conditions. Residents of New Orleans who remained
behind found themselves without water, food, shelter, etc. Several
died by thirst, exhaustion and violence in the days that followed.

Fast forward from Hurricane Katrina to the evolving housing crisis and the government response is almost like déjà vu. We find the
U.S. government again being criticized for their inadequate response
to the collapse of the housing market thus far. In one account back
in 2007 a woman took her own life at the prospect of her home being
foreclosed on. In another account, a 62-year-old man tells us his wife
cried herself to sleep every night because their home was going into
foreclosure in February 2008, "and there's nothing I can do," he said.
Anecdotal vignettes like that, which highlight the increasing stresses
borne by marginal homeowners, are popping up everywhere.

## THE BLAME GAME

In March 2008, Joe Mason, a former economist at the Office of the Comptroller of the Currency and current professor at Drexel University had just returned from an overseas trip. Institutional Risk Analyst Chris Whalen had the opportunity to catch up with Joe and grab a brief interview. It went as follows:

> **The IRA**: You just returned from an overseas trip. What are the impressions of the U.S. response to the subprime crisis among your foreign contacts?
>
> **Mason**: I've been meeting with a combination of regulators, legislators, attorneys and investors. Worldwide, people are looking at the situation in the U.S. and are asking "what did you people do?"
>
> **The IRA**: So what do you tell them?
>
> **Mason**: Well, they ask "Did you people really screw up that bad?" And my response is "Yes, we did." [13]

Ad hoc government measures to keep people in the homes that the same government sought so hard to put everyone into are coming up incredibly short. Their response has done almost nothing to stem the tide of roughly 1.5 million home foreclosures estimated in 2008 and roughly another 1.5 million or more home foreclosures anticipated in 2009. The rapid acceleration in home foreclosures led to banks carrying substantial amounts of troubled assets [mortgage loans] on their books. The rise in home foreclosures is largely what is driving down inflated home prices back toward their long-term historical mean. But, as 2008 comes to a close, home prices are still above their long-term historical mean. And as home prices continue reverting to their historical mean, the more problematic those toxic assets [mortgage loans] become that financial firms are carrying on their books. It's a debt-deflation spiral, the likes of which the economist Irving Fisher described so eloquently back in the 1930s.

Bright minds, such as Josh Rosner, Peter Wallison and Jerry O'Driscoll, were in attendance at Institutional Risk Analyst Chris Whalen's GSE (Government Sponsored Entities) roundtable over the weekend of July 19, 2008. They shared their thoughts with us on the deteriorating plight of our government mortgage lenders Fannie Mae and Freddie Mac and what their impending failures could do to the United States. Unfortunately, there was little confidence expressed in our U.S. Secretary Hank Paulson or the Federal Reserve, and they are concerned no one is at the helm of this listing ship. Rosner viewed Paulson's proposals to date for the rescue of the GSEs "as one of laziness and a lack of creativity." Peter Wallison concurred, "Yes, I am very disappointed in Paulson."[14] Rosner worried even more about the Fed, pointing out that:

> The Fed is the safety and soundness regulator
> that has failed us worst in this crisis. In terms
> of the leverage ratio, in terms of the allowance
> of changes in what constitutes bank capital, in
> terms of the Fed's prudential oversight of their
> institutions, I find it very worrisome.[15]

## PERMISSIVENESS AND GREED UNDERMINE THE SAFETY AND SOUNDNESS OF OUR FINANCIAL SYSTEM

My purpose here, however, is not to point the finger at the reckless lending and borrowing, nor the shortcomings and the flaws of the U.S. government, the Federal Reserve and regulators. We take that as a given in this book. As BlackRock CEO Laurence Fink related, "we were far too permissive: we allowed leverage to reach obscene levels. We allowed the securitization of assets [read subprime mortgages and the like] that historically were never allowed to be part of the securitization package. So now we're paying the costs of all those excesses."[16]

Financial engineering of Wall Street alchemists over the past 20 years, combined with lobbying efforts to deregulate the financial markets, conspired to unhinge the safety and soundness of our financial system. "At the end of the day we are here because we have moved from sound fundamentals of doing business to shady get-rich- quick programs. It is very discouraging that we have come to this point through gross mismanagement and greed and the wrong kinds of regulatory rules changes over the last several years,"[17] said Nucor Corps CEO Dan Dimicco.

Folks are justifiably angry at the captains of our ship responsible for sailing us into a Force 10 storm. As Republican House minority leader John Boehner put it, "The American people are furious that we're in this situation, and so am I." [18] We are now all very "unwilling participants" in this housing-related recession, but casting blame won't be a very productive use of our time and energy. Collectively, we are in for a very rough ride, and just getting through the storm should supersede the blame game in the interim.

## BUDGET SHORTFALLS ~ "WE'RE BROKE"

Nationwide, state and local economies will be faced with some very tough budget decisions that will trickle down to and negatively impact their constituents. To cite a few cases in point, the state of New York will be facing a $26 billion deficit over the next three years, according to New York Governor David Paterson, who had to call in his lawmakers for an emergency session in August 2008 to address widening deficits as revenue declines.

Budget deficits in New York City are projected to more than double in fiscal year 2010, to $5.96 billion from $2.3 billion in 2009, says NY city comptroller William Thompson. "We still haven't come to grips with how deep will be the impact on New York City's and the state's economy and budget resulting from this credit crisis,"[19] said the president of the Partnership for New York City, Kathryn Wylde, New York City Mayor, Michael Bloomberg elaborates:

> When the state government says they are going to cut back, they are fundamentally going to shift that expense downstream to us, so it is the mayors or county leaders, in all 60 counties, that are going to have to deal with where the revenue goes, I'm not preaching doom and gloom. I am preaching that it is likely to be difficult and trying, and we have to work together.[20]

I am sure that after Mayor Bloomberg said that, the collapse on Wall Street a few months later had a multiplier effect on the downside risks for the NY city budgets. That means Governor Patterson's and Mayor Bloomberg's outlooks have darkened considerably since. What is beginning to happen in New York State is a micro-economic view of what is taking place in all other states throughout the country, and which will almost inevitably worsen as the economic downturn extends into 2009.

On May 7, 2008, the city of Vallejo, California, declared bankruptcy in a 7-0 vote. On August 21, 2008, Tyrone, Georgia's finance director Mary Sturm told her town council "We're broke." [21]

Jefferson County, Alabama, strapped with $3.2 billion of sewer debt and soaring interest rates, was contemplating filing for bankruptcy on September 1, 2008, if they couldn't work out a solution with their creditors. The short story with Jefferson County is that some JP Morgan bankers helped them finance their sewer projects with some, shall we say, dubious instruments. For all intents, the county has been bankrupted by these loans. The U.S. Justice department is investigating JP Morgan for conspiracy to overcharge and price-fixing, and five JP Morgan bankers are targets of a grand jury investigation. This paints JP Morgan in what is deservedly a bad light, but if the bankruptcy does happen, it would be the largest county bankruptcy ever, far exceeding the $1.6 billion Orange County, California, bankruptcy in 1994. These are just a few of the growing litany of vignettes that highlight the worsening crisis as it evolves. [22] By October 2008, 34 states were already in a recession, the other 16 were at risk of falling into a recession. And pockets of the economy such as Detroit were clearly already in a Depression.

## STATE TAX REVENUES ARE DRYING UP, UNEMPLOYMENT FUNDING AT RISK

According to the Center on Budget and Policy Priorities in August 2008, "at least 29 states face $48 billion in combined budget shortfalls for fiscal 2009. The total U.S. deficit will widen into the trillions of dollars in fiscal 2009 and 2010 because of the shrinking tax receipts and government spending keeps increasing. "The long-run budget picture looks very poor, notes Moody's Economy.com. [23]

And the *NY Times* was reporting by December 14, 2008, many states are having difficulty funding unemployment claims. This would be something of a first, I believe.

Thirty states are at risk of having the funds that pay out unemployment benefits become insolvent over the next few months, according to the National Association of State Workforce Agencies. Funds in two states, Indiana and Michigan, have already dried up, and both states are borrowing from the federal government to make payments to the unemployed....

"You don't expect the loans to happen this early in a jobs slump," said Andrew Stettner, the deputy director of the National Employment Law Project, an advocacy organization for low-wage workers. "You would expect that the states should, even when they are not well prepared, to have savings."[24]

Government spending will be exceeding the real or inflation-adjusted GDP growth rate and this will only worsen when retiring baby boomers begin to increase the Social Security and Medicare outlays. Hence, the timing of this particular U.S. recession/depression couldn't be worse from the standpoint of future expectations on the U.S. budget deficit. Economic stimulus packages designed to spend our way out of this recession, as has been our usual course of action ever since the Great Depression, could be fraught with risks and consequences that we can not claim are unforeseen or unintended.

Total U.S. deficits going forward will be off the scale of the chart shown above. "We already have $3 trillion of debt as far as the U.S. government is concerned, [and] these debt figures across the U.S. economy are rising very sharply," noted Martin Hennecke, senior manager of Tyche on September 11, 2008. For this reason, Hennecke is expecting "a depression in the United States, very possibly also in Europe" before this crisis fully plays out.[25]

Recognizing that state and local municipalities are going to have an extremely difficult time over the next several years, Goldman Sachs, one of the top underwriters for municipal bonds, began advising investors in September 2008 to short municipal credit in 11 states that were either strapped with "current and worsening fiscal outlooks" or with "significant unfunded pensions."[26] Tossing aside Goldman Sachs' conflicts of interest for a minute (selling muni debt to investors and recommending other investors to short the same!), this is yet another indication that the risk of several states falling into a depression and defaulting on their general obligations is rising.

## UNCLE SAM MAY HAVE TO PLAY SANTA CLAUS WITH THE TAXPAYER'S MONEY

As more and more cities, counties and states slip into a recession and find themselves strapped for cash or otherwise bankrupt, the more likely it is that Congress will have to legislate Uncle Sam to bail them out as well. If we flash back once again to the Great Depression, this is exactly what happened 75 years ago. Chairman of the

United States Trade Surplus or Deficit

Source: Moody's Economy.com's Dismal Scientist

Reconstruction Finance Corp (RFC), Jesse H. Jones, illustrated well how dire the situation during the Depression:

> After the breakdown of the banking structure in 1933, numerous municipalities had been unable to borrow further on tax anticipation warrants. In some cases, the balances on such borrowings were frozen in closed banks.
>
> At the start it was not the intent of Congress that the RFC should ever play Santa Claus with the public's money. As unemployment and other maladies of a depressed economy became epidemic...hundreds of cities, towns, and counties sent politicians to Washington to plead for federal relief funds. What they wanted was money they wouldn't have to pay back.
>
> In response to their entreaties, Congress passed the Emergency Relief and Construction Act of 1932... That was the opening wedge for the siphon through which, later on, the New Deal poured billions in grants, gifts, and doles. Between 1933 and 1937 more than $2 billion mostly earmarked for relief was funneled by Congressional direction to other government agencies.
>
> That money was not recoverable.[27]

If Jefferson County, Alabama, Vallejo, California, and Tyrone, Georgia, are any indication of the impending financial risks that lie ahead - and they are - appropriations for federal relief by many state and local municipalities similar to the Great Depression are just around the bend. That ensures a large and growing budget deficit is inevitable for the foreseeable future.

Many communities suddenly finding themselves financially distressed are populated with thousands of distressed homeowners already unable to pay not only their mortgages, but their taxes as well. With the looming prospect of many more local municipalities going broke, paying our civil servants such as teachers, police officers, firefighters, etc., will become an ever-increasing challenge over the course of the next few years.

Channeling our time and energy to keeping the collateral damage down to a minimum seems the most prudent course of action while we ride out the storm. Restitution and reparation, insofar as it is humanly possible, hopefully will follow once the storm has subsided. As Warren Buffett told CNBC's Becky Quick and Joe Kernen, "I understand where they're very mad above what's happened in the past, but this isn't the time to vent your spleen about that. This is the time to do something that gets this country back on the right track." [28]

## HISTORICAL DETERMINISM

Regardless of what the U.S. government or Federal Reserve does and in spite of our "unflinching belief" in these authorities' omnipotence, there is an unavoidable inevitability or historical determinism to the crises that now confront us in the U.S. economy. Once the course was set and we failed to trim sail and alter our course as the impending storm approached, we passed a point of no return. There is nothing of an omnipotent nature our authorities can do for us now. This happened as certain as night follows day. At best, we can now only work with our legislators and government agencies to help them get us through the storm and soften the blow, but the storm and the blow itself still has to be absorbed. The nightmare must still be endured.

I would suggest, here as in any crisis, we do not look only to our elected and appointed officials and expect them to have ready-made answers for all of us. We can not and should not expect them to have a Johnny-on-the-spot disaster recovery plan or easy-to-use blueprint to tidy up this mess we are in. They may be our "lenders of last resort," our legislators and our government agencies, but this is not equivalent to them being anything close to being a safe refuge or "safe harbor" for us.

They, like us, are in unchartered territory and face considerable challenges ahead. They have made mistakes in policy, and they may not even be able to execute or respond all that well to our future challenges. It is very possible we will just have to muddle through the mess that has been created. As prominent institutions began collapsing one day after the next in mid-September 2008, Senator Charles Schumer complained on September 17, 2008, "The series of ad-hoc interventions in the market over the past 10 days were important to avoid a systemic disaster. But we can not continue to act in such an uncoordinated and ad-hoc fashion." [29] *Bloomberg News'* Kathleen Hays likened the interventionist responses to the collapsing financial system as akin to the "whack-a-mole" game. As we look back, we would have to conclude that the ad-hoc, whack-a-mole strategies did not fare so well in avoiding the systemic disasters Schumer had hoped would be possible.

## THE RFC AND NEW DEAL RESPONSE TO THE GREAT DEPRESSION

One of the more successful disaster recovery plans known to us, a facsimile of which seems to be being resurrected for our own predicament, was President Herbert Hoover's creation of the Reconstruction Finance Corporation (RFC) in January 1932. The creation of the RFC, chaired by the estimable Jesse H. Jones, was President Hoover's response to the devastating forces of the Great Depression "that wrenched the well-being of almost every inhabitant of the earth...but it was a year too late," observed Jones.[30]

Had a few billion dollars been "boldly but judiciously lent" by an agency such as the RFC in 1931-1932, Jones believed the entire breakdown of business, agriculture and industry could have been avoided and "saved the fortunes [and] morale and self respect of thousands of Americans who had never before bowed their heads in adversity." Jones was speaking with the benefit of hindsight twenty years later when he wrote that, and with the authority of being Chairman of the RFC, whose incredible and stupendous efforts did succeed in whipping back the forces of Great Depression of the 1930s.

> In the struggle against the depression, the Corporation used $10.5 billion dollars, without a loss to the taxpayers. To the contrary, that money was all returned to the Treasury with approximately $500 million [in net profits after operating expenses]... Looking back, I don't see how we accomplished all the myriad things we did. [31]

Unfortunately, agencies like the RFC tend to never get created in the first place unless precipitated by a crisis spiraling out of control. Even after 9/11 occurred and new never-before-thought-of homeland security measures were implemented, or even when Hurricane Katrina hit four years later, our government response was wholly inadequate. Plans and provisions to evacuate residents of the city of New Orleans proved to be both delayed and inadequate. As a result, many residents suffered a fate much worse than was necessary as a result. And why? The simple answer is that governments can not pre-plan for every unforeseen disaster or for the magnitude of their potential devastation. Time and again, by the time our government safety nets are eventually cast and drawn around a disaster, the collateral damage has already proven to be quite extensive.

## THE FORGOTTEN MAN

If our elected and appointed officials are the captains of the *Andrea Gail* (the name of the boat in the movie *The Perfect Storm*), we are their crew. I know many of us never expected to be in this predicament or that this could or would happen. Nevertheless, this is where we are and we had better recognize that we simply can't rely solely upon our government to bail us out. One of the most important lessons that we can take away from the Great Depression and which Americans learned in the 1940 elections was American citizens can and do make a difference.

"A government might help, when necessary, but a government was secondary, not enough," wrote author of *The Forgotten Man*, Amity Schlaes, in the economy. "What [the Forgotten Man] wanted us to remember was his chance, his right, to take part in our great American adventure," said the 1940 presidential candidate Wendell Wilkie. The forgotten man "was the force who pushed the economy forward," and not the government.[32] Our modern day sense of entitlements must neither diminish nor obscure the fact that we must still push the economy forward, and can not lay it all at the feet of the government. The forgotten man must not forget his role!

The mistake in the 1930s was for the New Deal to put the government and its centralization plans before business, and before its constituents. President Obama will be walking a fine line pushing forward his agendas. Obama told *Ebony* magazine in a December 2008 interview that he will be tapping the millions of e-mail addresses he compiled during his election campaign to mobilize his agendas:

> If I'm trying to move health-care reform through Washington, then the fact that we have 10 million people on an e-mail list who are ready and willing to get activated and to help educate their friends and neighbors and co-workers about the issue, that's incredibly powerful.[33]

Obama also acknowledged the crisis that is building at the state level when he met with state governors on December 2, 2008, six weeks ahead of his inauguration. Obama communicated to the governors that he would not be cramming his own economic agenda onto state legislators as he tries to work on a two-year economic plan to create 2.5 million jobs. Rather, he is asking state legislators for their help drafting a two-year economic plan. This is a positive indication we won't be getting an FDR-crafted cram-down of his New Deal.

> This administration does not intend to delay in getting you the help that we need. I'm not simply asking the nation's governors to help implement our economic plan. I'm going to be interested in you helping to draft and shape that economic plan.[34]

## EXPRESSION OF OPTIMISM

In a crisis, crews work cohesively and interdependently. Like Mayor Bloomberg, I see the American people coming together as they always do in a crisis to face the challenges ahead and work for the benefit of everyone in their local communities. In fact, this is starting to happen throughout the country. I expect our resolve and community spirit will be both visible and indispensable over the course of the next few years. This expression of optimism is not simply altruistic platitudes abstracted from some famous movie like *It's a Wonderful Life*, where do-gooder George Bailey rallies the residents of a local town to raise a few dollars to rescue a small savings and loan.

Actually, the averted run on George Bailey's savings and loan may have been grounded in the real-life story that originated in the troubled banks of Bangor, Maine, back in April 1933. Upon learning that their banks were facing insolvency, the local citizens formed a civic committee and launched a drive to 'save our banks,' holding public meetings and running advertisements in the local newspapers, noted RFC chairman Jesse H. Jones. [35]

Rather than stampeding the bank out of fear to withdraw their deposits, in a very unusual move, no one panicked. Instead, about 5,000 local citizens raised about $3 million and the RFC kicked in another $2 million to save the bank. "What this proved is that if you tell the American people the truth they can stand anything and take it," exclaimed a very satisfied Mr. Jesse H. Jones.[36] Without knowing the merits of the Bangor, Maine, bank, Mr. Jones raises an excellent point: if folks are told what the problem is and given a chance to solve it themselves, they can do so.

One of the more troubling challenges we face today as American citizens is that our policymakers have taken it upon themselves to tackle the crisis in a sideways manner instead of head on. Their operations are aimed at helping zombie banks stow away their declining assets [non-performing loans] for some 10 years or so in the hope that after these loans are done deflating, they will reflate back to their initial values at the time of loan origination. Many of the loans were written at inflated values in 2004-2007, so this will be problematic on the backside and could prove to be quite unrealistic.

That also makes these strategies and initiatives questionable, and therefore counterproductive to moving the economy beyond the morass we find ourselves trapped in! These mistaken goals do nothing to help restore the confidence of Americans. If they truly wished to move the economy toward a recovery, they would be best served if their strategies and initiative were aimed at restoring public confidence, first by injecting capital into good banks that are not in trouble, while at the same time making the bad banks take the hit/loss on those non-performing loans that have gone sour already. This would be the straightforward and proper thing to do, because there are many more sour loans in the pipeline yet to come over the next three to four years! Yes, taking a hit would contribute to the debt-deflation spiral and worsen it in the near term, but this would be partially offset by the good banks extending credit and lending in the real economy.

## HANK PAULSON'S PLAN FOR THE GSES TRIGGERS UNINTENDED CONSEQUENCES

The U.S. Secretary of the Treasury Hank Paulson successfully lobbied legislators in July 2008 to grant the U.S. Treasury full authority to rescue our government mortgage lenders Fannie Mae and Freddie Mac — the two government-sponsored entities or GSEs. And on September 8, 2008, Mr. Paulson used that same authority, through the collaborative effort of the Federal Reserve and the FHFA (a new regulator called the Federal Housing Finance Agency) to take control of Fannie and Freddie and place them into a "Conservatorship."

Under U.S. law, a conservatorship provides the U.S. Treasury and

FHFA with legal and protected guardianship of these agencies. This "nationalization" of the largest financial institutions in the world, for all intents, "officially" wiped out the common and preferred shareholders. Wiping out the shareholders was a serious misstep on Paulson's part. The GSEs and virtually every other large bank with troubled assets on its balance or off-balance sheets had been encouraged by the federal regulators to raise capital in 2007 and 2008. To that end, the GSEs did successfully raise $20 billion through preferred offerings. By wiping out those new preferred shareholders of Fannie and Freddie, all the other banks in dire need of raising capital lost a very important funding source to raise capital. Without an ability to raise additional capital, these other financial firms' risk of insolvency skyrocketed and their illiquidity became imminent.

Former *Financial Times* journalist Anatole Kaletsky was fairly incensed and referred to Paulson's plan as "the biggest expropriation of private property undertaken by a government outside the former communist world [and was astounded that] there was absolutely no protest about the terms imposed by the U.S. Treasury."[37] At first glance, Kaletsky's rhetoric regarding the "expropriation" might seem a bit harsh and overblown when one considers that shareholders of any company are always at risk of being wiped out when the company is no longer a viable business concern. Shareholders are always the first to go when a company runs into trouble, subordinated to the senior creditors of the company.

Strictly in that sense, the existing shareholders of Fannie and Freddie hadn't anything to really gripe about; as their insolvency had already wiped out the capital they provided Fannie and Freddie. Paulson was simply the county coroner pronouncing these shareholders "dead on arrival." However, in so doing, he inadvertently sparked a flight of capital out of most every other financial firm in the country, similar to an old-fashioned bank run. Except this time, the flight of capital was not just one bank, but the entire financial system.

Trying to protect the taxpayer had evoked the evil law of unintended consequences. It triggered an immediate liquidity crisis for almost every major firm on Wall Street. The entire financial system was imploding. It demanded a massive response from our policymakers. And the only solution that our policymakers could think of at the spur of the moment was a massive government bailout package. I believe this is primarily because this is the only response they have become comfortable with over the past several decades. They call this behavioral conditioning, acting in a manner that would be suitable for Pavlov's dog. Perhaps it is high time Pavlov taught his dog a new trick or two!

## DOMINO EFFECT STRIKES THE HEART OF OUR FINANCIAL INSTITUTIONS

Paulson's plan to wipe out the shareholders of our GSEs Fannie Mae and Freddie Mac triggered a huge chain reaction of failures among our most prominent institutions. The crisis at Lehman Brothers was more acute than any other financial firm on the ropes. The word on the street was that JP Morgan gave Lehman an ultimatum to file bankruptcy. JPM told Lehman that if they did not file, then JPM was going to put them out of business by closing down their clearing account.[38] The 158-year-old Lehman Brothers filed bankruptcy on Monday, September 15, 2008.

That same day, Merrill Lynch's CEO, John Thain, seeing that his firm was about to suffer the same fate as Lehman Brothers if he did not act quickly, wedded the Merrill Lynch firm to Bank of America. The shotgun wedding of Merrill and Bank of America came out of left field. And it was a forced marriage to be sure, as Bank of America "had its foot firmly on Merrill's windpipe" noted *Bloomberg News*. Thain later explained to his employees how Bank of America had cut their "trading lines" for several days prior.[39] In short, JPM and BAC had bullied Merrill Lynch and Lehman into taking a long walk off a short pier.

The insurance firm AIG also came under attack that week. But AIG's "tentacles" were deemed by our policymakers to be far too deeply ingrained into the fabric of our financial system to be 'allowed' to fail. They fell into the "too big to fail" category. "A disorderly failure of AIG could add to already significant levels of financial market fragility," read a Fed statement on September 16, 2008.[40]

To resolve the AIG crisis, Paulson and Bernanke had arranged that Tuesday night to place AIG into a "conservatorship" under the Federal Reserve. For an $85 billion bridge loan that they believed would be more than enough to float the company, the Federal Reserve took an 80% ownership interest in the insurance firm AIG. Former Treasury counsel Peter Wallison, commenting on the AIG rescue, said:

> It's extraordinary, I am floored. No one could
> have possibly imagined this a few months ago.
> I can't imagine why the Fed would do this un-
> less they were sure AIG's failure posed systemic
> risk. It does speak to the fears in the market.[41]

Still, even $85 billion to AIG bridge loan only provided momentary relief for the financial markets. The initial outlays proved woefully inadequate less than a month later. In hindsight, many market observers, including your humble author, feel AIG was one of the more undeserving entities of taxpayer monies. And to this day, no one is quite clear on why Lehman was allowed to fail on Monday, and why AIG was rescued on Tuesday, the very next day!

Oh, wait, we have some breaking news. This just in: it looks like it was a bailout not so much for AIG as it was a bailout for AIG's counterparties, namely Goldman Sachs and other dealers in the credit default swaps market. Credit default swaps act like an insurance policy, which offers downside protection in the event that a company files bankruptcy. As an insurance company, AIG sold a lot of these credit default swaps, or so-called insurance policies, but they were never properly funded—until of course the taxpayer against his will backstopped AIG with that initial $85 billion. Dealers like Goldman Sachs bought these swaps to hedge against their counterparty risk exposures. Shining a light on these dark affairs, Institutional Risk Analyst Chris Whalen finds a bit of cronyism at work in the bailout of both AIG and Bear Stearns (back in March 2008, which I address in chapter 7):

> We've got a big problem with Hank Paulson's proposal to bail out the remaining dealers like his former firm Goldman Sachs. Indeed, the rescue of AIG was clearly not a bailout for the shareholders of that firm, but rather for the dealers in credit default swaps who were counterparties of that firm in the credit derivatives market. As one IRA reader said this week.[42]
>
> We think that the bailout of Bear [Stearns] and AIG were horrible errors and that these two names should be in bankruptcy along with Lehman Brothers. The idiocy of the Fed and Treasury rescuing Bear, but then letting Lehman go bankrupt and finally propping up AIG is monumental. At the time [March 2008] we felt bad for Bear, but now that $10 per share

[they received] seems like quite a gift. We think
these and other issues deserve discussion.[43]

Clearly, a capitalist government is not supposed to be in the business of who arbitrarily gets bailed out and who doesn't; the government has clearly been losing sight of its role in this crisis.

Unfortunately, the rescue of AIG still did little to ring-fence the
widening liquidity and solvency crisis of our most prominent financial institutions in September. More financial dominoes remained
under attack, namely the independent investment banks Morgan
Stanley and Goldman Sachs. Fed Chairman Ben Bernanke readily
solved/disposed of their problems with the stroke of a pen at 9:00
pm Sunday September 21, 2008, by approving their applications to
become "commercial banks."

This provided the two firms with the "ability to take out direct
loans from the central bank against a wider pool of collateral."[44]
That is, as commercial banks, they would now be allowed to take in
deposits as collateral. Morgan Stanley and Goldman Sachs were the
last two standing independent investment banks. Just like the story
about the ten little Indians: "and then there were none."

Overall, the dominoes tumbling in our financial system in mid-
September 2008 proved to be far too much strain on the financial
markets and our regulators. This led Senator Charles Schumer, Federal
Reserve Chairman, Ben Bernanke, and U.S. Secretary of the Treasury,
Hank Paulson on Wednesday, September 17, 2008, to propose sweeping market interventions called TARP — or the Troubled Assets Relief
Program. TARP, it was hoped (however woefully by their creators),
would provide a permanent solution to the clogged financial system
and allow banks to return to their primary business of taking deposits,
but more importantly, extending credit and lending. That hope would
later prove to be quite misplaced as TARP fell well short of lawmaker

expectations, and of everyone else's expectations, for that matter.

The "permanent solution" called TARP that these regulators hatched was perhaps first proposed in print by Pimco's Paul McCulley back in July 2008. He argued it was "time to lever up Uncle Sam's balance sheet."[Ä] With that very thought in mind, U.S. Secretary of the Treasury, Hank Paulson and Fed Chairman, Ben Bernanke took it upon themselves to meet with Congress on the evening of Thursday, September 18, 2008. Their goal was to request lawmakers create a new government agency that would buy up to $700 billion of illiquid assets on the balance sheets of all U.S. banks in order "to stabilize the financial markets." The plan Paulson and Bernanke hatched may not have been quite what Paul McCulley was thinking...

Senator Chris Dodd called that Thursday evening meeting "as sobering a meeting as any of us have ever attended in our careers." Bloomberg's Peter Cook noted that whatever was said to Congress by Fed Chairman Ben Bernanke and U.S. Treasury Secretary Hank Paulson that night, it was "alarming enough" that they were willing to accept the most sweeping market interventions proposed since the Great Depression.[46]

To even propose such sweeping measures led investment advisor and economic consultant Gary Shilling to note it "reflects the Treasury and Fed are very scared [and coming] in a little too late."[47] According to Senator Charles Schumer, what Bernanke actually told Congress that Thursday evening was that banks had stopped their usual overnight lending money to each other after Lehman's bankruptcy triggered a money market fund to lose $785 million dollars and "break the buck." The bankruptcy of Lehman Brothers had shattered what little trust was left in the banking system. Our policymakers were going to have to act decisively and in a very big way (so they felt).

"The credit lines in the American financial system, the lifeblood of the economy, are completely frozen. You could have massive failures within days," cried Bernanke.[48]

## HENNY PENNY CRIES, "THE SKY IS FALLING"

The scene in Washington was surreal. Picture, if you will, a facsimile of a Mother Goose tale: Henny Penny rushing to the Capitol crying: "the sky is falling, I must go and tell the king!" Paulson intimated that the "consequences would be far worse" if lawmakers did not heed his warning and rubber-stamp his TARP plan. If something wasn't done immediately, Bernanke added, the crisis would spread beyond the banking systems to "large name-brand companies."[49]

Well, it did take some jaw-boning and arm-twisting on Capitol Hill, but eventually lawmakers did cave in to the fear-mongering cries of Paulson and Bernanke. A few weeks later, legislators enacted a $700 billion bailout plan to save the banks and stabilize the financial system. They called it the Emergency Economic Stabilization Act of 2008 or EESA for short. But the sky had already fallen and the much-feared contagion spreading to large name-brand companies happened anyway.

Those companies were Ford, GM, and Chrysler. And they wound up on Capitol Hill in front of lawmakers a few months after Paulson and Bernanke, on November 19-20, 2008. After watching lawmakers stuff $700 billion into the U.S. Treasury with no strings attached weeks earlier, it was somewhat farcical to watch lawmakers who were no longer panicked read the automakers the riot act for asking for a mere $25 billion.

The problem was the serious missteps lawmakers had made forking over $700 billion in an expedient fashion to the treasury without any oversights. The actual implementation of TARP went extremely poorly. This meant there would be no more cram-down bills legislated. So, they had to be much tougher on the automakers demanding many concessions and, most importantly, a viable business plan. We can't fault the lawmakers for being tougher on the automakers; we just wish they had been as tough on Paulson and

Bernanke asking for $700 billion. The tact of toughness was a necessary one to take, and one that should have been implemented long before legislating away $700 billion of taxpayer dollars to save the banks. However, for the automakers, it became a sad circus affair that dragged out for the better part of two months.

## THE PROBLEM WITH TARP WAS THAT IT HAD TO BE IMPLEMENTED

Once the TARP plan was legislated to stabilize a moribund financial system, it then had to be implemented. In its original form, TARP was supposed to buy illiquid assets from banks in what they called a "reverse auction." The details of the original plan are of little consequence today, because the Treasury Secretary repurposed the TARP funds to recapitalize the banks by buying preferred stocks in the troubled banks. This seemed at the time like a more workable approach than buying up troubled assets at artificially high prices at the taxpayers' expense. However, the TARP funds injected into the comatose banks did not elicit the hoped-for response. Rather than snapping out of the coma, the zombies remained comatose.

In effect, the initial TARP outlays will ultimately prove to be a very costly burden to American taxpayers, as it effectually did nothing to unclog the clogged financial system. At least Drano when applied to a clog actually works on the clogged plumbing, but these Drano-dollars tossed into the TARP plan went to work anywhere but on the clog itself! The end result was worse than doing nothing to unclog the system. *Quelle surprise!* This was much to the chagrin of lawmakers who subordinated themselves to Paulson and Bernanke's fear-mongering and were eager to avoid the systemic economic collapse fretted about so greatly.

A minority of congressional leaders and market observers, however, held to the view that the market interventions by Federal Reserve Chairman Ben Bernanke and U.S. Treasury Secretary Hank Paulson would only worsen the crisis. Without question, the Paulson Plan supported by Ben Bernanke had significant flaws as originally structured and later revised. Opponents were vehement in their criticisms of the whole plan, and their criticisms proved to be spot on. In an interview with Bloomberg's Peter Cook on September 19, 2008, Senator Jim Bunning commented:

> The way we are going right now, Peter, is that we are going deeper into a recession if we follow the policies of Ben Bernanke and Henry Paulson.[50]

Overall, the sweeping measures of the U.S. Treasury and the Federal Reserve to backstop the entire clogged financial system, by cramming capital onto the balance sheets of our "zombie" financial institutions to prevent their insolvencies can hardly be said to commendable. Yes, they propped up the zombie banks that slipped into a coma after the collapse of the financial system in September. With our tax dollars, they are now on life support. Thanks be to us!

Maybe with time, they will one day awaken from their coma and maybe they won't. And worse, there is no foreseeable timeline for such an uncertain eventuality. Can we take comfort knowing that the Treasury has their back? Yes, cold comfort we can. But at the same time we also know that these zombie institutions are in no condition to fulfill even their most basic roles as financial intermediaries to the broader economy. No one is proud of the results, so it behooves us all to find other solutions and forge ahead without them.

In short, these ad-hoc prop-up measures, including the "permanent solution" called TARP, in 2008 have failed to provide credit into the real economy where it is most needed and failed to inject capital into solvent financial firms who had the capacity to extend credit into the real economy. These measures also failed to liquidate the toxic assets sitting on the balance sheets of our financial institutions. Broadly speaking, these measures have done next to nothing to cleanse the financial system of its toxins—up to this point. As Institutional Risk Analyst Chris Whalen pointed out as 2008 drew to a close:

> Strong banks and companies can support a strong economy, but zombie banks with balance sheets polluted by OTC derivatives, subprime debt and other toxic waste are a drag on the taxpayer and the economy. The prime solution of driving the bad banks out of the system means a quicker recovery from the spreading economic malaise.[51]
>
> Egregious and unnecessary systemic risks were placed upon the U.S. economy and the American public by our financial system. However welcome these new sweeping market interventions of Bernanke and Paulson may be greeted by some Wall Streeters and some members of Capitol Hill, there are many other folks inside Senator Jim Bunning's camp who found the Paulson plan for a so-called permanent solution to the troubled toxic assets quite distasteful. As Graham Fisher's Josh Rosner quipped on September 15, 2008:
>
> Today, in Washington, there are active discussions about the "need" for the government to buy up the distressed mortgage-backed securities and CDO assets that a year ago everyone knew were being hidden, overvalued and mis-

> marked by financial companies. Let us be clear,
> it is not citizen groups, private investors, equity
> investors or institutional investors broadly who
> are calling for this government purchase fund
> [of toxic assets]. It is almost exclusively being
> lobbied for by precisely those institutions that
> believed they were "smarter than the rest of
> us," institutions who need to get those assets
> off their balance sheet at an inflated value lest
> they be at risk of large losses or worse.[52]

Critics also will argue correctly that to rescue the banks privatizes the profits and socializes the losses. Still, that is merely a descriptive and academic gesture, since the crisis has moved far beyond that point. For better or worse, in the end, the majority of our congressional leaders on Capitol Hill believed Paulson and Bernanke's efforts to "save the banks" were necessary steps in the right direction. Even as the results of their efforts fail—at least to themselves, they can take cold comfort knowing they were doing something as opposed to doing nothing.

The minority of lawmakers worried, rightly so, that these policies would undermine our capitalist society. These legislators are to be much commended, in particular Senators Richard Shelby and Jim Bunning. "Where do we stop, where do we draw the line? I don't know what road [the Fed] is going down. If they don't watch what they are doing, they are going down a path of no return," said Senator Shelby in an interview on Friday, September 19, 2008.[53]

> I am concerned that Treasury's proposal is nei-
> ther workable nor comprehensive, despite its
> enormous price tag. In my judgment, it would
> be foolish to waste massive sums of taxpayer
> funds testing an idea that has been hastily

crafted, and may actually cause the government to revert to an inadequate strategy of ad
hoc bailouts.[54]

Looking back, these measures certainly have the appearance of being ad hoc bailouts, and the same lawmakers that lobbied so hard to legislate the U.S. Treasury's Plan later cried foul when the funds were re-purposed from what lawmakers legislated and intended. Oh well, say I! Senator Shelby was spot-on that the Treasury proposal was hastily crafted and not workable. Regarding our policymakers' ongoing efforts to prop up our zombie financial institutions, Eric Hovde, CEO of Hovde Capital Advisors, had this to say in December 2008:

> I think that the Fed and Treasury have to aban-
> don this mistaken belief that they are going to
> resurrect the Street and its role in the credit
> creation machine. And they have poured so
> much of the Fed's balance sheet and so much
> of the Treasury's money down this hole called
> AIG to prop up the Goldman Sachs, Morgan
> Stanley's and Citigroup's of the world. I think
> we would be much better off focusing federal
> monies on the regional and smaller institu-
> tions, build them up with new capital, because
> these banks have actual credit underwriting
> skills in their organization. They have less risk
> assets and more capital to begin with.[55]

The question that looms large first and foremost in my mind as we enter the next stage of the crisis is both the trajection and the tardiness of the responses. The responses began in ad-hoc fashion, attempting to put out one fire at a time. Then when the one fateful misstep came along in September, our policymakers, taken by surprise, were not prepared. The permanent solution they sought did not pan out. For 2008, the permanent solution was the wrong solution and headed us in the wrong direction. A new administration will be on board in 2009, and hopefully, they will try a new tack beyond pumping more money into all-but-dead banks.

In 1932 Jesse H. Jones felt the RFC agency, which moved quickly to inject capital into good banks, the ones that were solvent and capable of providing new leverage and liquidity into the real economy, had come a year too late to the aid of the Great Depression. But President Hoover, who had the smarts enough to create the successful RFC, knew that if the financial system had never been allowed to exceed its role to the real economy, agencies like the RFC would never have been needed in the first place. As President Hoover wrote in his memoirs, *The Great Depression*:

> If we had possessed adequate banking laws and a sound financial system, we should never have needed the Reconstruction Finance Corporation, the Home Loan Banks, and the half dozen other government props to credit, which we were compelled to introduce later on.[56]

Looking back upon our own crisis, both Hoover and Jones were right. The response of our regulators and government agencies is a bit late in coming and with little to show for their efforts. Our policymakers have been putting out fires anywhere and everywhere for 16 months now, to no avail. It leads me to believe that the systemic risks of our tightly coupled, highly over-levered financial system have been too overwhelming. The processes of a boom-bust cycle inevitably lead one day to a Great Unwinding. Like the great rivers in springtime after the snowmelt, they just destroy whatever gets in their way within their floodplains. If you try to stop it, the river just crushes you like a bug. Had we not shredded sound banking laws and regulations over the past 30 years, however, the magnitude of the bust cycle we are now enduring could have been largely mitigated.

For many of the victims of the housing crisis and the record wave of foreclosures that this crisis has already caused, the deepening recession for the American people, there can be little solace taken in the measures implemented by the Federal Reserve, the U.S. Treasury, and the U.S. Government. One of the biggest shortcomings of all was our regulators lack of foresight, and for failing to recognize the scope and severity of this crisis once it got underway. Certainly, the interventionist measures have failed to adequately reach out to the millions of Americans who either have lost their homes, their jobs or both.

## HOUSING CRISIS LEADS TO CRASH IN STOCK MARKET AND MAIN STREET PORTFOLIOS

Eight-five-year-old Joseph Granville, born in 1923, lived through the Great Depression years. Granville grew up to be a financial newsletter writer and has been writing a daily stock market newsletter for 51 years, since 1957. On Monday, October 6, 2008, Joe said "This is the worst financial experience in world history."[57] Just four days later, by Friday, October 10, 2008, the SP 500 had fallen another 21%.

By the time the SP 500 had bottomed on November 21, 2008, the overall decline from peak to trough was 53%, worse than any stock market crash in the U.S. since 1929. The effect on the mass psyche was devastating and led the Oracle of Omaha, Warren Buffett, to say "this is an economic Pearl Harbor...I don't think I've ever seen people as fearful economically as they are now." [58] There was no place for an investor to "hide out" anywhere in any stock index market in the world. A few defensive stock sectors such as consumer staples may have lost only 30% from their peak valuations, but the point is—you still lost substantially.

Obviously, the housing crisis has already seeped into and proved quite damaging to both Main Street portfolios and home values. Their home values and portfolios will continue to be adversely impacted by these gale force headwinds for awhile longer. The question at large is how can Mom and Pop protect their portfolios against these once-in-a-lifetime headwinds? How can they hedge their bond and equity portfolio risk exposures against a potentially deep and prolonged recession that will almost assuredly be followed by a bout of escalating inflation?

Generally speaking, portfolio risks will abound to the downside for the foreseeable future as long as the debt-delevering process continues. Foreclosures and unemployment are rising and home prices are declining. A recessionary and deflationary economy can make for a dangerous environment for a bond and equity portfolio. Here I can only urge you to seek out an experienced, very trustworthy financial advisor who really understands the abnormal risks we face in today's abnormal markets and economy.

There are no easy answers and we still face many perils and challenges ahead. It is high time to sit down and discuss with an experienced advisor who can help you construct a diversified portfolio of non-correlated assets to hedge against the future foreseen and unforeseen risks. Another extremely important discussion to have with your advisor a plan that has mechanisms in place (using simple tools like the P/E model I discuss in the final chapter) to strategically rebalance your portfolio to reduce risk exposure and volatility. A suitable advisor will incorporate these asset allocation and risk management elements into the products he or she offers.

Realistically, investment expectations must be in line with economic realities. Until manufacturing picks up and businesses begin hiring aggressively again, our economy will almost certainly continue to "list," keeping our stock market limping along. Because the non-farm payroll reports are a lagging indicator, only when the Bureau of Labor Statistics announces that businesses have begun to add north of 300,000 jobs to payrolls will it be fairly safe to say we are out of the woods and the coast is clear. Strong job creation hopefully accompanied by some wage growth will signal the wind is at our backs again. But the timeline for a sustainable economic recovery is largely unknown, other than to say it will certainly not happen in 2009. And wage growth fantasies may be just wistful thinking. We live in a new era where global trends are now the great leveler of wages. The $30/hr to $50/hr employee in the U.S. must compete with the $15/hour laborer in India or $5/day laborer in China. These global wage imbalances will take a few generations to work-out.

The best we can hope for is that the housing foreclosure crisis and recession abates sometime in 2009. Ideally, job growth will be spurred sometime thereafter. Because I am a financial newsletter writer, and many readers may be interested in how I saw and related to my clients the growing market risks in real-time during 2007-2008, please check out the link to *Letters From The Crash* at www.financialfuturesanalysis.com.

Risks in the equity markets on balance appear to be to the downside for the next few years, but yes, some recovery is possible in the first half of 2009, and it may be fairly substantial. It might be prudent to reduce risk exposures if you felt your risk tolerances were exceeded in the crash, after some meaningful recovery. Be careful not to entertain any false hopes or delusions. Be realistic, do your homework, and make adjustments accordingly. Some stocks may be priced above their fair valuations for a short time, but in a recession we can not expect rich valuations to be sustained for long.

## THE FUTURE AIN'T WHAT IT USED TO BE — YOGI BERRA

Economically, it seems the U.S. economy today has much in common with Great Britain in the 1930s. Back in the 1920s, the U.S. was the net exporter to the world, a producer of everything. We exported the production part of the business cycle to China. The scary thought is we don't produce enough of anything now to get out of the mountain of total U.S. debt to GDP, which needs to shrink to become manageable. In 1929, for a reference point, the total debt to GDP was 270%; today it stands at 350%. Smoot-Hawley tariffs worsened the economic crisis in the 1930s by impeding U.S. export business until the Bretton Woods agreement in 1944 and the GATT in 1947. And the thought that we have to shrink our auto industry is not very comforting. America needs to become more productive to get out of this mess, not less so!

Gearing up for WWII was what it took to get the unemployment (UE) rate out of double digits for both Great Britain and the U.S. This did not happen until 1937 for GB and 1941 for the U.S. Short of a world war, I expect UE rates in the U.S. to be generally high over the next decade. Yes, Obama will fast-track about 2.5million jobs in the next two years, but we have already lost 1.9 million jobs. And FDR created job programs up the ying-yang in the 1930s, and still unemployment could not be abated. At best, Obama will partially offset the jobs being lost today. Still, our debt is not manageable.

And policymakers' only solutions to date have not been to shrink the humungous debt/credit but to expand it even more towards the wrong financial intermediaries. That is problematic when the ailing banks don't want to lend, ailing consumers don't want to borrow, and ailing businesses don't want to invest. What will make such an environment disappear? Fiscal stimulus and accommodative monetary policies will only go so far. To a great degree, the consumer is but a sponge, and can only soak up so much credit and debt. And right now, the consumer is waterlogged with debt, and must be wrung out to dry.

We now face the specter of almost one in ten workers being displaced from their jobs during this recession, so there won't be much opportunity for many Americans to even begin to dig their way out of debt until after the recession phase. Until that consumer debt is wrung out, businesses will be reluctant to invest aggressively, as our economy is far too reliant on the consumer (accounting for 70% of GDP) that is now in a serious retrenchment mode. In the long run, consumers will be paying down debts more and consuming less. Businesses will be reticent to invest until the overall consumer debt has shrunk to manageable levels. None of this is even possible until after the slack in labor resources has been reabsorbed by the market place. But all that is on the other side of the valley! We are still de-

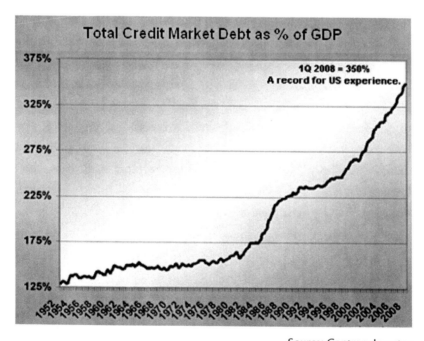

Source: Contrary Investor

scending into the valley, so we are talking about years here, possibly half a decade. Consider this: it took almost four years for the slack in labor resources to be absorbed earlier in this decade. And we are only accelerating the UE rate at the moment.

I am attempting to write about the messy details of this financial crisis as it has been subjectively experienced and expressed by the high-profile major players while the events have been unfolding—not afterwards. In other words, beyond the factual chronicling of events, this is also a retelling of an epochal moment in our financial history as it is actually taking place. By this means I hope to capture to some small degree the emotional and cognitive responses of some of the biggest players in the game as the proverbial s### hit the fan.

For example, events like the sudden demise of Bear Stearns imploding virtually overnight in March 2008 without much, if you can believe it, advance warning. This has been happening almost on a daily basis in 2007-2008. How are the major market participants reacting to unforeseen rapid-fire Uh-Oh crises such as that? As the financial turmoil unfolds, new crises seem to arrive on the shores of the U.S. economy almost on a daily basis. If these crises are predictable and imaginable at all, they tend to be so only in the way that these events are predictably unpredictable and unimaginable. The Nobel Laureate Kenneth Arrow once said, "Vast ills have followed a belief in certainty."[61] When the future ain't what it used to be, then it might be fair to say we are experiencing a "Minsky Moment in Time"—which is the subject of the next chapter.

# Experiencing a Minsky
# Moment in Time

The late Hyman Minsky was a monetary theorist who believed all financial systems are "unstable, fragile and prone to crisis." According to Minsky, events that precipitate a financial crisis start with some exogenous shock or "displacement" that triggers the end of a boom and beginning of a bust.

Minsky's summation of our financial systems is not unlike the descriptions of why catastrophes happen, laid out by the emerging science of nonequilibrium physics, or what is called historical physics. The science of non-equilibrium physics is the "science in which history matters"—where the history of all things matter. Non-equilibrium physics or the science in which history matters introduces elements of historical determinism. To briefly summate the overlap of historical physics with Minsky's model of economic history: historical physics posits that "fingers of instability" build up within all closed (historical) systems, ultimately leading up to a "self-organized criticality or "critical state." Once a system reaches a critical state, it only takes one spark, or one seemingly insignificant event to trigger a catastrophic event, such as the Yellowstone fire of 1988. Mark Buchanan illustrates historically catastrophic events like the Yellowstone fire in 1988 in his book *Ubiquity*, published in 2000.

Similar to Minsky's paradigm of our financial system being in-

herently unstable and prone to crisis, Buchanan's paradigm of historical physics asserts that "our world is at all times tuned to be on
the edge of sudden radical change."[1]

## ZERO TOLERANCE, SAFETY NETS AND THE YELLOWSTONE EFFECT

When a forest fire starts, no one knows how big it will become or
how far it will spread. This is largely a matter of chance, but it seems
undeniable that the U.S. Bureau of Land Management's policies had
a role in helping the Yellowstone fire of 1988 reach catastrophic pro-
portions. The U.S. Forest Service spent the previous 100 years suppressing natural wildfires. In spite of their zero tolerance, wildfires in
recent years, such as those seen in California in 2007, have become
more numerous, severe and difficult to control. What happened?

Apparently, in their infinite wisdom of "zero tolerance" to suppress every fire, there were some unintended, undesirable and nefarious effects. As Yellowstone aged, old trees were not replaced by
younger trees and more deadwood and brush accumulated on the
forest floors. The fuel available for a gigantic and catastrophic fire
laid waiting for just the right spark. The Forest Service had unwittingly driven Yellowstone Park into what Buchanan and other phys-
icists call a "supercritical state." With a high density of burnable
material everywhere throughout Yellowstone, the Forest Service had
created the "equivalent of a doomsday device. The protected woods
have built up an enormous fuel load"[2] of combustible material so
that just one match, one lightning strike....

The U.S. Federal Wildland Fire Policy now recognizes how their
"zero tolerance" policies of the past century compromised U.S. wild-
lands, today stating: "Catastrophic wildfire now threatens millions of
wildland acres, particularly where vegetation patterns have been altered by...a century of fire suppression."[3] Ergo, the policies of the past

century are in large part responsible for the frequent raging wildfires, the likes of which were seen throughout Southern California in 2007.

If natural wildfires should be allowed to run their course and burn out of their own accord as the U.S. Federal Wildland Fire Policy suggests, should our financial policymakers not take a cue from them and allow our financial crises to burn out of their own accord too, since, as Minsky posits, our financial system is unstable and prone to crises anyway?

Could over a century of financial bailouts by U.S. policymakers be unwittingly contributing to our financial system finally reaching a "supercritical state?" Could it be that government policies of providing backstops and bailouts, thereby suppressing all financial crises over the past three quarters of a century, have compromised and threatened our financial system today? Have we already arrived at the Supercritical State, and has the match already sparked a financial catastrophe? This is precisely what First Pacific Advisors are beginning to suspect or at least worry about:

> This country has been on a course of raising the safety net so that the market's discipline in a capitalistic economic system has been truncated. We have witnessed a growing level of decisions that are based upon expediency rather than sound long-term decision making. Each time these expedient decisions are made, the level of risk within the U.S. economy has been increased. The market's discipline is not allowed to work for fear of the potential economic fallout.[4]

First Pacific Advisors wrote this note two weeks after the March 14, 2008, so-called "rescue" of Bear Stearns Corporation by the Federal Reserve. Roughly 50 percent of Bear Stearns business model was predicated on mortgage-related business. The rescue of Bear Stearns by the Fed pushed the legal limits of what the Federal Reserve is chartered to do by law. This particular rescue of Bear Stearns may have stretched beyond the strict legal limits of their charter, or at the very least, they have broadened the interpretation of those legal limits. In fact, many of the Fed's rescue efforts during this crisis have broadened the legal limits of their charters.

## CASTING A NET UNDER THE FAILING FANNIE MAE AND FREDDIE MAC

By July of 2008 our government-sponsored mortgage financing agencies Fannie Mae and Freddie Mac were also failing. This time, it fell to the U.S. Treasury to draw their safety nets under these agencies. The U.S. Treasury relies either on its tax receipts or borrowing for its funding. To borrow, the Treasury can turn to the Federal Reserve, which can buy Treasury debt out of thin air in return for Federal Reserve notes or U.S. dollars. This process is often referred to as "printing money." Ultimately, this debt funding is born by the taxpayers. How many hundreds of billions of dollars this will cost taxpayers is unknown and unquantifiable. But what is known is that the burden of risk explicitly shifts away from the senior bondholders of the GSEs to the American public.

As Secretary of the Treasury Hank Paulson put it when he announced that FNM and FRE would be placed into a "conservatorship" on Sunday, September 7, 2008, "In the end, the ultimate cost to the taxpayer will depend on the business results of the GSEs going forward."[5] In other words, there are risks involved for the taxpayer that can not be entirely decomposed. There is no insurance to taxpayers. It all depends on how bad Fannie's and Freddie's balance sheets are and how much further they will deteriorate as more and more houses end up in foreclosure. The early indications are that the costs will be quite substantial, as their assets (declining mortgage values) are not performing very well at all amidst the ongoing decline in home values and rising unemployment aggravating the escalating foreclosures.

## AN UNMITIGATED DISASTER: CAROL MASSER, ELLEN BREITMAN INTERVIEW JIMMY ROGERS

Some critics were understandably up in arms at the thought of the Treasury backstopping the GSEs. On Monday July 14, 2008, the day after it Paulson announced that Congress had authorized the U.S. Treasury to backstop/guarantee Fannie and Freddie's operations, Bloomberg's Carol Masser and Ellen Breitman interviewed the outspoken Jimmy Rogers. Rogers and George Soros were the co-founders of the Quantum Fund in 1970 that returned 4200% in 10 years.

> **Masser**: Jim, good morning. So, what do you think about what the government is doing or proposing to do with Fannie and Freddie?
>
> **Rogers**: It's an unmitigated disaster. I don't know where these guys get the audacity to take our money, taxpayer money, and buy stock in Fannie Mae. I mean, what is this? If that is what they are doing with our tax money, why don't they ask us? I didn't say, take my money, my tax money, and buy Fannie Mae. And what are they doing guaranteeing their debt?
>
> The people who bought debt in Fannie Mae and Freddie Mac can read a prospectus. They can read it. It says it is not guaranteed by the government. Anybody who can read a balance sheet knew that both of those companies were a sham.

And it ruins the Federal Reserve's balance sheet, and it makes the dollar more vulnerable, and it increases inflation, and it drives down the dollar. Other than that, good morning!

**Massar**: So where do you think this is all leading us to?

**Rogers**: It is leading to more and more rampant inflation. It is leading to a decline and the eventual demise of the United States dollar.... It is going to mean the debt of the United States is going to be downgraded over the next few years....

**Massar**: Jim, I mean, did we have a choice though with Fannie and Freddie? I mean, could we have let them fail?

**Rogers**: Carol, I know you always like to print money, you always like to bail out everybody in sight. But that is not the way capitalism is supposed to work. That is socialism for the rich. That is what that is. Welfare for the rich! Of course not!

**Massar:** Are you still negative on the dollar at this point?

**Rogers**: The dollar is a terribly flawed currency, Carol.

**Massar**: So, Jim, how do you think this is all going to be playing out?

**Rogers**: Well, the United States is in a recession. It is going to be the worst recession we have had in a long time, perhaps since the Second World War, because the federal government keeps making mistakes. The central bank makes mistakes, the Treasury makes mistakes. Everybody keeps making mistakes.

**Braitman**: Jim, I want to ask you a question I asked an earlier guest today, how does this play out in terms of the level of history that is being made?

**Rogers:** Well, it's a very good question and the answer; I don't think I want to give you the answer because you will probably cut me off the air. What is happening here is they are ruining the value of the U.S. dollar. They are ruining the Federal Reserve. They are ruining what has been one of the greatest economies in the world, bailing out everybody in sight.

This is a disaster for America. This is a disaster for the world. Ben Bernanke and Paulson are bailing out their friends on Wall Street, but there are 300 million of us Americans who are going to have to pay for this and there are six billion people in the world who are going to have to pay for this. And they are doing it with no authorization from anybody.

Paul Volcker said a couple of weeks ago that perhaps what the Federal Reserve has done is illegal. I would submit it is illegal what

they have done and what they are doing. They
are saddling all of us with hundreds of billions
of dollars of debt that they have no authorization to do.[6]

## THEIR SENSE OF ENTITLEMENT IS APPALLING

That dollar cost to the taxpayer has since ballooned into the trillions
even before 2008 comes to a close and before President Obama
kicks off his economic recovery plans in 2009. What is legal and not
legal to do does seem to change at epochal moments in America's
crisis history. The Jimmy Rogers interview took place in July 2008,
three months before Paulson asked Congress for the authority to
buy up to another $700 billion of bad assets/toxic waste sitting on
the balance sheets of various other failing financial firms. The Rogers interview also took place months before the government decided
to backstop another institution that failed for its egregious risk-taking in the notable wild-west market - the credit default swaps (CDS)
market. This was the insurance company called AIG.

The government provided AIG with an initial $85 billion loan in
September 2008 with taxpayer money. AIG then received another $37
billion dollar loan through one of the Fed's new lending facilities. As
2008 comes to a close, aid to AIG with taxpayer money had mush-
roomed to $152 billion. Apparently, given the trajectory of events that
later transpired, we find that the U.S. Treasury Secretary Paulson and
Federal Reserve Chairman Ben Bernanke had agreed to just about unlimited funding for AIG with very little if any controls or oversight.

AIG repeatedly went back to the government saying that they
needed more, more, more money in the months that followed the
original $85 billion loan they all thought would be sufficient to see
them through the rest of the storm. On one occasion, November
8, 2008, they went back to the U.S. Government not only seeking

yet more bailout money, but also complaining about the onerous terms of the first loans and seeking to renegotiate them. Observers were both shocked and taken aback at AIG's new demands. Financial blogger Yves Smith at www.nakedcapitalism.com had this to say about AIG's November 8, 2008, proposal:

> Man walks into pawn broker. He says to the person behind the counter, "You know that watch I brought in two weeks ago? I know you lent me $85, but now I need another $50. And I will tell you why you will give it to me. I have a gun with me. I will blow my brains out here, right now. With your nice carpet, I guarantee it will cost you more than $50 to clean up your store. And that's before we get into the cost of keeping your store closed while you clean my grey matter off your walls." Oh, and we forgot to mention that the man in the story above pulled the same trick last week and it worked like a charm.
>
> The other bit that is offensive is (separately) that AIG is unhappy that it is paying more for its bailout than banks did for theirs. The arrogance is breathtaking. Banks and securities firms are regulated by Federal agencies. The fact that they came close to going under says the oversight was defective, and one can argue that the government was required to prevent a disaster that happened on its watch.
>
> The federal government has NO oversight over AIG. Its mess was SOLELY AIG's own do-

ing, and they should consider themselves incredibly lucky that they were so big that the
Fed felt it has to intercede.

Now they think they are entitled to demand an improvement of terms? They should
be told to take a long walk off a short pier (the
management that is). If we are merely going
to salvage random about-to-fail-that-might-
hurt-the-financial-markets players, I'd much
rather rescue GM. They at least have a better
attitude. And I have far more sympathy for
blue collar workers than AIG executives.[7]

At the time, General Motors (GM) was also in need of a rescue before year-end to avoid bankruptcy. In this one vignette, financial
sleuth Yves Smith eloquently expresses the rage we have all felt as
Americans bailing out these financial firms. We are even more taken
aback because a major dictum of the capitalist society we supposedly live in is that we allow entities that have failed to actually fail.
Propping up our financial firms and socializing the losses is a frontal
assault on American sensibilities and values. As members of a capitalist society, Americans have every right to question and challenge
the constitutionality and legality of the government funding and socializing the losses of our financial system. (FYI- In times of crisis, the
Constitution tends to get thrown out the window, and that is when
it needs to be most protected and defended by its citizens.)

But why should AIG (and other financial firms, by the way) have
stopped their abuses on the taxpayer? In fact, they didn't! On November 26, 2008, the *Financial Times* reported that AIG announced
in a regulatory filing that they made after the $85 billion bailout
that they were going to be paying 130 AIG executives "retention bo-

nuses." No one had ever heard of such a thing before. When pressed, the company said that "retention bonuses would be necessary to maintain continuity and value."[8]

Such semantics, one observer noted, should remind us of former President Bill Clinton's definition of what "is" is.

But more to the point, rewarding AIG executives for their failure as an entity with bonuses paid with taxpayer money is a grotesque act. Yet, some market observers argued that these bonuses were deserved. Their line of reasoning was as follows: AIG has a few so-called "rainmakers" who were instrumental in bringing in a great deal of revenue to the parent company. Proponents of these retention bonuses also point out that some AIG subsidiaries were still profitable as a result of these rainmakers, such as their life and annuity businesses. They further point out that most of the blame for the failure of the company ultimately falls to the parent AIG holding company, and not the subsidiary rainmakers. Collectively, however, the company has failed from the top down, and should therefore have been allowed to be reorganized under Chapter 11 bankruptcy under which no employee would be receiving any salary. In closing, Yves Smith added:

> In the old days on Wall Street, when the house had a bad year, everyone took a hit and accepted it, even the performers that had done well. And if I am finding virtue in an older Wall Street compared to now, you know our values have gone down the toilet.[9]

The so-called "rainmakers" are AIG's only assets. But AIG does not own the rainmakers. The rainmakers can come and go as they please with due allowances made for non-compete clauses. Non-compete clauses notwithstanding, these AIG rainmakers would eagerly have been picked up by AIG's solvent competitors had AIG been allowed to fail as should have happened to any proper entity in a capitalist system. As or when a failed entity is reorganized and liquidated, superior employees should immediately be seeking greener pastures and new opportunities. This is precisely what all employees of failed and insolvent entities like AIG and other financial firms should have been doing instead of sticking around for their year-end bonuses.

In fact, do not be surprised when AIG loses these rainmakers in 2009 - after they have received their year-end "retention bonuses" of course. They are not indentured servants or chattel of AIG. There is nothing stipulated in their "retention" bonuses that says they "must stay." Retention bonuses are not contractual obligations. So, in the end, it has all been another flush of taxpayer dollars down the drain. It is unnerving to say the least.

AIG's statement about maintaining continuity is as disingenuous as it is fallacious. Beyond the so-called rainmakers, most of the so-called talent at AIG are lucky to even have a job and would be extremely hard-pressed to even find another job within the financial industry - now that the industry is shrinking after the financial system blew up. The shrinkage in the sector will play out over the next several years.

It should be footnoted that our policymakers, lawmakers and regulators all failed put in place a mechanism to protect the taxpayers from this type of misappropriation of funds at AIG, in spite of the U.S. Treasury Secretary's exhortations about protecting the taxpayers. Worse yet, the practice of bonusing financial executives of failed firms in 2008 was not limited to AIG. Year-end bonuses went out to executives at all the other failed financial firms. In fact, in the midst of attempting to secure funding for the financial crisis, the U.S. Treasury Secretary defended the salaries and bonuses of financial executives. Thus it was that through government sanctioning, 2008 year-end bonusing became a widespread phenomenon in the failed financial industry.

During the boom years, the *New York Times* reported that Merrill Lynch's record $7.5 billion earnings in 2006 turned out to be nothing but smoke and mirrors. "The company has since lost three times that amount, largely because the mortgage investments that had powered some of those profits plunged in value."[10] What is more, most of the $7.5 billion 2006 profits accrued directly to management and not to shareholders. Merrill disbursed over $5 billion dollars in bonuses that year. Come rain or come shine, every year is a windfall year for financial executives. A crisis is a very small matter for these executives when the taxpayer is available to backstop their bonuses when they lose money for their egregious risk-taking.

When American citizens got wind of the fact that these financial executives would still be receiving 2008 year-end bonuses, their anger was evident. As Vietnam veteran Ken Karlson put it, "I may not understand everything, but I do understand common sense, and when you lend money to someone, you don't want to see them at a new-car dealer the next day. The bailout money shouldn't have been given to them in the first place." And retired merchant marine Patrick Amo added, "Even really sober people are saying this is the worst financial crisis since the Depression, and they're saying bonuses are just going to be reduced? Oh my God, you read that and your jaw drops."[11] Another veteran said:

> My friends [American soldiers in combat] died
> doing their job so jerk offs can pull the kind of
> shit that's going on now in Wall Street and DC.
> How do they feel over there now and when they
> come back to a system that has never looked
> after them for their sacrifice? I have blood

on my hands that will never wash off and for
what? So rats can bilk the blood out of others
to massage their fragile egos?

Am I incensed? YES I am, and until this
country has a national mentality that goes beyond wealth and ignorance of what transpires
in the ivory towers of politics and industry
we're screwed.[12]

The losses on Wall Street in 2008 have been so substantial that they
exceeded the total earnings of 2004 through 2007. Given the scope
of the losses in 2008, the earnings during the prior three years were
nothing but fairy tales. They were bubble earnings, an illusion created by a speculative scheme that comes to nothing. Even though
the earnings were make-believe, the bonuses doled out during 2004
through 2007 were real. For that reason, Baltimore lawyer Woods
Bennett argued for a clawback:

The executives in companies that get bailout
money should have their base salaries reduced
by 10 percent for 2009 and they should pay
back a substantial portion of their 2007 bonuses to the government for the financial devastation they oversaw, fostered and, in some
cases, directly caused. Their sense of entitlement is appalling.[13]

I see nothing wrong with Bennett's clawback argument, except that
it does not go nearly far enough. These executives should be paying back a substantial portion of their bonuses since 2004, not just
2007, given that the earnings were part of an illusion created by a
speculative scheme. And indeed, their sense of entitlement is ap-

palling. After the earnings illusion bubble popped in 2007-2008, they still rationalize and cry for their bonuses. They can cry for their undeserved bonuses all they want, but shame on us the taxpayers for allowing Congress to give them our money (though we did try to stop them)! Their sense of entitlement is even more outrageous when you consider the total cost of the bailout to the failed financial system through 2008. Bloomberg reported that the total U.S. government outlays to rescue Wall Street and stabilize the financial system through November 2008 totaled $7.76 trillion. To put that in perspective, Bianco Research and CNBC did some historical number crunching. On an inflation-adjusted basis, the bailout to date is more than equivalent to the total cost of the Invasion of Iraq ($597 billion), S&L crisis ($256 billion), Vietnam War ($698 billion), NASA ($851 billion), Korean War ($454 billion), New Deal ($500 billion est.), Louisiana Purchase ($217 billion), WWII ($3.6 trillion) and the Marshall Plan ($115 billion). All these previous government outlays only reach $6.59 trillion.14 Richard Kline describes the government outlays disparagingly: "For the most part, the first year of response by the public authorities from Aug 07 to Sep 08 was largely wasted effort, sandbagging a dyke which was overtopped, undermined, with the crest of failures yet to come."15

One has to wonder what the colorful and spirited Mr. Rogers might have to say just five months after his July 2008 interview after all the other developments that have since transpired. The bottom line is that Jim Rogers' pointed remarks underscore the very real and growing risks to the American people that our have policymakers have been creating as the crisis evolves. There is a great deal of uncertainty about what the actual outcomes and costs will be. Certainly, what the actual costs will ultimately be cannot be calculated. Government outlays for this financial crisis are still rising and will considerably exceed $7.76 trillion.

Some of these outlays will undoubtedly come back to the government when the economy recovers, and this may well be considerably less than $7.76 trillion. But why are the taxpayers bonusing out the executives of financial firms again after wiping out more than four years of make-believe earnings? There isn't any defensible response to this question, no matter how these executives semantically slice or "tranche" it. One thing is certain: the abuses heaped upon the taxpayer to save the flawed financial system are both reprehensible and galling.

## TARP – A TROUBLING ANSWER TO A TROUBLING PROBLEM FOR THE TAXPAYER

Speaking of protecting the taxpayer, Paulson and the lawmakers were quite vocal on this point with the GSEs and TARP. To Paulson's credit, during the restructuring of the GSEs and placing them into a conservatorship on Sunday, September 7, 2008, Paulson did mention that he felt very strongly and rightly so about protecting the taxpayers' interest as much as possible. In his statement, Paulson said that the "conservatorship was the only form in which I would commit taxpayer money to the GSEs."[16] Unfortunately, the scope of the financial crisis broadened considerably after Lehman Brothers failed on September 15, 2008. Things began happening too fast. There was little to nothing Paulson would be able to do now to protect taxpayers' interest.

Lehman's demise, which sparked the financial collapse, prompted Paulson and Bernanke to seek a "permanent solution" they called the TARP plan. The justification Paulson offered to taxpayers this time was that the consequences of not buying up the illiquid assets would be far worse for the economy and the American public. "This is not a position where I like to see the taxpayer, but it is far better than the alternative," Paulson said.[17] In short, Paulson's plan, he said, would carry real costs to the American people.

The "sky-is-falling" fear-mongering was not well received by market observers who recognized this bailout plan went against core traditional values upheld and cherished by millions of Americans. The American public was incensed they were being asked to bail out the failed banking system and railed against it.

Over the long haul, Mr. Paulson said that he expects both the conservatorship of the GSEs and the TARP program to eventually turn a profit for Uncle Sam and the U.S. taxpayer. While it is extremely doubtful that that will turn out to be the case given the foregoing, such an argument never should have been put forth to support Uncle Sam's extracting monies from the taxpayer. That said, had Paulson chosen to, he could have cited historical precedents in which the government did not lose money. One such case, which bears similarity to the newly formed TARP, was the RFC lending agency 75 years ago. One of the many accomplishments of the RFC lending agency under Jesse H. Jones' leadership was to eventually turn a profit on most everything they put onto their balance sheets. But it certainly did not happen overnight for the American public.

Because of historical precedents of the government not losing money when they went in and took over financial firms, such as the RFC agency, it was not necessarily surprising to see that Hank Paulson's placement of the GSEs into a conservatorship was initially fairly well-received overall by many on Wall Street—even if Jimmy Rogers correctly viewed the whole affair as an unmitigated disaster. When Paulson had initially mentioned the shareholders would be wiped out, it seemed to have the right ring to it. Indeed, it seemed that Paulson had struck a happy balance—that he had found *"le juste milieu"* and for this, his actions were initially applauded. The stock market also gave its nod of approval by rallying 5% over the weekend. As Chris Whalen, director of the Institutional Risk Analyst summarized the news September 8, 2008, regarding the conservatorship:

> But all things considered, Secretary Paulson's
> actions deserve our support... Reports of the
> impending takeover of the GSEs by the Trea-
> sury and the creation of a conservatorship...
> are great news for the markets and the tax-
> payer... A scaled down GSE operation that
> sheds the retained portfolios...and focuses on
> the historic role of secondary market maker for
> U.S. mortgage lenders actually will generate a
> stable profit for taxpayers.[18]

Viewed in this light, the conservatorship of the GSEs could have been interpreted as a net positive. However, Whalen made these comments immediately after the announcement and I think well before he and others realized that wiping out the preferred share-holders meant that would slam the door on other financial firms needing to raise capital through preferred stock offerings. Paulson's decision has been devastating to the market. "We all thought they would never help exacerbate the banking crisis and that's exactly what they did,"[19] said Marilyn Cohen, President of Envision Capital Management.

A week later, Paulson and Bernanke hauled in their safety nets and decided to let Lehman go bankrupt. That was a dark day that would precipitate the need to save the rest of the banks. Hence, the immediate TARP plan was resurrected to bail out the rest of the U.S. financial system. TARP, in its original form, was intended to save what was left of Wall Street. There were no obvious net tangible benefits that would accrue to Main Street. TARP was later revised and funds were "repurposed." To provide capital to our financial firms, the Treasury bought preferred stock with the TARP funding. Even the revised TARP provided no obvious tangible benefits to Main Street.

Paulson's TARP plan has always been under intense and heavy criticism. In its best light, TARP was intended to reduce the threat of the collapsing financial system to the rest of the economy. In reality, it was already too late to prevent contagion and spillover into the real economy. However, the government's rescue efforts to stop the profuse bleeding of our financial system through the TARP, the Federal Reserve's lending facilities, and conservatorships has been intended to act as a tourniquet around a gaping wound. Of course, it is extremely difficult to place a tourniquet around a gaping wound, and the bleeding in the financial system will continue until home prices stop declining. And this won't be happening until sometime in late 2009 or 2010, say some experts. But at least we have a government that can lay claim to be doing something about it, even if they are going about it the wrong way!

## TARP GOAL TO BE A HUGE FIREBREAK TO FIRMS BURNED BY TROUBLED ASSETS

TARP was another governmental intrusion into the financial markets. These intrusions were lagging indicators that the financial crisis was spreading like wildfire and that a huge firebreak was required. Still, the government measures under TARP would not do anything to relieve the record wave of home foreclosures on Main Street in 2008-2009 as estimated by Economy.com and others.

At best, this new legislature would only cushion the blow to financial firms caused by a combination of egregious risk-taking in the mortgage markets and regulators/lawmakers who were either asleep at the wheel or lacked the political will to do anything absent a financial crisis. As was the case in the 1930s, the intermediate outlook suggests the well-being of most U.S. citizens will be wrenched still further as they endure the spate of record foreclosures, the ongoing asset deflation, job losses and debt liquidation, not to mention footing the bill for our failed and insolvent financial institutions exposed to the illiquid and toxic assets on their balance sheets.

## DOLLAR DEVALUATION MAY ESCALATE UNDER TARP AND OTHER GOVERNMENT SPENDING PROGRAMS

The costs of the U.S. Government's expansion of the money supply will be borne by the American public not just through higher tax burdens and the like, but also through the continued depreciation of the U.S. dollar. Indeed, this is exactly the same question raised by the *Washington Sunday Star* cartoonist C.K. Berryman as Franklin D. Roosevelt and Jesse H. Jones sought to readjust the value of the U.S. dollar to 60% of its old parity to gold as part of the New Deal.

Source: Jesse H. Jones, Fifty Billion Dollars, My Thirteen Years at The RFC, C.K. Berryman, Washington Sunday Star

On April 5, 1933, the U.S. forbade its citizens to hold gold in monetary form; it could be held as artwork, jewelry and dental work. As extreme and crude as this New Deal measure was on the American constituents, President Roosevelt's aim was simply to restore deflating commodity prices from their depression-blighted lows. Once all the gold had been removed from circulation and the dollar devalued in consequence, the U.S. government was the first to profit — and profit handsomely it did. Some believe that President Roosevelt's experimental meddling with the gold currency was successful in helping prop up commodity prices and stimulating exports.

## Price Fixing the Cotton Market

I am not so sure, and I question how quantifiable that executive policy was, because other major countries were in the race to devalue their own currencies as well, offsetting the intended FDR benefits. But from Jesse H. Jones' own account, the RFC lending agency, through its subsidiary the Commodity Credit Corporation (CCC) was measurably successful in restoring commodity prices in that era.

In Jesse H. Jones' view, what really saved the farmer was the creation of the CCC on October 16, 1933, after Agriculture Secretary Wallace's missteps. Wallace had paid cotton farmers to destroy every third row of crop to reduce supply in order to prop up prices, but cotton farmers still brought in a bumper crop that year.

The cotton farmers faced the prospect of bringing to an already depressed market a huge new supply, which would depress prices further. Cotton at the time was selling for 6 to 9 cents a pound. Roosevelt told Jones, "Jess, I want you to lend 10 cents a pound on cotton."[20] In essence, FDR was implementing his own TARP plan to artificially inflate or price fix farmers' most troubled asset — cotton. Cotton, it can be said, was a lot less toxic than these mortgage-backed securities that are defaulting left and right because of the subprime borrowers' inability to service the mortgage.

Like FDR, Jesse H. Jones felt cotton prices were too low and believed cotton was worth more than 10 cents a pound, on the premise "that to lend on that amount would be very helpful and entail no loss to the govt."[21] Paulson's TARP plan to buy troubled/toxic assets at marks above the market stole a page out of the CCC script.

"For long periods we carried a large paper loss on our farm-aid program," said Jones. "Whatever the season, whatever the size of the crop or the loan, the interest rate to the farmer remains the same 4% for several years. Then it was reduced to 3%."[22] In 1934 FDR jumped the price of cotton to 12 cents. The cotton was stored in the 12-cent loan warehouses instead of being taken to market. Effectively, the government had taken over the supply of cotton production, and in doing so was able to manipulate the price of cotton higher. From this, we can infer a direct relationship between the rise in commodity prices being due to government controls and less to the overnight 40% devaluation of the U.S. dollar.

## FDR's GOLD CONFISCATION

When all was said and done, even the RFC chairman Jesse H. Jones looked back years later and took a noted pause at the many angry Americans who adamantly believed the Roosevelt Administration's tampering with the gold currency was "illegal and dishonest, a fraud upon every pocketbook in the land."[23] In fact, the constitutionality of Roosevelt's gold policy had to be ruled upon by the Supreme Court. While the Supreme Court did not rule against it in 1933, Justice McReynolds did speak out against it, arguing that the New Deal's "flippant approach to currency manipulation [was dangerous]. This is Nero at his worst. As for the Constitution, it does not seem too much to say that it is gone."[24] And so it was that the dollar was successfully devalued, which served to reflate the price of everything against the dollar. From all appearances, many Americans felt this act made the FDR administration look like a bunch of kleptocrats.

Right or wrong, the same delegation of angry American citizens remains every bit as adamant today that our government continues to deflate and debase the dollar every time they find it expedient to do so. To a large degree, when we look at the taxpayer-funded bailouts of Fannie, Freddie and AIG today, we observe another form of expropriation taking place that puts the U.S. Treasury in a very unfavorable light, even if they have the blessings of the administration, Congress and the Federal Reserve.

It might be easier to take had any measurable economic good come from their efforts thus far. But they haven't. First, Wall Street firms used taxpayer dollars to pay out egregious bonuses. Second, the taxpayer monies that the U.S. Treasury crammed down on the failed banks to recap them in 2008 are not being used to extend credit as intended by lawmakers (Ludicrous to think it would work in a debt-deflationary spiral and uncreditworthiness run amok!). And third, no cleansing process of the financial system has occurred, primarily because that was not even a policy goal. Under the original Paulson plan, the goal was to purchase the troubled assets, sweep 'em under the TARP and hide/hold them there until maturity at artificial, fictitiously high and fraudulent prices. Moreover, they would be carrying those toxic assets on their balance sheets at a very large paper loss for a very long time.

It's been a blessed mess out there, and no one with the power has had the *cajones* to clean up the collateral damage. Instead, the original response to blowing up the financial system we got from the U.S. Treasury was akin to the following: "Psst, I am going to create this huge TARP with taxpayer monies that all you banksters can hide your crap under until maturity or made whole." However, by the time Congress appropriated funds for the U.S. Treasury's TARP plan, the Treasury had already decided to redirect or repurpose the TARP appropriations.

## MISAPPROPRIATION OF TARP FUNDS

The TARP plan had been so unsatisfactory and distasteful after it was first implemented, even the lawmakers who supported it in the first place began complaining about it. So too are the banksters who received TARP funding, alleging that they never asked for it. On October 31, 2008, the House Financial Services Committee Chairman Barney Frank complained that banks used the cash from their $700 billion bailout plan for bonuses, acquisitions and other purposes unrelated to lending (supposedly the aim of TARP, according to Frank). "I am deeply disappointed a number of financial institutions are distorting the legislation. Any use of these funds for any purpose other than lending, bonuses, acquisitions, is a violation of the terms of the act."[25]

Barney Frank, who was an early and outspoken proponent of Paulson's TARP plan, acted surprised to see the funds being misappropriated and repurposed. But should he and other lawmakers who were in favor of TARP really have been surprised? There had been plenty of dissent from other lawmakers and economists to think it through and modify the plan before legislating it. In its original form, TARP was a bill just three pages long asking for $700 billion. Lawmakers, under the cram-down urgings of Treasury Secretary Paulson, felt that something (whatever that was) must be done now, immediately, and decided the most expedient thing to do would be to pass the bill. To do so, they needed to buy the rest of the votes from other lawmakers who were opposing the bill. By the time the lawmakers felt they had enough votes to pass the bill, they had added $150 billion of pork to it.

In its bloated $850 billion pork-laden form, the bill was now 449 pages long! Just a spoonful of sugar may have helped the medicine go down for the other opposing lawmakers, but taxpayers and many other market observers found the whole charade offensive and in bad taste. With the TARP funds being misappropriated, due to lack of controls and oversight, (even though something clearly had to be done — just not that!), the TARP legislation was another misstep in a series of missteps. It would behoove legislators to have listened more carefully to the inputs of private market participants, economists and other experts who more than willingly had offered their wisdom towards establishing appropriate legislation that would have yielded better outcomes.

As it now stands, the TARP plan, under the Bush administration and U.S. Treasury, in both its original and revised design, has only managed to keep a moribund banking system on life support— good for bonuses, acquisitions and the like. TARP is simply "draining assets away from the productive economy" says the author of *Web of Debt* Ellen Brown.[26] A working paper on systemic banking crises done by the International Monetary Fund (IMF) shows that the TARP plan was consistent with what the IMF study found to be the least effective policy response to systemic financial crises:

> Existing empirical research has shown that providing assistance to banks and their borrowers can be counterproductive, resulting in increased losses to banks, which often abuse forbearance to take unproductive risks at government expense. The typical result of forbearance is a deeper hole in the net worth of banks, crippling tax burdens to finance bank bailouts, and even more severe credit supply contrac-

tion and economic decline than would have
occurred in the absence of forbearance.[27]

The TARP plan behaved precisely as the IMF's empirical research indicated it would. A more intelligent use of $850 billion dollars of
taxpayer money under the fractional reserve banking system would
have been injecting the capital into well-capitalized, solvent financial
firms (for example, local credit unions and local community banks)
that were strong and did not have troubled assets on their balance
sheets. Under the fractional reserve banking system, roughly every
dollar of capital allows a bank to make $10 worth of loans. Then
had we placed the capital into healthy financial institutions, the
$850 billion taxpayer dollars could have been stretched to roughly
$8.5 trillion with the pork—and $700 trillion without the pork.

If the American Banking Association (ABA) executive director Ed
Yingling is to be believed (take with the usual large grain of salt) in a
letter he wrote to Treasury Secretary Paulson on October 30, 2008:

> It is completely unfair to ask thousands of
> banks across the country — and they are be-
> ing explicitly asked by their regulators — to
> participate in a program when the impact of
> the program on those banks is unknown. [ABA
> member banks] run the risk of being labeled
> falsely as needing government support, or of
> appearing to be asking for a handout. This is
> not a program the banking industry sought.[28]

Mr. Yingling was stating that a sacred element of the banker's code
had been violated: banks never willingly give the appearance of needing a handout or a rescue. They will go to the grave before seeking
financial help. Banking is a game of confidence, and the appearance

of always being a strong bank must be vitally protected. Mr. Paulson violated that element of the banker's code when he crammed down those handouts, causing banks to lose face. Mr. Yingling was expressing this displeasure in so many words to Mr. Paulson.

The U.S. government and policymakers have chosen policies to lend and spend aggressively to stabilize the financial markets in an effort to protect the collapsing economy from the adverse headwinds of debt-deflation and prevent slipping into a depression. Lawmakers and the new administration should lend and spend taxpayer money more wisely than what happened with the failed TARP as originally implemented.

Policymakers and legislators can look back to some of the successes of the RFC model and FDR's New Deal back in the 1930s to grasp the significance of how any "new," New Deals that will be structured by the new Obama administration and lawmakers should be done. The RFC model ensured good banks and good business entities were solvent and provided with liquidity. The model adopted some of the principles of Keynesian economics. To a substantial degree, the RFC provided a key solution to John Maynard Keynes "Paradox of Thrift" that so defined the Great Depression, a paradox which also defines our present day circumstances of debt-deflation and delevering.

## APPLYING KEYNESIAN ECONOMICS TO THE PARADOX OF THRIFT

Under the Paradox of Thrift, when everyone collectively liquidated assets and saved what was left of the proceeds in the 1930s rather than reinvesting or spending them, the capital markets collapsed and assets deflated in a downward spiral. This is why it then became necessary for the government in the 1930s, under Keynesian economic principles, to spend aggressively and to provide the RFC a blank check for lending purposes. Under the RFC, the U.S. government became the world's lending agency and the lender of last resort in order to re-liquify the frozen capital markets.

The RFC had "zero tolerance" towards the forces of the Great Depression. To counter those forces, they literally did whatever was necessary and politically expedient to spend their way out of it. Although the U.S. Forest Service has adopted policy changes in response to outdated "zero tolerance" forest fire management, our government and Federal Reserve by and large still employ a Keynesian response, or "zero tolerance" policy, to the myriad financial crises that have arisen since the Great Depression. Commenting on the present state of affairs, former St. Louis Fed President William Poole, who retired in March 2008, said on May 2, 2008, "It's appalling where we are now. The Fed has introduced a backstop for the entire financial system."[29] Seventy-five years later, the U.S. government has once again become the lender of last resort, poised to save all the banks and buy up all their unwanted assets. Derogatorily, financial commentators have called the newly legislated TARP program devised by Paulson and Bernanke the "No Bank Left Behind" Act.

In effect, we have come full circle. Not only are the banks being recapped by the U.S. Treasury under TARP and the Federal Reserve's lending facilities, but so too are other vital industries. A case in point is the automobile industry. But after lawmakers' missteps enacting the flawed TARP plan, by November 2008 legislators had become a great deal more circumspect about handing out taxpayer money with little to no scrutiny and oversight.

That said, the government's willingness to spend in order to prop up the economy as businesses and consumers retrench, we are moving closer and closer towards where we were in the 1930s, under FDR's New Deal. One thing FDR did to prop up the economy during the Great Depression was to have the RFC extend credit and lend aggressively not only to the financial system, but to the entire agriculture, railroad, mortgage and insurance industries as well as cities and states. Creating the RFC as an instrument to whip the Depression was a winning strategy. In the long run, the affairs of the RFC worked out fairly well back in the 1930s. But it remains uncertain that this same strategy will work as effectively in today's economy, particularly with the level of debt in the system that needs to shrink.

Past performance is no guarantee of future results. There is always the possibility to consider that aggressive government lending and spending policies might undermine "price stability" in the markets. This is particularly so if policymakers do not or are unable to mop up the excesses until it is too late to prevent a great deal of inflationary pressures once we pass through the deflationary cycle. This would potentially expose our economy to a new set of risks, creating a situation similar to the hyperinflation of the Weimar Republic in 1923. Hence, William Poole's understandable apprehension towards backstopping the entire financial system.

It is worth pausing here for a moment to consider further the economic roots that have guided Federal Reserve and U.S. government policies for the last 75 years and to juxtapose that with the economic roots that guide the European Community Bank (ECB) monetary policies, which focus on "maintaining price stability" today. The former grew out of the 1930s Depression, and the latter grew out of the hyperinflation of the Weimar Republic in the 1920s.

John Maynard Keynes' macroeconomic theories grew out of the mass unemployment and Great Depression of the U.S. and Great Britain in the 1930s. Keynes' solution advocated stimulating the economies through government intervention and injections of capital. In Keynes' view, during periods of high unemployment, recessions and depressions, the government should legislate that government agencies intervene in ways that would offset the slack in demand or economic activity. That, in a nutshell, is what the RFC

was created for by President Hoover in January 1932 and implemented by FDR. FDR's New Deal embraced this element of Keynes'
economic theory as well.

Keynes' general economic theory was that government "utilization of resources" could be high or low, depending on whether economic conditions were good or bad. Keynes's ideas of economic stimulus worked very well in the 1930s. U.S. economic policies have been
greatly shaped and influenced by Keynesian economics ever since.

Too much utilization of government resources, however, could
have negative unintended consequences. And this is what much of
the brouhaha and protestations have been about this past decade.
To have the Federal Reserve artificially stimulate the economy with
negative real rates, those below the rate of inflation for prolonged
periods of time already have proven to be highly inflationary this
decade. By 2008, the U.S. dollar had plunged 40% from its peak
valuations at the onset of the decade. Additionally, as First Pacific
Advisors and former St. Louis Fed President William Poole worry,
when the Federal Reserve and U.S. government backstop virtually
everything, the safety nets are raised too high, which increases the
risks to the American public. The costs to the taxpayer are high. As
my good friend Robert Hitt both fears and contends, "Americans
are being held upside down and every penny is being shaken out."[30]

These well-founded concerns may well prove to be overblown
when all is said and done if the series of bailouts pan out like the
various RFC-directed bailouts and other FDR New Deal programs
implemented in the 1930s. However, we should not necessarily expect the same results. In the long run, it took WWII to get America
up and running again, not the New Deal. And certainly, we do not
want WWIII on our hands.

## Government Backstop Measures to Reflate the Economy May Ultimately Prove Inflationary

The logical consequences of the U.S. government and Federal Reserve policies intervening constantly to prop up the U.S. economy, assets and financial institutions remain a legitimate risk to the U.S. taxpayers and to inflationary pressures within the economy. If it is pushed too hard, the Keynesian model upon which our economy has been running for the past 75 years could blow up in our faces. Therefore, the Cassandra-like cautions can neither be pooh-poohed nor easily dismissed.

Even our legislators are beginning to wake up to the fact that our long-standing economic model might be broken. There is little "visibility" in Capitol Hill in discussions about necessary legislation. Indicative of the uncertainty on Capital Hill were Senate Majority Leader Harry Reid's comments on September 17, 2008, a time when fear and anxiety were at their highest level since 9/11:

> No one knows what to do. We are in new territory, this is a different game. Neither Federal Reserve Chairman Ben Bernanke nor Treasury Secretary Henry Paulson know what to do but they are trying to come up with ideas.[31]

One of those new ideas was the creation of a government agency to buy up all the "troubled" assets on the balance sheets of our financial institutions. But as Martin Hennecke of Tyche told CNBC on Sept 11, 2008, what worries him is the $3 trillion of U.S. debt that is sharply rising. "When the government can no longer pass the United States "immense debt" on to taxpayers, it will turn to holders of U.S. dollars, leading to the eventual downfall of the currency."[32] Hennecke's worst-case scenario would push the U.S. into hyperinflation similar to experiences of the Weimar Republic of 1914-1923.

With Uncle Sam borrowing more than $1 trillion dollars to shore up the economy, restore consumer and investor confidence and stabilize the credit crisis, other strategists concur. "The downdraft on the dollar from the hit to the balance sheet of the U.S. government will dwarf the short-term gains from solving the banking crisis,"[33] said Barclay's head of foreign exchange, David Woo. John Taylor, chairman of International Foreign Exchange Concepts, the biggest currency hedge fund firm, added, "as we get to the other side of this, the dollar will get crushed."[34]

## FLIPSIDE TO GREAT DEPRESSION IS THE HYPERINFLATION OF THE WEIMAR REPUBLIC

The flipside to the Great Depression in the U.S. is the hyperinflation of the Weimar Republic (Germany). The economic roots of the ECB are grounded in the hyperinflation experience of post-WWI Germany. If we are to understand the ECB and their focus on "maintaining price stability" over propping up economies and the like, we must understand a little about the depreciation of the German papiermark of 1918-1933.

The depreciation of the mark began in 1914, when the German government abandoned the link between its currency and gold at the onset of WWI. Specifically, the papiermark was a banknote printed and issued by the German government to pay their war debts. After the "London Ultimatum" demanded war reparations be paid in gold installments in May 1921, however, the situation got out of hand. "The total reparations demanded was $132 billion gold mark which was far more than the total German gold or foreign exchange."[35] As Professor Constantino Bresciani-Turroni, an Italian economist, author of *The Economy of Inflation – A Study of Currency Depreciation in Post War Germany* and member of the German Reparation Commission, wrote in 1937, the depreciation of the mark:

Source: Wikipedia/Hyperinflation—woman burning papiermarks

...is one of the outstanding episodes in the history of the twentieth century. Not only by reason of its magnitude, but also by reason of its effects, it looms large on our horizon. It was the most colossal thing of its kind in history: and next to the Great War itself, it must bear responsibility for many of the political and economic difficulties of our generation. It destroyed the wealth of the more solid elements in German society, it left behind a moral and economic disequilibrium, apt breeding ground for the disasters which have followed. Hitler is

> the foster child of the inflation… If we are to
> understand the present position of Europe; we
> must not neglect the study of the great Ger-
> man inflation. If we are to plan for greater sta-
> bility in the future, we must learn to avoid the
> mistakes from which it sprang.[36]

Note Bresciani-Turroni emphasizes the need to "plan for greater stability in the future." With the ECB's adamant focus on maintaining
price stability, we can sense the ghost-like presence of Constantino
Bresciani-Turroni rankling around in the halls of the ECB today. Too
much debasement of a currency to get out of debt, war-born or otherwise, is never a good thing. Currency debasement has contributed
not only to the destruction of wealth and decline in post-WWI Germany, but in all great societies. As Martin Armstrong of Princeton
Economics Institute put it back in 1987:

> History is littered with countless debt crises
> that have occurred regularly since the Babylo-
> nians right through into modern times. It ap-
> pears that the endless cycle of borrowing more
> than one can repay has sealed the fate of just
> about every government that has ever existed.[37]

It can be observed that some of the intervention elements of
Keynesian economics embraced by the Federal Reserve and the U.S.
government agencies have long aided and abetted the slippery slope
that we now face as we work through this debt-liquidation crisis.
The challenges ahead of us are substantial. It seems evident that
we must somehow strike a delicate balance somewhere between the
ECB's focus on maintaining price stability and the Federal Reserve's
focus on accommodating and fostering economic growth. Finding

that balance won't exactly be easy, but preserving the dialectical tensions that exist between the ECB price stability policies and Federal Reserve's accommodation policies will probably serve us well. Additionally, it is hoped that this dialectical tension can be maintained without necessarily disrupting or interfering with the need for organized and timely support from international policymakers in general.

## FINANCIAL CRISES ARE HARDY PERENNIALS

Charles Kindleberger illustrates the history of financial catastrophes in his 1978 book *Manias, Panics, and Crashes*. He termed financial crises "hardy perennials." If financial crises are not inevitable, they can be shown to "at least be historically common."[38] But still, even if financial crises are historically common, each of us individually living through one of these financial crises experiences at some emotional and cognitive level that Holy #!## feeling. They are almost always historically uncommon to the individual.

What we are all discovering as the credit crisis evolves is that "what we did not know is proving to be far more relevant than what we know".[39] Nassim Taleb eloquently proves that point in his new book *The Black Swan*. To cite a glaring example of Taleb's observation, the CEO of Bear Stearns, Alan Schwarz, and the Federal Reserve Chairman both alleged they had no advance warning of the imminent collapse of Bear Stearns just days before Bear Stearns filed for bankruptcy. You can't be any more of an "insider" than one of these two guys.

In the final analysis, none of their supposed inside info and financial modeling proved relevant in forecasting the ultimate and immediate collapse of Bear Stearns or in any of the dominos that followed Bear Stearns into the abyss. If these two guys don't know what is going to happen from one minute to the next at Bear Stearns, then who? What comes next? "God knows" comes to mind as the best answer to that question. As Yogi Berra would put it, "The future ain't what it used to be."

The Minsky model rests squarely on the fact that "bank credit is notoriously unstable."[40] Whatever the source of displacement or exogenous event, "if it is sufficiently pervasive, it will alter the economic outlook by changing profit opportunities in at least one important sector of the economy: displacement brings opportunities for profit in some new or existing lines and closes out others."[Ä]

## BEAR STEARNS PROVIDES THE SPARK TO OUR PRESENT DAY FINANCIAL CATASTROPHE

In our present crisis, it is pretty darn clear that it was the June 20, 2007, announcement that two of Bear Stearns mortgage-related hedge funds had collapsed, coupled with the announcement a month later, in mid-July, that these investors would be getting little if any money back that sparked the credit crisis of 2007. The revelation that high-yield investors could lose everything meant that the jig was up.

This led other hedge fund investors to seek redemptions, in effect causing "runs" on other hedge funds and eventually even runs on banks. Most significantly these runs were occurring within our unregulated "shadow banking system." Shadow banking is a term coined by Pimco's Paul McCulley to describe financial institutions that were not required to meet the capital requirements of our fractional reserve banking system. Not only did high-yield investors become reluctant to lend, so did the banks themselves shortly thereafter. In fact, as this credit crisis has continued to evolve, the *modus operandi* of banks has been to hoard cash rather than lend it, a condition that has persisted right through 2008.

The Bear Stearns hedge fund collapse, more than any other event, also triggered the drying up of leveraged buyouts (LBOs) and mergers and acquisitions (M&As). LBOs and M&As in particular were the other primary drivers of our financial markets and speculative activity during the 2004-2007 period. However, LBOs and M&As are highly dependent on debt financing. Once the credit dried up, the "animal spirits" of greed on Wall Street receded and the speculative fever driving the stock markets higher began to disappear.

## MINSKY'S REVULSION

The Minsky word for all this liquidation and hoarding is "Revulsion"—revulsion of our global financial system insofar as we know it. Heightened tensions in the credit markets have led to several panics along the way. The Germans call these runs on hedge funds and banks "torschlusspanik" or "door-shut-panic," where most investors are trying to get out the door of these now discredited institutions at the same time before it slams shut, leaving behind only the trusting souls and unsuspecting.

The problem with everyone rushing to get out of their risky assets at the same time is that it leads to John Maynard Keynes Paradox of Thrift (as we mentioned before), which has an inherently deflationary impact (as Pimco's Paul McCulley illustrates so well for us). The principle behind Keynes' Paradox of Thrift is that what is good for the individual is not necessarily good for the "community of individuals." While it may benefit the individual to sell his or her risky assets, if everyone tries to do the very same thing at the same time, which happens when the "door-shut-panic" occurs, there are never enough buyers to absorb all the selling pressure. Liquidity dries up under these conditions, and the overall effect is overwhelmingly deflationary on asset valuations.

The financial engineering of propping up and inflating asset values over the past 25 years worked wonderfully, until one day it no longer did. What happened? To answer that, we have to first recognize that the way our financial system has been crafted in the past

25 years has been built entirely upon a game of confidences with increasing counterparty and bilateral risks being taken along the way (more on bilateral counterparty risks later). When confidence in the financial markets fled in August 2007, so did the liquidity. Had the rationale for the crisis of confidence later been invalidated, perhaps all we would have had was a liquidity crisis. Unfortunately, there was good reason for the paradigm shift in investor expectations, so much so that the liquidity crisis evolved into a widespread solvency crisis as conditions worsened.

## CONFIDENCE GAME IN SUBPRIME LOANS COMES TO AN AWFUL END

Shake the confidence, the confidence game ends, and investors flee the financial markets like rats from a sinking ship. As the author Samuel Clemens penned in his 1873 novel *The Gilded Age: A Tale of Today*:

> Beautiful Credit! The foundation of modern society. Who shall say this is not the age of mutual trust, of unlimited reliance on human promises? That is a peculiar condition of modern society which enables a whole country to instantly recognize point and meaning to the familiar newspaper anecdote "I wasn't worth a cent two years ago, and now I owe two million dollars.[42]

Clemens wrote *The Gilded Age* during the stock market crash and Panic of 1873 when the railroad boom came to an end. The railroad bonds of the "Gilded Age" compare favorably to the subprime loans of 2007, when the subprime boom came to an end. The foundations of both societies were dependent on huge amounts of debt—debts that were ultimately too big to possibly be manageable. The Panic of 1873 was precipitated by the bankruptcy of the Philadelphia banking firm Jay Cooke and Company. It was the onset of a severe economic depression in the U.S. that lasted until 1877. Jay Cooke and Company suffered the plight of what happens when all booms go bust: liquidity suddenly disappears. As Bloomberg's Caroline Baum stated in June 2008: "The thing about liquidity is, it's adequate until it isn't."[43] In the midst of a railroad boom, Jay Cooke and Company suddenly found themselves unable to market several million dollars of railroad bonds. Their subsequent bankruptcy officially marked the end to the railroad boom.

Fast forward 144 years, and we can look to the failure of Bear Stearns' mortgage-related hedge funds as precipitating the official end to the U.S. housing boom, even though the housing boom had peaked about a year earlier. Suddenly, everything subprime-related became toxic waste. Toxic waste is the modern-day version of Minsky's "revulsion." No one would lend anymore to institutions holding mortgage-backed securities.

This led Pimco's Bill Gross to say on August 23, 2007, "the commercial paper market, in terms of the asset-backed commercial paper market, is basically history."[44] Gross turned out to be disturbingly right, but he certainly did not know how so! The commercial paper market started dying slowly in August 2007, perhaps by around 35% over the next several months. But the real death blow was dealt by the bankruptcy of Lehman Brothers in September 2008.

## THE DEATH OF THE COMMERCIAL PAPER MARKET

If you ever need to wonder why the Fed, the U.S. Treasury, and lawmakers were shaking in their boots in September 2008, all you need to do is consider the following chart illustrating the overnight collapse of the entire commercial paper market!

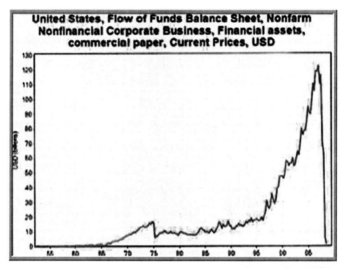

United States, Flow of Funds Balance Sheet, Nonfarm
Nonfinancial Corporate Business, Financial assets,
commercial paper, Current Prices, USD

Source: GaveKal Research

Based on this collapse, our policymakers' fears proved to be well-founded. The commercial paper market is indeed a vital source of short-term credit for American businesses. Without access to a short-term funding source, many businesses would certainly fail. The immediate policy response was to get the banks, our financial intermediaries, lending again, no matter what the cost.

Had they just taken a step back and thought it through beyond their moment of panic, and BREATHED, rather than cramming/forcing handouts into banks who said they did not want them, perhaps they could have created an RFC-type lending agency on a national level that all businesses could borrow from directly. That is, we could possibly have created a lasting and viable solution that did not require these mortally wounded financial intermediaries. Perhaps a national lending agency could have funded all the local credit unions and community banks that could then provide short-term borrowing needs directly to the local entities that needed them. We should have done something on this order, precisely because our financial intermediaries are mortally wounded (though they will not admit it), and because of this fact, they are still not lending. Moreover, they will continue be reticent to extend credit while the asset side of their balance sheets are still eroding, no matter how many TARP dollars are crammed down their throats. I say we just let them be, give the patients some much-needed rest and time to recover!

While I do not take credit for this alternative solution, this appears to be a fine alternative to continuing to try to push the lending needs of our economy through the financial intermediaries that failed us and will be handcuffed until home prices stop falling. Albert Einstein once said that "The definition of insanity is doing the same thing over and over again and expecting different results." If you stop and think about it for a minute, that is exactly what the U.S. Treasury and legislators expected with their TARP plan. Namely, that if they simply recapped our ailing financial institutions, these banks would and should go out and start lending again. Well, how can they possibly start lending again when the assets on their books are still declining and when the fear and mistrust about the creditworthiness of counterparties are so high that it caused a total collapse of the commercial paper market? Such a course of action, going around our financial intermediaries, would also help reduce the tight linkages in the financial system that increases the systemic risks and the potential for abuses.

## TRUST IS VOLATILE, AND NOT ALWAYS EASILY REPAIRED

Trust is a volatile commodity. Lose or otherwise break the trust and confidence in the financial system breaks down and is immediately zeroed. That perhaps answers best why Minsky viewed all financial systems as inherently unstable. This is all the more true as our government and Federal Reserve officials begin tampering with or modifying the sanctity of contractual obligations, such as freezing the adjustable rate mortgages (ARMs) in late 2007.

In early 2008, the Federal Reserve even went so far as to ask lenders to "write down mortgage principals." In essence, this request really amounted to asking banks and mortgage lenders to forgive a portion of the principal contractually owed to them by homeowners. By Q2 2008 the notion of "forgiveness loans" had suddenly become very appealing to many, although this Fed proposal was initially rebuked by U.S. Treasury Secretary Henry Paulson at the end of February 2008 as being a "non-starter." However, even though Paulson modified his views a few months later, modifying mortgage loans by reducing the principal amount owed has never really caught on as late as December 2008.

That said, reducing the principal owed, I understand, has been successfully tried in previous housing busts. But one of the major obstacles to successfully modifying loans this go-around is that we have securitized them and resold them all. The banks that originated the mortgage loans to begin with no longer own them. The original mortgages have been resold to holders of mortgage-backed securities, which greatly complicates any possibility of extricating or unwinding this subprime and ARM mess we have gotten ourselves into. So, while some loans have been and will be modified, the majority of homeowners in need of a loan mod will still eventually end in default and finally foreclosure. Worse, of homeowners who had their loans modified in the first half of 2008, more than half of them were already re-defaulting less than six months later. The fact that the re-default rate is so high in 2008 indicates this foreclosure crisis is far more insidious than any other since the Great Depression, and real solutions are not easily had.

## MINSKY'S "DISPLACEMENT" THEORY IN ACTION

So what actually triggered a Minsky displacement in the financial markets? It was the Bear Stearns July 2007 announcement that their hedge fund investors would be getting little to no money back that dramatically altered the global economic outlook and changed profit opportunities in the equity markets worldwide. Shortly thereafter, within weeks, the major credit markets froze up in the first half of August 2007. This would ultimately lead to a total collapse of the global financial system 13 months later, in September 2008. For all intents and purposes, the U.S. and several other stock markets also peaked in that July 2007 announcement—even though the actual final price highs were in October 2007, a few months later. The October 2007 equity highs were very short-lived and qualify as what we call a "false breakout" or "headfake."

While the credit and equity markets were imploding after August 2007, crude oil prices embarked on a campaign to go from $69 in August 2007 to $147 by June 2008, gold prices went from $643 to $1033, soybeans went from $7.89 to $15.70, and wheat went from $6.20 to $13.00. We will delve into the subsequent unravelings in the financial markets later on. These were characteristics of a true Minsky displacement in action. The final downward adjustments of the U.S. dollar within the global monetary system were being made.

As a footnote, it took the S&P 500 five years to double in price from the bear market low in 2002 to the peak in 2007. Crude oil prices more than doubled in ten months from August 2007 to June 2008 alone. If we go back a bit further to the start of the new millennium, we find that crude oil prices have risen more than tenfold over the past decade, while the U.S. dollar fell 40% and the U.S. stock market remained in a sideways trading range during the same time span. Truly, much of the first decade of the new millennium has been a boom in commodities and a bust in equities, until another

Minsky's displacement led to a debt-deflation spiral in the second half of 2008 that caused both equities and commodities to crash.

## POSSIBLE CULMINATION OF A 60-YEAR CREDIT BOOM

This particular financial crisis has been dubbed to be "the culmination of a super boom that has lasted for more than 60 years"[45] and which had its roots in the post-WWII economic expansion, according to George Soros. It is possible, with the benefit of hindsight, that Soros will be proven right. Only time will tell. Certainly the credit crisis so far has exhibited shades of the Great Depression of the 1930s, though a rerun of the 1930s is far from an inevitability. It should also be pointed out that many highly prominent economists such as Gave-Kal Research and the Bank Credit Analyst (BCA), among others, take exception to Soros's "Peak Credit" paradigm. One should never lightly underestimate government and central bank resolves to reflate sinking economies. They will die trying. Since Soros is not likely underestimating that resolve, he is probably indicating that he believes the central banks will fail to reflate the economy. The deflationary forces are leaning towards Soros' perspective, but the economy can probably begin to reflate after home prices stop falling at some point in 2009-2010.

## KNIGHTIAN UNCERTAINTY

All financial crises have an aura of "Knightian uncertainty" about them, which implies they are highly unpredictable and unquantifiable. That is the angst that confronts the financial markets and us as individuals today. Those who contemplate the worst-case scenarios recognize they are far from being remote possibilities. They carry the weight of that existential angst with them every day. And it is within this context that I write. "It is always a mistake for the historian to try to predict the future. Life, unlike science, is simply too full of surprises,"[46] notes Richard Evans.

In Kindleberger's assessment, what made the 1930s Depression so horrible was the absence of an international lender of last resort. Great Britain was "exhausted by the war and groggy from an aborted recovery of the 1920s"[47] and so was unable to act as a lender of last resort. The U.S. was simply unwilling, at least until it was too late. Seventy-five years later, it should be noted that the U.S. was already running a fairly substantial fiscal deficit to fund the Iraq war and such. This may limit its ability to act as a lender of last resort. Many economists advocate the creation of a Global Monetary Authority or central bank to assume that role. Thus far, the Federal Reserve and U.S. Treasury, with the organized help of other central bankers throughout the world, have been able to collectively act as the lender of last resort. But what this crisis has proved is that any one central bank, even if it is the central bank of the world's reserve currency, is too small a player to act successfully and independently as a lender of last resort, indicating others may join Kindleberger's call to establish a Global Monetary Authority in the coming years.

One of the "lessons our policymakers learned from the banking crises of the Great Depression was that governments should bail out depositors when banks fail,"[48] notes former International Monetary Consultant Richard Duncan and author of *The Dollar Crisis: Causes, Consequences, Cures*—a substantive and relevant tome. From that lesson, policymakers have extrapolated forward that the government ought to bail out any bank, insurance company or other financial firm deemed "too big to fail." We may find one day that this is a mistaken goal on their behalf. Duncan adds that:

> The lesson that may be learned from the current set of crises is that governments themselves may go bankrupt in attempting to bail out [not just] the depositors, but the banks

> themselves! Global economic stability will only
> be restored when policymakers implement
> measures that eliminate the disequilibrium in
> the international balance of payments that has
> caused these crises.[49]

Many analysts have been openly wondering and discussing the Fed's waning ability to effectively intervene in the financial markets throughout this decade: first in 2001-2002 and now again in 2007-2008. As I write this, the Fed and U.S. Treasury are working furiously to cushion the economy as it slips into a deep recession. They have cut short-term borrowing rates almost to zero, created all sorts of new lending facilities that accept as collateral all sorts of debt instruments of dubious character (toxic waste), and taken over some of our most prominent financial institutions. Shaky forms of collateral now sit on both the Fed's balance sheets (the troubled assets wound up on the Fed's balance sheet and not in the TARP program as was the TARP program's original intent). The financial risks to the U.S. are elevated. It has become a high-stakes poker game for the Fed and U.S. government. If all does not go according to plan — and what has for them in 2008—they may need a lifeline from a global lender of last resort in subsequent years.

## THE DANGER OF BELIEVING THAT THE GODS ARE STILL IN THEIR TEMPLES

The broad consensus/informed view is that our own central banks' efforts work most effectively when coordinated with other major central banks. Organized support is generally a good thing. The unfortunate reality is that other central bankers' objectives are not and will not always be the same as our own. In fact, the Federal Reserve's aggressive accommodation policies, which are inherently inflationary, left other central banks aggressively fighting those same inflationary effects to maintain price stability in their own countries during the first half of 2008. So, while at times the Federal Reserve may find and enjoy brief moments of organized support from various other central banks, it is dubious such organization can be synchronized or sustained over the long haul.

Investor confidence, which had been shaken badly when the credit crisis began in August 2007, did not crumble immediately. It worsened as the housing crisis evolved and morphed into a full-blown recession. Many informed people thought the Federal Reserve might pull a lucky rabbit out of a hat with a shift in monetary policy towards easing and aggressive fed funds rate cuts back in September 2007. However, with the benefit of hindsight a year later, we found there was no such rabbit in the magician's hat. Aggressive monetary easing did not manage to avert an economic meltdown.

Investor confidence is a resilient animal, and only relents slowly and unwillingly. This fact has its parallel in the stock market crash of 1929. The 1929 stock market peaked on September 3, 1929, at 386 points. John Kenneth Galbraith, author of the *Great Crash 1929*, noted that "confidence did not disintegrate at once." Through September 1929 and into October there were signs that indicated "the gods of the New Era were still in their temples." Chairman of National City Bank (now just Citibank) Charles Mitchell announced on October 15, 1929, that the "industrial condition of the U.S. is absolutely sound, that too much attention to broker loans...nothing can arrest the upward movement."[50]

## THE MYTH OF ORGANIZED SUPPORT

As late as Sunday, October 20, 1929, with the stock market down just 13% from its peak valuation of 386, investor confidence remained high in spite of a declining market. In fact, investors speculated that the next day the "market would receive organized support. Never was there a phrase with more magic than "organized support." Almost immediately it was on every tongue and in every news story about the market,"[51] says Galbraith. Organized support is intended to bolster the financial markets and instill confidence in the gods still sitting on their thrones.

We also hear this theme of organized support echoed throughout the financial crisis of 2007-2008. Moody's Economy.com's chief economist Mark Zandi found himself "encouraged" that "global policymakers" were working together in August 2007. Market participants were also relieved to see Bank of America raise capital for Countrywide Financial in August 2007 and January 2008. When banks like Citigroup, Merrill Lynch and others needed to raise capital, investors were heartened to see sovereign wealth funds provide much-needed funds to meet their capital requirements. The same went for the bond insurers MBIA and AMBAC throughout the first half of 2008, for the rescue of Bear Stearns by the Fed and JP Morgan, and for the government guarantee and bailout of Fannie Mae and Freddie Mac. Unfortunately for Lehman Brothers, the safety nets were unexpectedly pulled out from underneath them on September 15, 2008. Not a buyer in the world could be found to prevent their bankruptcy filing.

Throughout the 2007-2008 banking crisis, there has already been an unprecedented amount of organized support coming from all corners of the world, with no end in sight. And while this is generally a good thing, this support has as yet only managed to prop up the moribund house of cards upon which our financial institutions have been built. Moreover, our economy and the global economy continue to sink ever deeper into a recession. Without such support, of course, the financial system would have already entirely collapsed.

Typically, during substantial and prolonged crises, it takes a few years of corporate bankruptcies and the like before organized support begins to take effect. Getting there from here is no simple matter. Monetary and fiscal policies work with a lag, as they say. We are closer to getting there as 2008 comes to a close, but realistically the economic downturn could well push out to 2010-2011. As the theory goes, the strong swimmers that survive the recession/ depression are then in a better position to thrive as they are able to increase market share under much less competition. Since the current downturn is only a year old as we work our way through the second half of 2008, our weakening economy is still a year or more away before the economy begins to grow and GDP can even think of growing towards its potential again. We will need to get people working again to grow GDP.

## THE TAPE DOESN'T LIE/TRADE WHAT YOU SEE, NOT WHAT YOU BELIEVE

Investors and traders can believe in any myth they wish to, but the tape doesn't lie. The investment community must learn to do their due diligence and listen to the tape. Flipping back to the crash of 1929, if the market buzz is bullish, such as it was on the eve of Sunday, October 20, 1929, and the market gaps open lower (to new move lows no less) on Monday, October 21, 1929, listen up folks, the tape of the market is screaming at you to pay attention and take appropriate action.

Those investors who failed to take action on Monday, October 21, 1929, experienced the Dow Jones plunging another 36% to the intraday lows of 212 on Tuesday, October 29, 1929, little more than a week later. By Tuesday, November 13, 1929, the market had plunged to 195. In little more than three weeks time, the Dow Jones was down 49% rather than just down 13% from peak valuations. In a similar vein, the tape began screaming to market participants that something was wildly wrong with investor confidence on September 4, 2008. That was the fateful day the market signaled investor confidence had been totally shattered. Oh, the Fed and the U.S. Treasury tried valiantly to prop up the markets in subsequent weeks, but still they could not prevent the S&P 500 from falling 42% from the September 19, 2008, high to the November 21, 2008, low!

I must make a personal yet relevant digression for a moment. To trade what you see and not what you believe is a very, very important lesson to learn, and one that I have personally struggled with over my own investment/trading career. Forty-year veteran trader Larry Pesavento teaches this market precept religiously. In fact, "trade what you see, not what you believe"[52] is the shingle Pesavento hangs on the homepage of his website, tradingtutor.com. He is the author of nine books on trading, some of which I found to be quite excellent.

I can remember my first soybean option trade in 1993, long soybean calls, sitting at home with a six-pack each night, watching the Mississippi flood washing farm homes down the river. I had four calls on, and soybean limits were set at $1,500 a day, so that meant for every limit up day, I was making $6,000 on paper. Too bad I overstayed my welcome. My belief in there having to be a "5th wave up" according to the Elliott Wave model (a model used in technical analysis) was quite misplaced. As the flooding subsided, my profits began to wash away, too.

Again, this underscores what I have said above: trading or investing in something you really believe in can be a really bad investment whether it be the Fed, Elliott Waves or some financial alchemist's supermodel. The rule for a trader or investor to live by is to "trade and invest in what you see and know, and not what you believe," as Pesavento has invoked. This should be a market mantra for everyone managing risk. Even better, tape it to your computer screen if you like to remind you every day of the rule.

## Play Great Defense

It is far better to suspend one's beliefs (after all, our belief system may not prove to always be valid, so at least always question them) and embrace "Knightian uncertainties" knowing "Minsky moments" and "hardy perennials" are not really market aberrations after all, but actually part of the market processes. Doing so sharpens the wits when it comes to managing risk. Especially in times like this, it is best to heed the following Market Wizard and famed trader Paul Tudor Jones axiom: "The most important rule of trading is to play great defense, not great offense. Every day I assume every position I have is wrong."[53] In my own experience managing risk, I find it extremely helpful to trade and invest small or not at all. Generally, this allows you to be wrong in the short term, and it allows you to not obsess at the computer screen trying to be perfect, and still put the long-term odds on your side and make a little bit of money in the process. Adjustments to one's outlook and trading strategies have to be made occasionally. Or to quote John Maynard Keynes, who once queried long ago: "When the facts change, I change: what do you do sir?"

## Three Bear Markets in Two Months

The generally accepted definition about bear markets is that the stock market has to decline 20% or more to qualify. Under that definition, we saw three full-blown bear markets condensed into two months and almost a fourth between September 19, 2008, and November 21, 2008. This is the story of our stock market crash, the likes of which has been far worse than anything seen since 1929-1932. The first two bear markets followed lawmakers' September 18, 2008, proposal to permanently fix the foreclosure crisis with their "No Bank Left Behind" act. The plan was so ill-conceived and badly botched; the stock market fell 35% in 15 days by October 10, 2008.

A wild-haired, two-day short covering rally ensued that allowed the S&P 500 to rally 27% by October 14, 2008, but that was as ill fated as all the prior short covering rallies. As a footnote, that two-day short covering rally was the two-day largest short covering rally since the 32% two-day short covering rally that began on October 29, 1929. Both were bear market rallies, followed by new bear market lows two weeks later. After the 27% two-day rally into October 14, 2008, the S&P 500 fell another 22% in nine days to another new bear market low by October 27, 2008.

Not surprisingly, the stock market caught a brief presidential election bid and rallied from the October 27, 2008, low into the November 4, 2008, election. However, the failure of the financial system in September and October had by that time spread into the real economy. The majority of voters were happy Barack Obama had been elected. But by the time of the election, banks had stopped lending to each other or anyone else, for that matter, since September. The commercial paper market had died. Funding day-to-day operations had come to a halt. It is said that in October 2008, global commerce virtually collapsed throughout the world, the Baltic Dry Index crashed. The shipping industry came to a halt because a 400-year-old world trade practice based on Letters of Credit (LOC) froze. That moved the epicenter of the crisis out of the financial system and into the real economy in October and November. Nowhere was the impact on the real economy more evident than in the auto industry.

By November, it became clear the U.S. auto industry was on the brink of bankruptcy. The CEOs of the Big Three automakers flew hat in hand to Capitol Hill in their private jets—begging for taxpayer money. Congress was not amused, and on November 19-20, 2008, refused their request for $25 billion. The gravity off the automaker's plight created such investor angst that the stock market fell another

27% by November 21, 2008 from the election high. They kicked the can and told the Big Three CEOs to come back on December 2, 2008, with a "plan" that would be viable to get them through the storm. Eventually, lawmakers kicked the can back to the White House administration.

In what was a surprise move to me, our lame duck President Bush sat on approving aid to automakers until December 20, 2008. It was a stalling technique that escalated the risks of rising corporate defaults throughout the economy. By escalating the risks in the real economy like he did, this created an unprecedented "safe haven" bid in U.S. Treasuries, which greatly benefited every single bank that had failed months earlier and received capital from U.S. taxpayers. You see, those failed banks shifted all their illiquid and toxic collateral onto the balance sheet of the Federal Reserve. The beneficent hand of the Federal Reserve gave these banks U.S. Treasuries in exchange for their toxic collateral. This act, coupled with the Federal Reserve's rate cut to 0.25% on December 18, 2008, all came at great expense to fixed income investors depending on some sort of yields to live off.

Corporate credit spreads were said to be at record levels not seen since 1932 and 1938 in Q4 08. Risk of corporate defaults/ failure with the fate of the automaker industry hanging on a limb was about one in five, according to sources. The other good news is that the corporate default risk subsided slightly after President Bush decided to provide some sort of relief to the automakers. The downside to the record credit spreads is that it still signals that a lot of companies are slated to die, and unemployment will be going significantly higher. This will have negative consequences for the real economy over the next several years.

# It's the End of the World as We Know It

*I know from studying history that credit eventually kills all great societies...If the economy starts to go with the kind of leverage that is in it, it will deteriorate so fast that people's head will spin.*[1]

—Paul Tudor Jones

CREDIT CRISES ARE AT the root of all bear markets. The general view of most economists is that excess credit creation and overinvestment leads to recessions and depressions. Bad credit has always been the bane of any society. In our particular case, too many foreign-owned U.S. dollars coming back into the U.S. generated the reserve assets to fuel the credit creation and overinvestment in the housing sector. The reckless and widespread securitization and repackaging of subprime mortgage loans did us in. These loans were bad credit risks, making these securities at best a very risky asset class, which is better classified as shaky collateral. Our banking system pushed this securitization model way too far, causing the impact of this bad credit creation to be felt around the world!

The collateral damage wreaked upon the U.S. economy and local communities has been devastating. Homeowners, businesses, banks and municipalities are defaulting anywhere and everywhere throughout the country. The busting of this credit cycle may not quite kill us as a society, but the Nietzsche-ism "that which doesn't kill us, makes us stronger" certainly does not apply, either. As a society, this bust in the credit cycle seems to have accelerated the aging process of America.

## PEAK OF THE CREDIT CYCLE

By now, most everyone has heard of "Peak Oil." Peak oil is that point in time when the maximum rate of crude oil production is reached, after which the rate of production enters its terminal decline. Much in the same way, the first half of 2007 saw the peak of credit creation.

On July 10, 2007, Bloomberg mentioned that more than a dozen companies postponed or restructured debt sales. A few days later, several economists recognized the credit cycle was peaking. Incremental risk aversion in the financial markets seems to us that the liquidity spigot is starting to tighten," said Merrill Lynch's chief investment strategist Richard Bernstein. Colorfully, he added, "the childhood alliteration to remember how to turn a spigot is 'righty-tighty, lefty-loosey.' It's now righty-tighty time for the financial markets."[2]

## SHELF LIFE EXPIRES ON MORTGAGE-RELATED PRODUCTS IN SUMMER OF 2007

Much of this "righty-tighty" activity on the liquidity spigot came about immediately after it was announced in mid-June 2007 that two of Bear Stearns mortgage-related hedge funds had blown up. This ushered in the end of the credit cycle as we knew it in the new millennium.

Months earlier, things began to get a little worrisome for those two Bear Stearns hedge funds that blew up in mid-June 2007. These hedge funds, run by Ray Cioffi and Matt Tannin, billed their products to investors as offering low-risk high-grade securities (read mortgage-backed securities and collateralized-debt obligations a.k.a. CDOs) providing annual returns of 10% to 12%. In the second half of 2006 those returns began to fall below the hedge fund managers' expectations. Privately, Cioffi and Tannin were concerned. On March 7, 2007, Cioffi wrote in an email to a colleague on March 15, 2007, "I'm fearful of these markets." [3] Two weeks later, Cioffi withdrew one third of his $6 million in the hedge fund and transferred it to another Bear Stearns product, according to federal prosecutors.

Prosecutors also allege that Tannin e-mailed Cioffi on April 22, 2007 stating that the "subprime market looks pretty damn ugly and could be toast" and further suggested that they "should close down the funds immediately" if projections for the CDO market were "anywhere close" to accurate. Publicly however, on a conference call with investors three days later, Tannin said, "We're very comfortable with exactly where we are." As a consequence, prosecutors allege that both Tannin and Cioffi misled investors and misrepresented the fund's viability. Both Cioffi and Tannin were indicted for fraud and a variety of security violations in June 2008. [4]

## STOCK MARKET "ANIMAL SPIRITS" FLEE THE SCENE OF THE CRIME: SPECULATIVE FEVER BREAKS ON VERIZON BUYOUT RUMORS

Buyouts and mergers were all the rage. Every rumor or fact of a big buyout or merger drove the broad stock market indices higher. The last big speculative rumor that hit Wall Street on July 16, 2007, and drove the Dow Jones briefly over 14,000 was that Vodafone would buy Verizon for $160 billion.

"I think just the idea of the number floated—$160 billion—gets the juices running in the market again even after this big move. It would be the biggest deal ever. I think when this might pop is where one of these big deals can't get financing. Then the game is done," said Greg Church, chief investment officer of Church Capital Management. [5] On July 18, 2007, I remember e-mailing my own clients that the hype and mania behind the VZ deal was the stuff that stock market tops are made of and that the downside risks in the stock market would be increasing.

The stock market crested that very same week. The Verizon acquisition never happened. Ten days later the "animal spirits" on Wall Street had vanished entirely. While the hype drove the Dow to 14,000, Bloomberg was quietly reporting that high yield investors had shunned at least five takeover stocks in the past month. Commenting on these financing deals that were falling through, "Many of these things are beyond our risk desires," said Bruce Monrad at Northeast Investment Management.[6]

Monrad's risk averse behavior was made all the more comprehensible when Bear Stearns announced on July 18, 2007, that the declines in their subprime hedge funds were "unprecedented," and that there was "very little value left" that could be returned to the high-yield investors who participated in their hedge funds. There have been a lot of "unprecedented" events in the months that followed, to which investors have adopted an "Oh-No, Not Again" posture with a roll of the eyes and a shake of the head.

High-yield investors' skittishness caused the investment bankers Goldman Sachs and JP Morgan, who finance these takeover deals, to become "lenders of last resort." JPM and GS began writing "bridge loans" to cover these failed debt offerings to high-yield investors. When high-yield investors, for reasons of prudence, disappear, the banks that finance these takeover deals must provide a bridge loan to the borrower, tying up capital that would otherwise be used to finance more deals. This is precisely how liquidity begins to suddenly dry up.

"The underwriters are going to be forced to provide bridge loans and it's getting pretty ugly, but Wall Street deserves to get smacked around a little, it's been so easy for so long," said William Featherston, managing director in high-yield at J. Giordano Securities LLC.[7] Little did Featherston know how badly these firms would be smacked around.

## PRUDENT HIGH-YIELD INVESTORS PUT LIQUIDITY IN FINANCIAL SYSTEM AT RISK

Who'da thunk it? Just a few months before the August 2007 credit crunch, bankers were boasting that "demand for high yield assets was so great that they would have no problem raising debt for a $100B LBO." Now, "the cost of tying up their own capital may curb earnings and stem the flood of LBOs," according to Brad Hintz, former Lehman CFO.[8]

As Jim Caron put it that week, "the problem isn't that Bear Stearns has a hedge fund that lost money. The problem arises when the lenders of capital stop lending or charge higher rates."[9] In the first half of 2007, you couldn't find a prudent man in a crowd of lenders. In fact, the prudent man had been trampled to death by the stampeding herd of animal spirits. Suddenly, lenders got a whole lot of religion and became more than just a tad circumspect. Following their "Come to Jesus" moment prudent men began popping up everywhere.

This meant the takeover and merger mania would substantially subside from that point forward. This also meant that the takeover premium in the stock market would disappear. What we didn't know at the time was that the mergers and acquisitions (M&A) game would fall off a cliff entirely. The M&A game would later morph into a bailout and rescue (B&R) game.

## SENSING A "WATERSHED CHANGE IN INVESTOR PERCEPTIONS"

In a newsletter to my clients in July 2007, I opined that investor's glee with regard to takeovers, stock buybacks and earnings growth rates thus far in 2007, and in particular the Verizon buyout announcement, would reflect a peak in investor sentiment.

About the same time, Morgan Stanley's Richard Berner also commented that "the interplay of weak economic data, fears of a credit crunch, lingering inflation risks and rising energy prices, combined with the reduction in liquidity, are producing rapid changes in asset prices. And I sense that those factors are promoting a watershed change in investor perceptions."[10]

## SUBPRIME SPILLOVER RISKS BEGIN TO MOUNT

Economy.com also reported that same week that subprime risks were continuing "to mount" as the ABX index (a synthetic asset-backed security index for the 20 largest mortgage deals of the last six months) "takes a beating." The index had already fallen 50% by August 2007. The credit rating agency downgrades of mortgage lenders by Moody's and Standard & Poor's that month was a primary culprit for the extreme weakness in that index.

The problem, as Economy.com saw it at the time, was that "while the lowest rated [ABX] tranches are the first line of defense, there has been increased selling pressure in higher rated tranches." Tranches are a market euphemism that divides and categorizes low-grade mortgage securities from high-grade mortgage securities along a defined continuum. Increasingly, investors were concerned the troubles may not be entirely isolated to the subprime securities market. In other words, spillover risks into the prime market had grown, and Economy.com recommended keeping an eye on the ABC 07-1AAA. If this index deteriorated, they said, "it may foreshadow weakness in the prime market."[11]

## INVESTOR AND CONSUMER OPTIMISM REACH THEIR LIMITS OF ELASTICITY

The charts above show investor confidence peaked at the end of 2006 and consumer confidence peaked in late February 2007. Both these sentiment indicators acted as leading indicators five to seven months early. There was a mild rebound in sentiment that coincided with an upward shift in the economy, as reported by economists for Q2 07. However, it was a false signal. On July 26, 2007, Scott MacDonald, di-

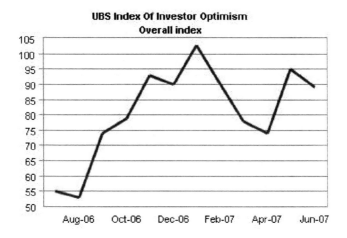

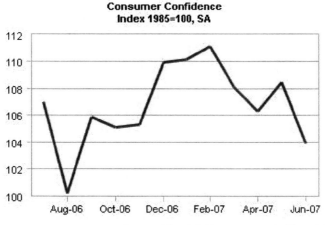

Source: Moody's Economy.com's Dismal Scientist

rector of research at Aladdin Capital, quipped "you have a stampede of the animals away from the watering hole. Right now, everything that smacks of financial risk is backing out through the door."[12]

By December 2008, with the entire global economy deep in recession and darkly pessimistic about the first half of 2009, the stampede away from the watering hole of risk took on new dimensions. Investor confidence plunged to a record low -31.5%. Likewise, consumer confidence fell to its lowest level on record going back to the inception of the index in 1969, indicating consumers feel their economic conditions are worse than they were in the 1981-1982 recession and the 1974 recession. There is a silver lining to the shift in sentiment to record lows: it is a contrarian indicator. The only question is when does it begin to turn back up? We don't know the answer to that yet.

## AUGUST 9, 2007—A FULL-BLOWN CREDIT CRUNCH ARRIVES—ECB RESPONDS VIGOROUSLY

Responding to the credit markets sudden demand for cash roiled by the subprime mortgage collapse in the U.S., the European Central Bank injected $130 billion into the money markets. "The ECB said it will launch an unlimited fine-tuning operation to assure orderly conditions in the euro money market. It intends to allot 100 percent of the bids it receives."[13]

"This is probably the most serious step of all taken since the subprime crisis started," said Glen Capelo, at RBS Greenwich Capital.[14]

## A HOLE IN THE BALANCE SHEET OF WORLD INC

"There seems to be a hole in the balance sheet of World Inc. that will have to be filled by government intervention. The ECB is treating this like an emergency," said Peter Lynch, chairman of Prime Active Capital.[15]

BNP Paribas had to halt withdrawals from funds that owned subprime loans that day because it couldn't value the holdings reported Bloomberg. "For some of the securities there are just no prices. As there are no prices, we can't calculate the value of the funds," said Alain Papiasse, head of BNP Paribas's asset management.[16]

"It looks hideous out there. The fear is obviously not that BNP Paribas has a problem, but that it's much more widespread," said John Wilson, co-director of equity strategy at Morgan Keegan & Co.[17]

"This is an old-fashioned credit crunch. This is not a small thing. A credit crunch, when the short-term credit markets seize up, is extraordinarily serious, almost always the precursor of a significant recession," said Chris Low, the chief economist at FTN Financial.[18]

The next day, on August 10, 2007, the ECB pumped another $83.6 billion into the banking system, and the U.S. Federal Reserve added another $35 billion on top of the $24 billion to the reserves on the previous day. The Bank of Japan chipped in $8.5 billion to the financial system, according to Bloomberg. All told, these three central bankers pumped $281 billion into the money markets in just two days. Moody's Economy.com's chief economist Mark Zandi, who is usually optimistically balanced, had the following thoughts on August 10, 2007:

> Pressure on financial markets is likely to remain intense. Global hedge funds and investors are forced to realize very substantial losses. Forcing this repricing are investor redemptions in the hedge funds, and margin calls by other financial institutions worried they won't be repaid by the faltering hedge funds...there is a significant amount of repricing yet to occur, and more hedge funds and investors will stumble.
>
> Financial markets broadly are panicked at this prospect. Investors, not knowing where the next problem will be, are increasingly unwilling to take any risk at all. Liquidity is thus evaporating in the riskiest markets, but increasingly in nearly all markets. Issuance of subprime, alt-A, and jumbo mortgage loans has come to a standstill; high-yield corporate bond issuance is a trickle.

With investor sentiment frayed, less and less separates the current liquidity problem from a full-blown credit crunch. The economic implications would be serious, as free-flowing credit is the mother's milk of a well-functioning economy. Policymakers must be prepared to respond more boldly unless markets quickly find their footing.

Most encouraging is that today's events show global policymakers are working together and will not make a mistake. The current financial market turmoil should thus ultimately prove to be no more than a therapeutic cleansing of financial excesses.[19]

Up until August 10, 2007, one could almost always count on Moody's chief economist Mark Zandi to find an optimistic spin to almost anything. But by then, even Dr. Zandi had adopted a much more circumspect point of view. We can say a change in expectations from a state of confidence to a lack thereof in the future had come about—organized support or not from global policymakers. It happened in a matter of several weeks. Zandi's sense of alarm that week was shared by several other market participants. Richard Berner's watershed change in investor perceptions was the new reality.

## AUGUST 10, 2007—MARKET PARTICIPANTS CHILLED BY PANIC AS CREDIT MARKETS FREEZE

"The market is in panic mode. It is a full-blown unwinding of the carry trade. This is just the beginning," said Michael Woolfolk, currency strategist at the Bank of New York.[20]

"There's panic in the market, that's the bottom line. There are now systemic issues and risk," said David Ader, head of U.S. government bond strategy at RBS Greenwich.[21]

"Data doesn't matter. This is all about the fear of the system ceasing to function properly," said Thomas Roth, head of U.S. government bond trading at Dresdner Kleinwort, a primary dealer.[22]

Money funds that had been buying corporate commercial paper "have all switched to the safe side. I'm sure their managers have all given them a Treasury-only mandate, at least until the dust settles," said Glen Capelo at RBS Greenwich Capital.[23]

ECB President Jean-Claude Trichet, in perhaps the most understated comment on the collapse of the subprime credit market that week, said on August 17, 2007, that the market tumult "can be interpreted as a normalization of the pricing of risk." To which Tullett Prebon economist Lena Komileva shot back, "The ECB should recognize that the process of risk normalization is threatening to become disorderly. It's becoming a textbook financial meltdown now."[24]

"As a practical matter, banks both here and abroad don't want to lend for any period longer than overnight. The 'term' market is virtually frozen," said a NY bank funding desk.[25]

In a footnote that same day Bloomberg mentioned in passing that the $1.1 trillion market for commercial paper used to buy assets from mortgages to car loans has seized up just as more than half of that amount comes due in the next 90 days, according to the Federal Reserve. This passing footnote implied there would be year-end funding needs approximating $550 billion that would need to be met by mid-November. As the credit crisis worsened in November 2007, the Fed would begin opening up new lending facilities to keep the ever-so-shaky credit system alive.

August 17, 2007, ended with FTN chief economist Christopher Low mentioning that the credit crunch is "getting uglier and uglier. This has moved beyond temporary," he said. "It's gotten beyond bailing out some hedge fund and into the broad economy."[26] Chris Low's comments gave us all food for thought as the first wave of panic began to subside. Little more than a year later, the credit crisis of August 2007 morphed into something far more nefarious than a simple normalization of risk as ECB President Trichet intimated. And it was no longer just a textbook example of a financial meltdown. The magnitude of the subprime crisis had morphed into something comparable to the South Sea Bubble, Tulip-mania, and the Great Depression.

## CONTRASTING THE PANIC OF AUGUST 2007 WITH THE PANIC OF 1929

The panic of August 2007, which was semi-arrested by August 17, 2007, had evolved into a mini-sized version of the panic that began on October 24, 1929. As described by John Kenneth Galbraith: "Measured by disorder, fright, and confusion, Thursday, October 24, 1929, is the day most closely associated with the panic of 1929. That day "shattered the dreams and hopes" of shareholders, said Galbraith.

> "Often there were no buyers, and only after wide vertical declines could anyone be induced to bid...By eleven o'clock the market had degenerated into a wild, mad scramble to sell... By eleven-thirty, the market had surrendered to blind, relentless fear. This indeed was panic."

On Monday, October 28, 1929, the day's decline "was greater than that of all the preceding week of panic. On this day there was no recovery... Support, organized or otherwise, could not contend with the overwhelming pathological desire to sell."[27]

One distinguishing characteristic that sets August 2007 apart from October 1929 was that the organized support and reassurances from central bankers and market participants in August 2007 actually worked for a spell. This may be because economists and market analysts could "credibly" point to the improved balance sheets of U.S. companies, the cushion from global growth acting as a boon to U.S. GDP in the form of increased exports, and the overriding belief that the toxic waste from subprime-related assets would not entirely spill over into the prime markets, etc. In short, the story in August 2007 had another side to it that was not entirely panic-driven doom and gloom. But still, the initial scare of August 2007 was very real and only morphed into an all-out nightmare 13 months later, in September 2008.

In October 1929, reassurances utterly failed to support the markets in any way whatsoever. Utterances from President Hoover that "the fundamental business of the country...is on a sound and prosperous basis" fell on deaf ears as did John D. Rockefeller's echoed sentiment that ran "believing the fundamental conditions of the country are sound, my son and I have been purchasing sound stocks."[28] Not only did these reassurances fail to inspire investors in any way, but worse, the fundamentals were actually "turning sour" notes Galbraith, as the "slump had extended to commodity markets. So the reassurances were disingenuous as well. Markets abhor false reassurances.

## REAL ESTATE LOANS AND THE STOCK MARKET CRASH OF 1929

In *Manias, Panics, and Crashes*, Charles Kindleberger points out that the real estate economist Homer Hoyt drew a connection to real estate and speculation in real estate. Unlike stock market speculators who wind up in trouble and just sell to square their accounts, "speculators in real estate initially feel no such compunction." Their debts are backed by real assets, "not just paper claims. They can wait out recovery which will come soon, or so they think."[29] We would all do well to remember that paper claims are a very shaky foundation, particularly the modern day mortgage-backed securities that have led to the demise of the financial system in the new millennium.

But when an economic downturn is accompanied by slack in real estate demand, the hoped for recovery doesn't arrive, but the "taxes and interest on loans go on without interruption," notes Kindleberger:

> Slowly but inexorably, so Hoyt writes with great prescience in a book that came out in 1933, the speculator is ground down. With him, moreover, suffers the bank. In 1933, 163 out of 200 [Chicago] banks suspended payment. Real-estate loans, not failed stockbroker accounts were the largest single element in the failure of 4,800 banks in the years from 1930 to 1933.[30]

## DANGEROUS SECURITIES WITH LONG FUSES

The havoc wreaked by real estate loans is accounted for in the thousands of letters received and testimonies taken by the Congressional Committee to Investigate Real Estate Bond Reorganizations. Guaranteed mortgages and real estate loans were far from being the .gilt-edged and ultraconservative investments billed and packaged by the promoters, i.e. bankers, underwriters and mortgage companies issuing them. They were actually explosive devices with long fuses certain to detonate three to five years later on conservative bond-holders, who had no legal recourse or other means to redeem their bonds for more than pennies on the dollar.

The chairman of the Congressional Committee to Investigate Real Estate Bond Reorganizations, Adolph J. Sabath, relates that "upwards of $8 billion of real estate bonds out of approximately $10 billion issued directly affected 4,000,000 and indirectly upwards of 20,000,000 of our citizens." These supposedly conservative mortgage investments were highly speculative vehicles being sold unsuspectingly to the

> thrifty hard working citizens of the nation. Many had placed their life savings in these real estate securities so that, in the evening of life, they might live pridefully independent of gratuities...only to be destitute today.
>
> The unfortunate feature is that a considerable portion of this vast fortune in real estate bonds represents the savings of very aged men and women, many of whom are living on the charity of friends and relatives or on public relief...[31]

As the American public continued to languish, so too did the banks eventually. And nowhere "was the banking crisis so prolonged or so tense as in Detroit." It was the closing of all the banks in Detroit on February 14, 1933, that precipitated the collapse of the "nation's entire financial system." [32] Detroit banks were the principal domino that triggered the U.S. government declaring a two-week banking holiday in the first two weeks of March 1933, during which the stock exchanges were also closed.

President Hoover telephoned Henry Ford at the height of the banking crisis to discuss a rescue plan. Mr. Ford agreed to listen to President Hoover's men explain Hoover's rescue plan at great length. Hoover's men conferred to Mr. Ford that if he proceeded with his intentions to withdraw his deposits from First Wayne National, First Wayne would go under. And if First Wayne went under, all banks in Michigan would have to close and then spread to all the other neighboring states and so on. Mr. Ford's reply was "All right then, let us have it that way, let the crash come." According to Jesse H. Jones, Henry Ford felt that if the entire system collapsed, there would be a blood letting and "cleaning up process and everybody would then have to get to work." Ford wasn't that concerned, figuring that whatever happened, he still had his millions to work with and "was sure he could again build up a business, as he still felt young." [33]

Tales of the 1933 banking holiday relate that the U.S. government was bankrupt. The Federal Reserve Bank, which was ostensibly created back in 1913 to end all bank runs failed in its mission to prevent bank runs that year. Things were so grim in February and March 1933 that the authors Bernard Reis and John Flynn of *False Security: The Betrayal of the American Investor* (circa 1937) relates:

> ...the fear and terror which seized the citizenry of this carefree country, as calamity upon calamity followed with such rapidity as to tread upon each other's heels, can readily be recalled...queues of people stood pitifully and helplessly before closed bank doors.[34]

Bernard Reis and John Flynn note that the calamity was not strictly limited to guaranteed mortgage loans and real estate bonds to mom and pop citizens, but also extended to foreign bonds, investment trusts, and the issuance of highly dubious stock securities.

The author of *House of Morgan*, Ron Chernow, concluded that the Foreign Bond Daddy peddlers of Wall Street in the 1920s had "badgered small investors into buying bonds issued in places they could scarcely pronounce...too many bankers again chased too few good deals, and credit standards eroded accordingly."[35]

Looking back at the train wreck of foreign bond defaults in the 1930s, Otto Kahn, a partner of Kuhn and Loeb, noted that American bankers were sitting around in South and Central American countries, "one outbidding the other foolishly, recklessly, to the detriment of the public."[36]

The blind faith of the trusting American investor of the 1920s in Wall Street bankers was literally rocked off its foundations by the time the U.S. government declared the two-week banking holiday in 1933. The modern day financial institutions of the new millennium can be likened to 1920 Wall Street banksters. Both were chasing too few good deals, sold and securitized the crappiest of loans and credit ratings eroded accordingly.

## STAN "THE MAN" O'NEAL'S RECKLESS INVESTMENTS IN SUBPRIME LOANS WITH LONG FUSES

Some of the better examples describing the attitude typifying the egregious errors of judgment and reckless risk-taking of Wall Street banks in the new millennium are found in statements by Citigroup's ousted CEO "Chuck" Prince and Merrill Lynch's ousted CEO Stan O'Neal. Chuck Prince told the *Financial Times* in July 2007 that "When the music stops, in terms of liquidity, things will be complicated. But as long as the music is playing, you've got to get up and dance. We're still dancing."[37]

To Prince's credit, he gave the impression of standing in the kitchen and taking the heat for his reckless risk-taking and for recognizing that when the music stopped, a disruptive event would ensue and the transition would be a difficult one.

O'Neal, on the other hand, lapsed into what may best be described as an episode of escapism on the golf course. We all have different ways of dealing with stress, and for O'Neal, a retreat to the links seemed to work best for him. At the height of the subprime meltdown, reported Bloomberg author Michael Lewis, O'Neal squeezed in 20 rounds of golf from August 12 through September 30, 2008— alone! Clues to O'Neal's escapist behavior were to be found, amazingly enough, on the back of his scorecards that Bloomberg's Michael

Lewis found on file with the USGA. How Michael Lewis ever came across these scorecards in the first place, I don't know. It's a mystery, but what a find! After shooting an 83 on August 31, 2008, O'Neal wrote, "Stan is the certainly the man!" On September 22, 2008, after shooting a round of 80, he wrote "Eighty makes me greaty!"

On his August 12, 2008, scorecard he wrote "All alone of the course. Had a thought: No one knows where I am! Really! Turned off cell phone. Five hours later, I wondered: Where did the time go? A perfect day."

On August 18, 2008, O'Neal had another thought: "Golf is like running Merrill Lynch. The trick is to keep it simple. Be a big-picture person. Note to self: smartest thing you ever did was to take firm away from the day to day drudgery and make just a few big bets—frees up time."

On September 22, 2008, O'Neal encountered a water hazard that prompted him to emote: "Freaking, freaking, water hazard!! Freaking, freaking, freaking water hazard!!! Remember: Bigger bets at ML mean less time having to think about the firm, and less time in office means more time to swim for balls. Best case scenario: Find ball. Worst-case scenario: $160 million payout."

By September 22, 2008, O'Neal's contemplation of the worst-case scenario implied he recognized his days were numbered and that he would most likely soon be fired. That said, O'Neal's worst-case scenario was everyone else's dream lottery ticket. The $160 million payout (read that twice) was his "golden parachute" that he would receive for his time and troubles at Merrill. All told, facing a $160 million golden parachute was not much downside risk for the CEO of one of Wall Street's largest financial firms taking recklessly big bets in the subprime markets and bringing the company to its knees. Given that Merrill Lynch's bubble earnings during the subprime securitization boom were entirely fictitious, there should be some sort of clawback provision that takes back O'Neal's golden parachute.

On August 26, 2008, O'Neal had forgotten to turn off his cell phone and it rang while he was chipping out of a bunker. Bitching about his day job, he complained, "Freaking markets! People saying subprime means subpar. Note to people: Subpar is good!"

As it turns out, we all know now, subprime is subpar and subpar is not good! O'Neal's perception of subprime and the risks surrounding subprime were flawed, and seriously so. Being bullish on subprime is not consistent with and does not equate with the Thundering Herd's (Merrill's nickname) long-standing slogan of being "Bullish on America." A year later, the subprime crisis brought America to its knees, and Merrill Lynch was forced into a shotgun wedding with Bank of America!

Losses that Merrill Lynch would incur from O'Neal's big bets in Q3 07 began to be tallied. As the quarter neared its end, the office called him "midswing" on September 29, 2008. Beside himself, he complained again: "On a Saturday! Why even bother to play alone???? 5.1 billion reasons to blame for this one. I think." The next day, on September 30, 2008, O'Neal modified that to "8.4 billion reasons to blame."[38]

In short, as Merrill Lynch was forced to begin unwinding the huge losses incurred from O'Neal's big bets in the credit and credit derivative markets, O'Neal discovered the first writedowns would approximate $8.4 billion in Q3 07 alone. In subsequent quarters, additional writedowns for Merrill Lynch would amount to tens of billions more losses.

July 2007 really became a game of musical chairs of subprime's "toxic waste" loans. On one hand, you found investors like Bruce Monrad finally taking a seat saying "many of these things are beyond our risk desires." On the other hand, you've got the Princes and O'Neals. According to Prince's mindset, he is thinking "Hey, if the music is still playing, I am going to be up dancing." The extremism in O'Neal's mindset was far more pronounced and is perhaps best summed as "Note to people: Subpar is good!" Monrad, by the way, is still in the game; Prince and O'Neal were both benched in the second and third innings.

## A MISLEADING AND FRAUDULENT MESSAGE FROM MR. HEARST IN 1930

Most notable in the issuance of fraudulent stock securities was the famed William Randolph Hearst. In 1930, Mr. Hearst became a stock promoter and ran a four-page promotional ad entitled "A message from Mr. Hearst" that was circulated throughout the country. This promotional ad was an announcement issuing $50 million of Class A Preferred Stock. Inside the announcement was the message from Mr. Hearst that:

> Having absolute confidence in the soundness of the plan and in the integrity of the structure, together with its earnings power...I feel Hearst Consolidated Publications has conclusively demonstrated...the soundness of its own conditions...the utmost consideration was given to the factor of protection...[to] the Class A shares.
>
> We have been and are determined to keep this security out of the class of speculative stock investment. We have seen millions of people in the U.S. engulfed by speculation in stocks which have been made a plaything of gamblers...this issue of Class A shares is not speculative.
>
> Very Truly Yours,
>
> William Randolph Hearst[39]

But Poor's (rating agency) in 1933 gave Mr. Hearst's Class A shares the lowest investment ratings grade that they provided at the time—

"B" speculative. Of course, no one ever read the Poor's investment rating, noted Reis and Flynn. (Seventy-five years later, however, sophisticated investors would soon discover they could not rely on modern-day credit ratings alone from the credit rating agencies. Far more due diligence would be required in the new millennium to understand credit and market risks. Had Reis and Flynn relied solely on credit ratings from the agencies in 2007 for their investment decisions, surely they, too, would have been fleeced.)

According to the authors Reis and Flynn, the net tangible assets tied to Mr. Hearst's Class A shares approximated $6 million, and included in that $6 million of net tangibles was a debt of $6 million due from The Hearst Corporation. The proceeds of the $50 million were to be paid to the Star Holding Company owned by Mr. Hearst to pay off various properties Mr. Hearst's holding company had purchased. It's the old borrow-from-Peter-to-pay-Paul story. Effectively, Mr. Hearst misleadingly and fraudulently borrowed from the public to finance his own debts.

The bottom line is that 75 years later, we have unlearned or learned very little from the lessons bestowed upon us from the speculative/fraudulent era of the 1920s. Credit defaults and the misleading or otherwise fraudulent investment vehicles of the 1930s have, as their modern day counterparts, credit defaults among the unregulated credit markets of today. Defaulting loans in the 1930s were popping up with "such rapidity as to tread upon each other's heels," noted Reis and Flynn.[40]

Citing the work of the late economist AG Hart, Fed Chairman Ben Bernanke wrote in 1983, "It was reported that the extraordinary rate of default on residential mortgages forced banks and the life insurance companies to practically stop making loans," according to Bloomberg author Caroline Baum.[41] Unfortunately, the observation made by Bernanke in 1983 of defaulting mortgage loans forcing banks to stop making loans during the depression foreshadowed the events unfolding in today's crisis. It is precisely the default rate of mortgages that have forced banks to stop making loans 25 years later. Reckless lending and securitization of these loans helped pave the way to the mess in which we now find ourselves.

Returning to Homer Hoyt's proposition, what we have here in 2007-2008 are banks, homeowners and every federal and government agency in the U.S. hoping they can ride out this housing slump through the implementation of myriad measures. But still, almost two years past the housing peak of 2006, demand for housing remains extremely soft, home lending has become far more stringent, a huge overhead supply of homes remains on the market, and all the while housing prices continue to fall. By the end of 2008, we find median home prices in the Case-Schiller 20-city Home Price Index have fallen roughly 20% from their peak valuations, and are expected to continue falling another 10% or more through 2009.

As a result of all these factors, many homeowners and banks find themselves upside down on their real estate properties and loans. Everyone wants the real estate bottom to be in, and everyone wants to say the worst is over, but the rising tide of mortgage defaults and foreclosures have yet to recede. And until then, the overhang of a housing glut will persist and pressure home prices even lower. The downward spiral of home prices is not expected to end until late 2009 or 2010.

Obviously, the U.S. housing slump in 2007-2008 is front and center stage for all of what ails the U.S. economy today. It is directly responsible for the insolvency and failures of household company names like Countrywide Financial Corp and Bear Stearns Corp, as well as hundreds of others firms. Slowly but inexorably, owners of subprime real estate holdings are being ground down. The odds of a sudden turnaround and recovery in the U.S. housing market to save these folks from being ground down is highly improbable, or akin to something of a Black Swan.

## SUBPRIME CREDIT SUFFER FROM FRAUDULENCE AND A LACK OF TRANSPARENCY

As alluded to above with BNP Paribas, many subprime-related credit securities actually had no prices to them and no way to value them. Bond Securities in August 2007 could not be "marked to market"— so BNP complained that no values could be assigned to them. It gets quite complex, but in our wonderful new financial engineering scheme of things, we created products that were either "marked to model" or "marked to make believe." As Consumer Confidence Chief Economist Gail Fosler noted, "The lack of transparency around risk creates an incentive for indiscrimate market turmoil because investors don't know how to selectively implement risk aversion."[42]

As early as 1892, the Queen's Bench in England stated in Scott v. Brown that:

> If persons, for their own purposes of specula-
> tion, create an artificial price in the market by
> transactions which are not real, but are made
> for the purpose of inducing the public to take
> shares, they are guilty of as gross a fraud as has
> ever been committed and a fraud which can be
> brought home to them in a criminal court.[43]

Unfortunately, what might have held true in an English court regarding fraud in 1892 had little bearing on the experience of the fraud perpetrated upon Americans in the 1920s and 1930s. The massive frauds of the 1920s and 1930s were almost entirely unregulated, and American investors were entirely without recourse. In fact, while the general public was reeling in financial ruin, corporate executives were of course still handsomely compensated throughout the entire fiasco! They profited by the fees paid creating these trusts and bonds and securities to be issued, they profited during the brief life spans of these issues, and then they profited again from the fees they charged during the bankruptcy reorganization process when these securities later defaulted at the bondholders' expense! Sucks, I know! The fraudulent and unregulated practices of the 1920s and early 1930s bear a great deal of similarity to today's fraudulent and unregulated practices in the real estate and financial markets.

Bloomberg author Caroline Baum succinctly and wittily summated the August 2007 credit crisis as "When things get dicey, the lack of transparency contributes to risk aversion. At times like these, the formula is simple: Don't Ask + Don't Tell = Sell." [44]

Bond investors clearly had adopted a more risk-averse posture in the summer of 2007, even if Wall Street firms hadn't. They intuitively understood Caroline's Subprime Devil We Don't Know = Sell and they acted upon that intuition. If you don't understand the risks – *Do Not Invest, Just Sell*! Ask questions later if you must, but not before. Far too many other investors and market participants failed to understand the credit and market risks that lay ahead in August 2007.

High-yield investors' sudden aversion to risk contributed to the virtual panic in the credit markets in the first half of August 2007. During the first wave of panic, the broad stock market as measured by the S&P 500 lost 13% of its value from its July 16, 2007, peak to its August 16, 2007, intraday trough.

Amidst the height of the panic in the credit markets on Thursday, August 16, 2007, the stock market would find a temporary bottom. Stock markets often bottom at the height of a panic, just before a crisis abates—even though the credit crunch we had just experienced in August 2007 would remain a serious overhang over the financial markets.

# THE SUBPRIME DEVIL WE DIDN'T KNOW SINKS COUNTRYWIDE FINANCIAL

*We are experiencing home price depreciation almost like never before with the exception of the Great Depression*

— Angelo Mozilo, July 25, 2007[1]

BLOOMBERG'S CAROLINE BAUM coined the subprime crisis as the "Subprime Devil We Didn't Know." This personification provides wonderful imagery for us. And in many ways, the Subprime Devil = Harry Potter's nemesis: Voldemort, or He-Who-Must-Not-be-Named. In a very real way, we are all collectively fighting and pushing back against this subprime devil now. And to that extent, we have all become Harry Potters. To get out from under the death grasp of this devil we are collectively being called upon to rely on our Harry Potter-like wits. Unfortunately for us, we won't be able to rely on any of Potter's magic or financial wizardry to disengage ourselves from the Subprime Devil's grip.

Hundreds of mortgage origination companies and hedge funds have collapsed under the weight of the Subprime Devil. The Subprime Devil has already forced millions of homeowners into foreclosure. Millions of other homeowners are also intimately familiar with this unassuming fellow and at risk of foreclosure. Because of the Subprime Devil, most all of our primary mortgage-lending institutions and financial firms have either failed or been bailed. One of the better known and earliest financial companies to collapse under the weight of this devil was the mortgage lender Countrywide Financial.

## NOBODY SAW THE DEVIL COMING

*Here he comes just a walking down the street,*
*Singing doo-wa-diddy-diddy-dum-diddy do.*

It is a bit farfetched to allege that nobody saw the housing crisis coming as it came a-whistling down the street. Yet, on July 25, 2007, the Countrywide Financial Corp's CEO Anthony Mozilo held a conference call for analysts and investors. At this conference call, this is exactly what Mr. Mozilo asked his shareholders to believe. Excerpts from that conference call reveal that he alleged that *"nobody saw this coming."*[2]

Mozilo must have been suffering from a case of extreme denial that day or was more than just a tad disingenuous with shareholders and analysts. Only a head-in-the-sand ostrich of one of the country's largest lending institutions would have said you could not see this coming. The housing crisis was *not* a highly improbable Black Swan event, as Mozilo would have us believe. The fact is a subprime storm surge was years in the making and widely telegraphed in advance to anyone with their eyes wide open. Only financial executives with their eyes wide shut missed it!

The subprime crisis, we know now, was certainly visible to Bear Stearns hedge fund managers Cioffi and Tannin and to many untold others in the spring of 2007, prior to the credit crisis in August 2007. Certainly, in the wake of Cioffi and Tannin's subprime hedge funds collapse in June 2007, the approaching subprime storm surge became quite evident to the general public as well. At best, the only legitimate thing in question was the exact timing of the moment the storm surge would hit land. Denial was not an option. Humorously restated by Institutional Risk Analyst Chris Whalen:

> Any investment manager or regulator who claims to be surprised at the subprime collapse is making a confession of gross incompetence, and more telling, ignorance of this country's financial history![3]

In the opinion of James Grant, publisher of *Grant's Observer*, the subprime chapter in U.S. financial history:

> ...began one of the wildest chapters in the history of lending and borrowing...
>
> Today's bear market in financial assets is as nothing compared to the preceding crash in human judgment. Never was a disaster better advertised than the one now washing over us. Housing prices stopped going up in 2005, and cracks in the mortgage market started appearing in 2006. Yet the big, ostensibly sophisticated banks only pushed harder.[4]

## WALL STREET ROLLS OUT ITS SUBPRIME TROJAN HORSE

*St. Louis Post Dispatch* cartoonist Matson aptly captured this laid-to-waste phenomenon of destructive subprime lending as Wall Street's Trojan House. Subprime literally morphed into a weapon of mass destruction, as it found itself falling into the wrong hands and misused and abused by the entire spectrum of the financial industry.

Denial was an essential component to the maintenance and then

the bursting of the subprime bubble. More than one notable CEO of a major financial firm made the claim that nobody could see this crisis coming. CEO Adam Applegarth of the failed Northern Rock Bank of England comes readily to mind. It is as if these executives took a page out of the script of former Federal Reserve Chairman Alan Greenspan, who alleged you can not forecast bubbles when the tech bubble burst in 2000. Denial functions as a defense mechanism through which the participants in bubble formations abdicate their role in the bubble formation process itself.

Responsibility and accountability is thereby disowned, and the risks transferred to shareholders and others are both intentionally and unintentionally masked. Even as late as September 2007, Alan Greenspan was reiterating the point that bubbles are an inevitable part of human nature, and that nothing can change that or prevent bubbles from happening.

We have been through this type of event innumer-
able times over the centuries. We get to a state
of extraordinary exuberance, which when confronted with reality turns to unrelenting fear...
It's essentially part of innate human nature...

We have never had the capacity to defuse
a bubble which is essentially what we've dealt
with, with respect to credit instruments.[5]

## NEGATIVE REAL RATES IGNITE ANIMAL SPIRITS

Greenspan's assumptions, we know now, were plain wrong. The key
phrase in the Greenspan quote above is *"We have never had the capacity
to defuse a bubble."* What Greenspan left unsaid is every bit as important as what he said. Bubbles require long fuses in order to form
in the first place at all. Once lit, the longer the fuse, the worse the
collateral damage will be when it finally detonates. In the particular
case of this subprime crisis/bubble, Greenspan himself lit the fuse
when he intentionally lowered short-term borrowing costs at the
Federal Reserve to 1%—well below the inflation rate.

When a primary central bank such as the Federal Reserve lets
other banks borrow at short-term rates that are well below the inflation rate (in financial parlance this is what is called a negative real
rate environment) and lend longer term at much higher rates for a
prolonged period of time, you most certainly ignite the animal spirits
of speculators and investors throughout the world who borrow short
term and lend long term at higher yields. Negative real interest rates
encouraged a response of perfectly rational exuberance and excessive
risk-taking in our financial and real estate markets. This wild episode
of excessive lending and borrowing never could have occurred were
it not aided and abetted by a central bank that had cut short-term
borrowing rates to 1%. I can almost hear Greenspan whistling:

*A long, long time ago...*
*I can still remember*
*How that music used to make me smile.*
*And I knew if I had my chance*
*That I could make those people dance*
*maybe, they'd be happy for a while.*

## BYE BYE, MISS AMERICAN PIE, I CAN'T REMEMBER IF I CRIED, THE DAY THE MUSIC DIED

It was Citigroup's CEO Chuck Prince who reminded us that *"when the music is playing, you got to get up and dance."* Greenspan certainly had his chance to make people dance and smile and be happy for awhile. Unfortunately, when the music died so too did the American Dream for millions of Americans. When short-term borrowing rates shot back up to 5.25% by June 2006, the jig was up, but we were only vaguely aware of it at the time. The music had stopped, but the actors and players on the stage went on dancing and partying for another year as if nothing had happened.

The reason the actors/players went on dancing for another year is simply because tightening Federal Reserve monetary policy always works "with a lag." Tighter monetary policy would impose grave risks to all the financial products that fueled the previous credit boom. When the short-term credit markets tightened, these sub-prime mortgages with interest rate resets became like financial time bombs—not unlike those Bouncing Betties that were responsible for the deaths of so many American soldiers in WWII.

When the eventual day came and the adjustable rate mortgage (ARMs) began resetting at higher rates, rising foreclosures and de-flating home prices had to come as surely as night follows day. This endgame result and their associated risks were entirely identifiable and predictable. They were therefore largely mitigable if not entirely avoidable, and not, as Greenspan says, inevitable. The music that made so many people smile and dance had suddenly died...

> *I can't remember if I cried...*
> *But something touched me deep inside*
> *The day the music died...*
> *I knew I was out of luck the day the music died.*

> *So bye-bye, Miss American Pie.*
> *Drove my Chevy to the levee but the levee was dry.*
> *And them good old boys were drinkin' whiskey and rye*
> *Singin', this'll be the day that I die.*
> *This'll be the day that I die.*

The only unanswered question not revealed to us beforehand would be the exact particulars of the collateral damage that the housing crisis would cause, such as when exactly this would happen, to what banks, to what mortgage companies, hedge funds and homeowners. Countrywide Financial Corp (CFC) was the first really big mortgage lender to be swept into the riptides. Straight from the horse's mouth, here is how Countrywide's CEO Anthony Mozilo answered questions from the analysts on his July 25, 2007, conference call:

> ...we are experiencing home price depreciation almost like never before with the exception of the Great Depression... I ask myself all the time as CEO...what should I have known and when should I have known it and what should I have done about it...?
>
> ...as I try to walk through what happened here, and [wonder whether] a lot of this [could] have been foreseen...as I do reflect on it, nobody saw this coming. S&P and Moody's

didn't see it coming...Bear Stearns certainly didn't see it coming, Merrill Lynch didn't see it coming, nobody saw this coming...*It would have been an insight that only a superior spirit could have had at the time.*

So far what we have seen in delinquencies to a great extent are not resets at all but people losing their jobs, loss of marriage, loss of health, and the problem is that they either can't refinance because the value of their homes have gone down, so they're under water, or the program that they used to get into the home is no longer available to them. So right now the delinquencies are being driven by more traditional issues then they are about concern about resets.[6]

Mozilo's final assertion that delinquencies were being driven by traditional issues and not resets also appears to be a stretch of the imagination. But what does ring true is that home prices were declining and homeowners could no longer use their homes as virtual ATM machines. Also, the programs that had been available to homeowners during the housing boom were no longer available. Lending standards and credit suddenly became tighter as everybody in the world became suddenly less creditworthy. That was one of the problems; because the homeowner's need to continually refi their home or obtain a second mortgage or home equity line of credit was as strong as ever and could no longer be supported by the marketplace.

Too many homeowners without any savings were constantly tapping their homes as ATM machines to fund their growing debt. Then the means to extract that credit disappeared at the very moment

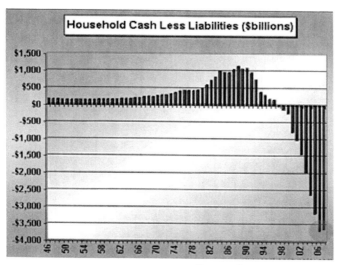

Source: Contrary Investor

they needed to fund those debts the most—when the adjustable rate mortgages (ARMs) reset at higher rates. To make matters worse, these ARM resets kicked in only after over-inflated home prices had been falling for a few years. Their homes in many instances were worth less than what they bought them for. Now they were upside down or negatively amortized on their homes. They owed more than their homes were worth as their over-inflated home prices began reverting to the mean. The chart below shows the year-over-year decline in home prices approaching 20% in 2008. Falling home prices coupled with ARM resets soon led to rising delinquencies, defaults and eventually foreclosure.

Rising mortgage defaults then made for a very poor environment for lenders to continue extending credit as they themselves became cash-strapped by the non-performing mortgage loans. The financial products that fueled the credit boom began to blow up everywhere, leaving dead soldiers in their wake wherever they were detonated. No one was immune: homeowners, mortgage lenders, banks.

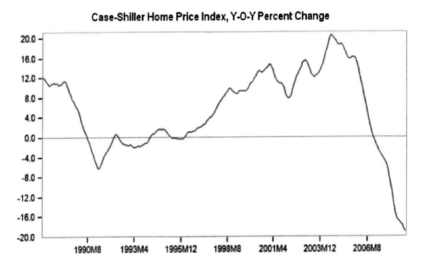

**Case-Shiller Home Price Index, Y-O-Y Percent Change**

Source: Moody's Economy.com's Dismal Scientist

The credit crisis led Countrywide Financial Corp (CFC), the biggest private U.S. mortgage lender, to tap their entire $11.5 billion bank credit lines on August 16, 2007. Bank credit lines are considered emergency loans. This happened a day after Merrill suggested that Countrywide could go bankrupt. Piper Jaffrey analyst Robert Napoli wrote in a report that same day that Countrywide Financial appeared to be "readying itself for a nuclear winter."[7]

> *Bad news on the doorstep,*
> *I couldn't take one more step...*
> *I met a girl who sang the blues*
> *And I asked her for some happy news,*
> *But she just smiled and turned away.*

Mortgage lenders like CFC were dependent on high-yield investors to continually refi their asset-backed commercial paper (ABCP) or mortgage-backed securities (MBS). The assumption on the street was that this cash would buy the company time to help get them through the freeze in short-term financing that was debilitating mortgage lenders everywhere.

## SUBPRIME LOANS MORPH INTO TOXIC WASTE

The problem was that mortgage-backed securities were souring assets at best, or worse—toxic waste. This froze the short-term credit markets. And the short-term credit markets would remain virtually frozen precisely because we were experiencing the worst home price depreciation since the Great Depression. With deflating home prices and rising defaults on mortgage loans, how could the loans on CFC's books not be in huge trouble as the crisis inevitably worsened?

Worse, the loans that CFC had bundled into mortgage-backed securities were beginning to default left and right, and the loan default rate was only just beginning to pick up steam in August 2007. It was quite early in the home-deflation and default game for CFC to find that it had already become a financially distressed company. They lacked any cushions to protect them as the deteriorating housing market spiraled viciously against them. Without any margin of safety, they had to reach for their credit lines at a very early stage in Great Unwind of the Subprime. Loan default rates were projected to escalate throughout the remainder of 2007 and not peak until sometime in 2008 or 2009.

With loan default rates projected to escalate over the next 12 months or longer, it is little wonder these mortgage-backed securities soon became popularly known as "toxic waste." Thus, it was no a surprise to see these securities being revulsed by high yield investors immediately after Bear Stearns' mortgage-related hedge fund investors were told they would be getting little to no money in July 2007.

From that day forward, there would be no short-term solution for the mortgage lenders and for other lenders of asset-backed commercial paper. Henceforth, the ABCP market would by definition have to shrink sizably. High-yield investors would flat out avoid the ABCP market for the foreseeable future. It was this risk aversion among bond investors that drove the CFC's need to prepare for their "nuclear winter."

"When a company draws on its bank lines, it just basically gives off the impression that it has run out of options. Typically these bank lines are there but not really meant to be used," said Christopher Wolfe at Fitch Ratings.[8] At the time, billionaire Wilbur Ross thought Countrywide, as a going concern, was still a viable company, stating "there is value there once you sort everything out."[9] Ross, a value investor by trade, was not the only one to make that mistake.

Had he actually taken the time to sort out each and every single one of Countrywide's securitized loans on their books, Ross would have found that Countrywide's book value was far less than its stated market cap—if the subsequent revulsion of Countrywide's share price is any indication.

A week later, on August 23, 2007, in another vote of confidence for CFC, Bank of America (BAC) claimed they actually went to the trouble to sort everything out. Bank of America's investor relations spokesman, Robert Stickler, found that "we were able...to look at their operations and their books. We determined the value is greater than what the market was giving them credit for."[10]

This stupendous bit of due diligence (DD) allowed BAC to rationalize a $2 billion purchase of CFC preferred stock, which could be converted at $18. The preferred stock also came with a 7.25% dividend yield attached to it. At the time, the stock was trading about $22, down about 50% from its peak valuation of $45 at the onset of 2007 just eight months prior.

Subsequent to the August 23, 2007 BAC assertion that CFC's assets were seriously undervalued, Countrywide Financials' share price plunged still further into the abyss. This begs the question: What valuation models could BAC have been using to derive its conclusions regarding CFC's tangible book value? What sort of "stress test" did they run on those valuation models amidst falling home prices and rising delinquencies and defaults? Or were they simply "talking their book" because the risks not to do so were far greater? These questions can't be answered, however, as BAC did not make any pertinent disclosures.

## CFC NO LONGER ON THE ENDANGERED LIST—OH REALLY?

Punk Ziegel's analyst Dick Bove, in a note to clients, excitedly wrote that Countrywide is "no longer on the endangered species list."[11] At the same time Dick Bove and others were cheering Bank of America's vote of confidence for CFC with their preferred stock purchase, Sean Egan of Egan-Jones Ratings felt that CFC assets were worth "less than its outstanding obligations" and feared CFC would need to raise yet more capital because "falling prices for home loans in the secondary market [had] pared the value of its mortgage portfolio."[12]

I echoed his warning that investors not be duped by BAC's bravado, as Countrywide was still in a world of hurt after tapping their credit lines and there was still an "avalanche" of bearish news coming down the pike, and that momentum would drive the stock price lower yet. If the $2 billion, 7.5% dividend CFC shareholder dilution hadn't been enough insult to injury, investors who listened to these reassurances and stuck around eventually watched their CFC shares plunge another 60%, from $22/share in late August to $8.72/share by November 28, 2007.

## COUNTRYWIDE REASSURANCES RING FALSE

By late November, it was evident that investor confidence in CFC had not been shored up one iota and investor confidence continued to wane. This prompted yet another round of false reassurances on

November 28, 2007, from Countrywide's managing director of investor relations, David Bigelow:

> We said it back in August, we said it in September, we said it last week, we'll say it until we turn blue in the face, but we have ample liquidity to fund our growth and operational needs.[13]

More denials from the firm; what Bigelow failed to consider was how Countrywide would fund their contracting growth and operational needs. Amidst the declining asset values on its balance sheets, Countrywide would continue to struggle against the headwinds of both accelerating home price declines and defaulting mortgages as it entered the New Year—despite Bigelow's pronouncements to the contrary.

## BACK ONTO THE ENDANGERED SPECIES LIST

At the end of 2007, more than 7% of Countrywide's $1.5 trillion mortgage servicing portfolio was more than 60 days past due. Taking note of that ominous figure, the once enthusiastic Dick Bove waved the white flag, noting that "there's a rule of thumb that at the 5% level of delinquencies, you are finished."[14]

Dick Bove's 5% delinquency rule, for determining whether you are finished or not, is worth pausing on for a moment. The national mortgage delinquency crisis escalated all throughout the first three quarters of 2008 and across all classes of mortgage loans. By the end of the third quarter of 2008, the total delinquency rate for all mortgages had risen to 6.99%. Delinquency rates are setting record highs and climbing as we enter 2009, according to the Mortgage Bankers Association. This is already almost 2% above Dick Bove's 5% rule and worsening in a parabolic rise. Banks and lending institutions simply cannot remain liquid and solvent with non-performing loans exceeding 5%, let alone 7% or more. In the late 1970s and early 1980s the

## U.S. -Total Mortgage Loans Past Due

Source: Moody's Economy.com's Dismal Scientist

savings and loans (S&Ls) lent far more money than was prudent, and was the last time that total mortgage delinquencies exceeded the 5% rule for any length of time. The pressures on our entire financial system as we close out 2008 are intense and intensifying!

*I went down to the sacred store*
*Where I'd heard the music years before,*
*But the man there said the music wouldn't play...*
*The church bells all were broken*

## CFC BANKRUPTCY RUMORS FLOATED

Investors continued to speculate the company would go bankrupt even after CFC specifically rejected that prospect on Tuesday, January 8, 2007. Countrywide spokesman Rick Simon said "There is no substance to the rumor that Countrywide is planning to file for bankruptcy."[15] That reassurance had zero impact on investor confidence. By the next day, January 9, 2008, CFC's stock price had plunged another 41% from $8.75 in late November to $5.12 on a closing basis. Unbeknownst to investors and other market participants at the time, Countrywide in fact had other plans in mind besides filing for bankruptcy.

Bank of America announced on January 10, 2008, that it was in "advanced" discussions to "double down" on their August investment and buy the distressed mortgage lender, Countrywide Financial. "From Countrywide's perspective, it is their best chance for salvation," said Sean Egan, of Egan-Jones Ratings. "At the end of the chaos that is going to transpire over the next two years, it gives Bank of America a terrific position in mortgage financing."[16]

## A STROKE OF THE PEN WAS SUPPOSED TO SOLVE ALL OF COUNTRYWIDE'S ILLS

Analyst Kathleen Shanley at Gimme Credit wrote that the BAC buyout of Countrywide Financial "would solve the company's funding and liquidity problems with the stroke of a pen and make bankruptcy concerns moot."[17] Kathleen Shanley was the most optimistic analyst responding to this announcement.

"I hope Bank of America isn't throwing good money after bad. They struck a deal that wasn't very attractive. Hopefully they can get it right the second time around," said Eric Schopf, at Hardesty Capital Management.[18]

The most circumspect comment on this BAC announcement came from Hayman Capital Partners' Kyle Bass: "The worsening housing market makes BAC's timing questionable. The collateral for their loans is depreciating at over 20% a year, losses are spiking and there's a big potential 'fat tail' to Countrywide's legal liabilities."[19]

In many respects, the so-called "buyout" of CFC presented a whole array of headaches for the acquiring BAC. By doubling down on their already ill-advised August 23, 2007, investment in CFC, Bank of America's CEO Ken Lewis effectively averaged down his initial investment. Averaging down on a losing investment is generally considered a Bozo No-No in the world of portfolio management. Always has been. This fact was recognized as far back as 1932, when Jesse H. Jones approached his old cattleman friend Dick Coon:

> "Dick, I said, "why don't we buy some of these
> cheap stocks?" "Hell no," he said. "Never rope a
> steer going down hill: he'll kill you every time."[20]

Effectively, Ken Lewis was pulling a Stan O'Neal over at Merrill, who was an advocate of "concentrated risks." Remember, O'Neal was the CEO who said the smartest thing he ever did for Merrill was make just a few big bets—"frees up time."

## SHOCKER—COUNTRYWIDE ASSETS MAY BE WORTH LESS THAN LIABILITIES TO BAC

Institutional Risk Analyst Chris Whalen recognized by May 2008 that the steer was still headed downhill and presented both CFC and BAC shareholders and bondholders with growing risk factors. These risk factors, Whalen felt, might preclude BAC's deal to buy the CFC—the distressed mortgage lender. At the time the takeover deal was announced in January 2008, BAC did not state an offer price to CFC shareholders, nor had they made any commitment to stand behind CFC's debt.

In fact, on April 30, 2008, BAC filed an S-4 form with the Securities and Exchange Commission (SEC) detailing the terms of BAC's offer to purchase CFC. In that form, BAC stated that "Bank of America has made no determination...and there is no assurance that any of such debt would be redeemed, assumed, or guaranteed." [21] One banker who had spoken to Whalen back in January said "the BAC strategy is reportedly to manage the orderly liquidation of CFC..."[22] In other words, CFC creditors remained at risk of ruin. That revelation probably came as a surprise to many market participants. It almost goes without saying that CFC shareholder equity had long ago been all but ruined.

Whalen also pointed out that Bank of America's CEO Ken Lewis could be "considering a bankruptcy filing for CFC as a strategy after the transaction closes,"[23] should the home prices continue to deflate as anticipated and reduce the value of the mortgage paper even lower. By allowing a period of months to go by, as home prices deflate, Whalen figured BAC's management could get a better handle on what remaining book value there was to CFC's declining assets, not to mention the growing litigation risks. However, liability risks might be so large as to prevent the BAC deal from getting done at all, felt Whalen. "Without a re-organization to address the litigation and other off-balance sheet, contingent claims, [the extent of the pending litigation against CFC is so vast] there seems to be no way for BAC to quantify the downside risks of CFC"[24] for Bank of America shareholders.

It was evident to Whalen that the growing downside risks at CFC had evolved or otherwise morphed into being unquantifiable, especially with regards to the litigation. These new realities were a far cry from Robert Stickler's illusory findings back on August 23, 2007, determining that the value of CFC was "greater than what the market was giving them credit for."

Further confirming that CFC shareholders and creditors were still in a great deal of trouble (at this point, however, investors that had overstayed their welcome had already lost a lot of skin in the game) was a note written on May 5, 2008, from Friedman Billings analyst Paul Miller saying that Bank of America will probably have to reduce its per-share offer for CFC to the "$0 to $2 level." Bank of America, Ramsey also noted, "may have to write down the value of

Countrywide's loans by $20 billion to $30 billion when it closes the takeover deal. Bank of America should completely walk away from the Countrywide deal."[25] Given the foregoing litigation risks above, however, many market participants deemed the value of CFC's equity at $0, regardless of whatever settlement is determined and regardless of its marked to market price.

## WHAT WILL CFC'S ASSETS BE WORTH TO THE SHAREHOLDERS AND CREDITORS AND BAC?

Sean Egan speculated in January 2008 that when the chaos ends sometime around the end of 2009-2010, Bank of America will be well positioned in the mortgage-financing sector. Well positioned for what, I ask? When all is said and done, one has to ask: will the mortgage lending business even be a viable business model? It may be impossible for private mortgage lenders to compete against the government-sponsored enterprises (GSEs) going forward. The GSE business models that are now explicitly backed by the U.S. government make them almost risk-free monopolies and will be very tough to compete against. Furthermore, the government intends to make 30-year fixed mortgage loans available at 4.5% in 2009 through Fannie Mae and Freddie Mac. These low rates will be the lowest rates ever, and will be exceedingly tough for private lenders to compete against!

No matter how the dust settles for both BAC and CFC, investor confidence towards CFC's stock price continued plummeting into the blowup of Bear Stearns on Monday, March 17, 2008. After the collapse of Bear Stearns, CFC shares did stabilize around $4.50 even though the equity value of CFC shares may ultimately be deemed worth nothing. Repriced at $4.50, CFC had lost 90% of its $45 value in Q1 07, so I am sure it already feels like a zero to shareholders, regardless what pennies on the dollar they end up with.

Many CFC shareholders had chosen to hang in there throughout this Great Unwind in the housing market. The only reason I can imagine that they chose to gut it out was they found some sense of false security in the company's beguiling reassurances that they could cling to. Unfortunately, investors have become the bagholders, holding nothing more than a pig-in-a-poke. Conceivably, the false security offered by management and wishful analysts had left many investors and creditors with some semblance of belief, expectation or hope that management could and would somehow right their sinking ship. Yet "hope deferred" only sickens the heart. Hope founded upon false reassurances, while regrettably understandable, still can't right a wrong marriage. Investors were betrayed by these false reassurances.

## BAC's Ken Lewis Ropes in Two Bum Steers in One Year!

BAC's CEO Ken Lewis may well have roped himself two bum steers. When BAC took its initial stake in CFC on August 23, 2007, its stock trading near $52 was within striking distance of its record highs near $55. The stock price plunged to $19 eleven months later. The purchase of CFC added to the woes confronting BAC, creating a whole new set of uncertainties and risks that they probably would have been better off leaving alone. Ostensibly, they could have made this whole crisis easier on themselves simply by avoiding CFC. One has to wonder, too, if BAC wasn't set up to be the fall guy for CFC amongst the bankers. More likely, it was just Ken Lewis's huge appetite for making acquisitions.

On September 14, 2008, BAC bought Merrill Lynch, possibly roping in what would be the second bum steer in a year! Lewis at the time called the purchase of Merrill "the ideal long-term fit." But, as a former Merrill Lynch broker related a few months later, "There are some hand grenades on the balance sheet that are going to blow up on Bank of America. The cost savings are going to be nowhere near what they've

already promised." Looking in the rear view mirror after a year of acquisition binging, Ken Lewis admitted on December 3, 2008, that his
"banks outlook was too optimistic. If someone had told me a year ago
that things would be worse in December 2008 than in December 2007,
I would have thought that person was half crazy."[26]

By December 2008, no longer were BAC spokesman crying that
they had "ample liquidity to fund [their] growth and operational
needs." Confirmation that Ken Lewis had bagged two bum steers in a
year was confirmed by the media in January 2009 when the Wall Street
Journal and Bloomberg News reported Bank of America went begging,
hat in hand, to the U.S. Treasury in December 2008 for yet another taxpayer handout because of Merrill's larger than expected fourth quarter
losses. Note the blame shift to Merrill Lynch and not the reckless acquisition of Merrill of Lynch or of Countrywide Financial Corp.

The fact that Bank of America is broke and looking to the Treasury
for a taxpayer handout does not point back to Merrill Lynch per se.
The blame points squarely back to Bank of America's tomfoolery to
acquire two bum steers. Ken Lewis made two big bets in 2008, just like
his counterpart Stan O'Neil, that concentrated the firm's risks on the
worst investments one could possibly make in 2008. Effectively Bank
of America's strategy in 2008 was to average-down on two of the biggest losers of the year.

So much for any emphasis on non-correlated risk exposures, from
where I come from: the trading pits of Chicago, a risk management
strategy that averages-down is a bozo no-no. Averaging down is a
game of Russian roulette. Play it long enough and one day the cham-
ber will squeeze off a bullet. Ken Lewis squeezed the trigger of his ba-
zooka aimed at Bank of America's head, not once, but twice. The slow
motion bullet blew the bank's brains out in less than year's time. And
all the time, Lewis thought he was buying cheap stock and not shaky
collateral loaded with sub-primordial ooze worth less than nothing.

Commenting on the sub-primordial ooze Bank of America was hell-bent on acquiring in 2008 Richard Kline says:

> Here's a lesson for those who feel that they
> are qualified to executor a money center finan-
> cial administration: you don't eat the Blob,
> the Blob eats you. So one had better be sure
> that one is shaking hands with someone/thing
> which is definitely NOT a Blob. Lewis twice—
> TWICE—broke that rule, and he has just about
> killed his firm therefore.[27]

## ANTHONY MOZILO: CAPTAIN OF THE TITANIC'S GOLDEN PARACHUTE

At the time of Bank of America's announcement that it was going to buy out Countrywide Financial on January 11, 2008, CEO Anthony Mozilo stood to earn a whopping $83 million in severance pay, or three times his annual salary and three times his average bonus "in the event of a takeover." This buyout clause was just a bit too much to swallow for some investors and drew the ire of Frank Glassner, CEO of Compensation Design Group:

> The boards of both companies are well within
> their right to question these arrangements,
> [because the] circumstances are flat-out egre-
> gious. [It's like] paying the captain of the Ti-
> tanic buckets of money for sinking the ship.[28]

There should be some sort of clause that prevents golden parachutes if the firm being sold is failing and at risk of bankruptcy. Yet, Bank of America's CEO Ken Lewis thought that Mozilo will "want to have some fun" after the deal closes![29] Mozilo was one of several other big-name executives who had been bonused out for their failed or failing enterprises. Another abusive golden parachute provision example was Merrill Lynch's $160 million payout to oust Stan O'Neal for his egregious risk-taking.

At last count in May 2008, 262 financial companies like Countrywide have been laid to rest by the credit crisis thus far, according to one unidentified source. The moral of the story for investors: view corporate reassurances with a high degree of skepticism. If in doubt, and you can't sort it out, get out! It could be ruinous to your financial health. Rumors, believe it or not, can often have far more substance to them than those shoddy corporate reassurances and denials.

Countrywide's story goes straight back to earlier lessons: Trade and invest in what you see, learn to know what you can or can not trust, not what you want to believe or what others want you to believe! Insiders, company spokesmen and CEOs have separate agendas from interests of their shareholders and are often only "talking their book." As Pierpont Morgan, perhaps the most legendary of American bankers, once told an associate: "A man always has two reasons for the things he does—a good one and a real one."[30] Shareholders do not want to be caught on the wrong end of the unknown but real reasons why a company does what it does and says what it says.

Even billionaires like Wilbur Ross, who hadn't done any due diligence and was simply talking off the top of his head back in August 2007. Wholesale trust is never warranted. If Ross had done his due diligence and then put his money where his mouth was, that might have been a bit different, but that isn't what Ross did at all. For every household name like Countrywide, there have been hundreds of other similarly publicly traded companies offering and echoing the same false reassurances to their investors while they have been failing.

There are no shortcuts in the game of investing. Investors must simply learn to do their own due diligence. It often turns out to be the case that after a fair amount of due diligence an investor still can't make heads or tails out of a company's merits. If instead of green flags, red flags start appearing within the first few minutes of a superficial glance at a company's financial statements, just walk away and assign it an "Avoid" rating. This strategy has the benefit of saving the investor a lot of both time and money.

## SHADOW BANKING SYSTEM MEETS THE SUBPRIME DEVIL IT DIDN'T KNOW

Paul McCulley and Bill Gross have been instrumental in introducing us to the dark side of the "Shadow Banking System." The products and investment vehicles in the Shadow Banking System are largely unregulated. Many market participants have little exposure to the products peddled in these unregulated markets. Although I have followed the regulated exchange-traded markets for over 20 years, I am not an "insider" as to how the shadow banking system operates on a day-to-day basis.

The shadow banking system deals primarily in products that are bilateral. This means they are traded between two parties. That is, buy and sell orders are not routed to a central exchange where products traded are "marked to market." Price discovery and prices are transparent on exchanges. Products that do not trade on exchanges are considered "opaque" or non-transparent. You will never find them quoted in the financial papers much less ever hear about them in the news—until they happen to blow up like they did in 2007-2008.

As a market participant, I have been immersed in the trading and market research side of the business relating to exchange-traded products such as stocks, bonds, commodities, etc. As such, this rather precluded me from having much more than a vague awareness about the "financial engineering" and shenanigans going on in the opaque world of the credit markets.

Strange, alphabet soup-like names that I had never before heard of such as SIVs (structured investment vehicles), conduits, and monolines suddenly became *en vogue* and quickly became a part of my everyday vocabulary!

## MARK-TO-MAKE-BELIEVE PRODUCTS

Bloomberg's Jonathan Weil quipped that these shadow bankers were booking "profits based on pure guesswork" in what he called a game of "Fantasy Financials." Instead of products being "marked to market" as we say in the business, these products were either "marked to model" or "marked to make-believe."[31] Yes, part and parcel of the subprime bubble was to create fantasy products and then assign make-believe prices to them that drove the fictitious earnings capable of producing multibillion-dollar bonuses to financial executives during the subprime boom years.

## LEVEL ONE, LEVEL TWO AND LEVEL THREE

There are three tiers of assets on the books of various financial institutions. The industry assigns these assets classifications as Tier One, Tier Two and Tier Three, or Level One, Level Two and Level Three. Basically, Tier One assets can be marked to market as would be for exchange traded products. Tier Two was "marked to model" and Tier Three was "marked to make-believe." As Jonathan Weil explains, for Level One, you just go to the exchange that product is traded on, find the quote and mark it to the market price on your balance sheet—simple enough. Level Two is mark-to-model and that means there are no exchange traded quotes available. In this case, financial institutions "estimate the value using other inputs that are observable in the market." By using shaky models to determine estimated valuations, there is room for broad interpretation and things are already getting dicey. Level Three assets "are based on unobservable inputs reflecting a company's own assumptions about the assumptions that market participants would use in pricing the asset or liability."[32]

Financial firms like Morgan Stanley, Goldman Sachs, Lehman Brothers and Citigroup, along with all the others, were making assumptions about assumptions to determine valuations on their balance sheets. By definition, Level Three assets would appear to violate generally accepted accounting principles, or GAAP, developed by the Financial Accounting Standards Board or FASB—specifically their principles of sincerity and prudence. It is amazing that these assets were ever allowed by the FASB under GAAP, at all. Hence, that is why these products have become popularly known as "marked-to-make-believe."

Earlier, we demonstrated how exceedingly difficult it is to wholesale believe or trust anything coming out of company management without a huge amount of skepticism. It is that much more so when it comes to Level Three pricing. FASB member Tom Linsmeier understates the difficulty assessing Level Three valuations:

> There's a reason you want to be more skeptical
> about those [Level Three] numbers. But it doesn't
> necessarily mean those numbers are more biased.
> There's just more uncertainty about them.[33]

And that's precisely the problem with these Level Three products— the uncertainty of them. So many of these Level Three products are bundled securities that have declining asset values attached to them, be they subprime loans, CDOs, CDSs etc., and other products most people have never heard of—and for that matter, never will.

## THE RUDE AWAKENING OF FASB RULE 157 FOR BANKS—FAIR VALUE ACCOUNTING IMPOSED ON WALL STREET

FASB Rule 157 was created to streamline into a single definition the multiple definitions of fair value used in GAAP. The rule was intended to increase consistency and comparability in GAAP statements.

The definition focuses on the price that would be received to sell the asset, not the price that would be paid to acquire the asset... This statement emphasizes that fair value is a market-based measurement, not an entity-specific measurement. A fair value measurement should include an adjustment for risk if market participants would include one in pricing the related asset even if the adjustment is difficult to determine. Therefore a measurement (for example, a mark-to-model measurement) that does not include an adjustment for risk would not represent a fair value measurement.[34]

This rule was issued to be effective beginning November 15, 2007.

As noted above, it is extremely difficult to quantify the risks in asset values when an asset class begins to decline in value. This has been found to be especially true when all the previous pricing models for real estate had built-in assumptions that this asset class would probably never actually decline in value! Imagine the gall then, and the impertinence of home prices actually declining, and then the chagrin of all those financial wizards and engineers operating within the confines of the shadow banking system when their once sound collateral erodes to being shaky collateral. The situation is further worsened for the shadow banking community when the homeowners stop servicing their loans.

Structured products, conduits and what not take on an element of Knightian uncertainty to them when their asset-backed loans decline in value and are no longer being serviced. No wonder, then, that the financial community would shudder at the need to reprice these assets significantly lower even to the point of assigning a zero valuation to reflect an "adjustment for risk," as would be required by the accounting changes that took effect on November 15, 2007, under FASB rule 157.

In a nutshell, Rule 157 was an accounting change requiring "all the crappy paper on the balance sheets of various funds, banks and brokers—RMBS, CDOs, CDSs, etc.—[to] be 'carried at fair value on a recurring basis in financial statements,'" as The Big Picture financial blogger Barry Ritholtz described it.[35]

## JUST HOW BIG A HEADACHE IS RULE 157 TO FINANCIAL INSTITUTIONS?

After the subprime credit meltdown in August 2007 caused several billion of writedowns amongst financial institutions, the implementation of Rule 157 in November 2007 threatened to cause hundreds of billions more writedowns. Royal Bank of Scotland's chief credit strategist Bob Janjuah, who actually first coined the "mark-to-make-believe" terminology, wrote to clients that Morgan Stanley had the "equivalent of 251% of its equity in Level 3 assets, Goldman Sachs [had] 185%, Lehman Brothers 159%, and Citigroup 105%."

It is understandable that applying FASB Rule 157 to these financial institutions would be a hellacious undertaking and have bankers bristling. Throwing FASB Rule 157 at them was the equivalent of throwing Harry Truman at them, who once said about his opponents, "I never give them hell. I just tell the truth, and they think it's hell."

## REPEAL OF FAIR VALUE ACCOUNTING OR RULE 157

In the wake of Lehman's bankruptcy on September 15, 2008, and widespread loss of confidence on September 30, 2008, the final day of Q3 08, the SEC repealed Rule 157. It is no coincidence that this rule was suspended before the end of Q3 08. Barry Ritholtz, author of The Big Picture noted, "Suspending mark-to-market accounting, in essence, suspends reality."[36]

The reality of the matter is that there isn't a sophisticated investor in the world that trusts the mark-to-make-believe asset valuations sitting on the balance sheets of these financial firms. Even if we grant the obvious fact that marked-to-market prices do not = value, mark-to-market valuations do more or less accurately reflect the untrustworthiness of these mark-to-make-believe valuations—no more and no less. Since financial firms refuse to clean their own houses, preferring to let the U.S. Treasury sweep their dirt under a TARP or lay it off on the balance sheet of the Federal Reserve as they have done, investors have rightly chosen to walk away from these illiquid and troubled assets. And Uncle Sam's and the Federal Reserve's big TARP only hides and perpetuates the problem. It does not go away because Uncle Sam and the Federal Reserve artificially mark them back up to where the banks want them marked. Ritholtz elaborates:

> Suspending FASB 157 amounts to little more than an attempt to hide this broken business model from investors, regulators and the public. It's not just getting through the next few quarters that matters; rather, it's allowing the market place to appropriately reallocate this capital to where it will serve its investors best. That is what free market capitalism is, including Schumpeter's creative destruction...suspending the proper accounting of this paper is the refuge of cowards. It reflects a refusal to admit the original error, it hides the mistake, and it misleads shareholders. I find it to be a totally unacceptable solution to the crisis.[37]

## IF YOU WANT A FRIEND, GET A DOG

Harry Truman also once quipped: "If you want a friend in Washington, get a dog."[38] The same maxim applies on Wall Street. The last thing in the world financial executives wanted to have to do was to carry all their toxic waste on their balance sheets at "fair value." In fact, Barry Ritholtz points out that as a result of the Financial Executives International's lobbying efforts, they almost caused the seven-member FASB to not require fair value reporting under rule 157. It only passed 4-3. After passing, Rule 157 went into partial effect on November 15, 2007.

"That is a reminder of exactly how pathetic and shareholder unfriendly the corporate infrastructure remains,"[39] said Ritholtz. Barry could well have added "and always has been" to reflect the general trends of the past 100 years. While corporate structures and managements are not always shareholder unfriendly, the historical record on balance does not merit an investor's wholesale trust.

## HOW THE ALCHEMY OF STATEMENT 159 TURNED WALL STREET LOSSES INTO PROFITS IN Q1 08

Even while the resurrection of Rule 157 by the FASB in November 2007 intended the toxic paper on the balance sheets of financial institutions be carried at fair value on a recurring basis, banks had begun to take advantage of another new rule (Statement 159) that allows them to juice their net income and earnings. Statement 159 allows Wall Street firms a new accounting technique by which they can take a negative number and turn it into a positive one.

Statement 159, formally known as the "Fair Value Option for Financial Assets and Financial Liabilities," was adopted by most Wall Street firms back in February 2007. The rule was enacted by the FASB after the successful lobbying efforts of Merrill, Morgan Stanley, Goldman Sachs, and Citigroup. In letters to the FASB, these firms contended that it wasn't fair to make them mark their assets to market value if they could not at the same time also mark their liabilities.

"We do not believe it would be appropriate to let investors consider creditworthiness when valuing bonds if the issuing company couldn't do the same,"[40] wrote Goldman Sachs accounting policy director Matt Schroeder in an April 2006 letter. Countering Schroeder's concerns, Standard and Poor's credit rating agency worried that Statement 159 would lead to "diminished analytical transparency"[41] of banking institutions financial statements, statements on which they base their credit ratings.

## IN GOD WE TRUST, IN BANKS WE MISTRUST

Statement 159 essentially allows Wall Street firms to book their "writedowns" in an accounting category known as "other comprehensive income." This allows the banks to let these losses "bypass" their income statements. For example, if $100 million of bonds decline from 100 cents on the dollar to 80 cents on the dollar when marked to market, the company gets to book the "$20 million on the presumed savings that you have on your liabilities" explains Ladenburg Thalmann analyst Dick Bove. "In the real world you didn't save a dime," he said. "You still owe the $100 million. It's another one of these accounting rules that basically takes you further and further away from reality."[42]

Once again, like FASB Rule 157, some regulators at the FASB found the Statement 159 accounting rule distasteful. Two of the seven-member board voted against the adoption of Statement 159 in February 2007 on the grounds that it would "provide opportunities for entities to report significantly less earnings volatility than they are exposed to."[43]

Through May 2008, these "liability savings" had already helped financial companies "offset more than $160 billion of writedowns" taken by various Wall Street firms.[44] As these distressed bonds continue to lose value as corporate and homeowner credit defaults continue rising, these firms will recognize even further "liability savings" over the next several quarters. Expressing even further concern to the FASB regulators, Standard and Poor's Chief Accountant Neri Bukspan wrote "Equity may be overstated as a result of these illusory gains that may never be realized, hindering the analysis of the equity cushion to absorb losses."[45]

The illusions Wall Street firms are capable of creating with Statement 159 calls to mind the shadows cast in Plato's cave, whereby the only reality known to the prisoners in Plato's cave are the shadows of objects cast upon the wall opposite them. Thus chained and sequestered from reality, they are forced to live with the delusions provided them by these shadows. Truth and enlightenment eludes them.

One important lesson this whole financial turmoil of 2007-2008 should teach all investors, if it has not already done so, is to carry a healthy dose of skepticism with respect to corporate management. Trust is something a company must earn every day. From the foregoing, investors should realize they can not go blindly into Wall Street's den of wolves and expect everything to be hunky dory!

## FASB STATEMENT 140 POSTPONED

FASB Statement 140 is an off-balance sheet rule that replaces FASB Statement 125.

> This Statement requires that liabilities and derivatives incurred or obtained by transferors as part of a transfer of financial assets be initially measured at fair value, if practicable... This statement requires an entity that has securitized financial assets to disclose informa-

tion about accounting policies, volume, cash
flows, key assumptions made in determining
fair values and sensitivity of those fair values to
changes in key assumptions.[46]

The securities industry fought the adoption of this FASB statement tooth
and nail, too. And their lobbying efforts were successful. The FASB announced that it would postpone this rule until November 15, 2009.

"The risks of too much haste are high. The abrupt consolidation
of off-balance-sheet structures is likely to swell the balance sheets
of the affected entities," said the Securities Industry and Financial
Markets Association (SIFMA) in a July 16, 2008, letter to the FASB.
SIFMA further argued that Statement 140 "could affect as much as
$11 trillion of off-balance-sheet entities [making] companies appear
short of capital to regulators and lenders."[47]

"The proposed changes would serve only to further chill an already frozen real estate and other asset backed securities markets"
complained Dottie Cunningham, CEO of the Commercial Mortgage
Securities Association, in a July 21, 2008, letter to the FASB.[48]

The FASB approved in a 5-0 vote to postpone this requirement on
July 30 2008. Commenting on the 5-0 vote, FASB member Thomas
Linsmeier said "It's not practical to begin requiring companies to put
assets underlying securitizations onto their books this year."[49]

## DELAYING THE DAY OF RECKONING FOR FASB 140 IS FRAUGHT WITH DOWNSIDE RISKS

By waiting until November 2009, the hope is that the underlying
assets will be worth more than they were in July 2008. However, the
trend does not favor delaying FASB 140 until November 2009. The
Case-Schiller median home prices had already fallen roughly 15%
from their peak valuations by July 2008. They fell another 5%, to

20%, by December 2008. And the trend in home prices suggests they will continue to decline at least through most of 2009, if not beyond. The parabolic rise in mortgage delinquencies going into 2009 indicates foreclosures will put strong downward pressures on home prices ahead of November 2009. What then, Charlie Brown? There is fat chance these assets will be worth anything but even less in November 2009.

Short of the Federal Reserve and U.S. government putting an artificial floor under falling home prices, the implication is that this $11 trillion market of off-balance-sheet entities will still be negatively affected and appear short of capital to both regulators and lenders when the time comes.

Commenting on the lobbying efforts of these security firms, author of The Big Picture Barry Ritholz notes: "The longer they wait, the worse it ultimately will be. The long Japanese Recession (1989-2003) was caused by precisely this refusal to take the markdown, and engage in all manner of delays, excuses, procrastinations. Eeediots -- This only will make it worse!"[50]

## PROCRASTINATION IS BOTH A SYMPTOM AND FUNCTION OF DENIAL

Unfortunately, the Japanese procrastination and refusal to acknowledge or take a loss on the books is not likely a cause but rather a symptom of a recession related to declining real estate values and our flawed belief system related to the tangible values of real estate. Call it a function of denial, if you will. Because the promulgated myth throughout time has been that real estate is not a speculative asset class as such, and therefore not subject the volatility and vagaries of other asset classes such as the stock market. But as Homer Hoyt showed us back in 1933, the real estate investor was slowly and inexorably ground down!

Thus viewed, our situation in the U.S. can be seen as not much different than the Japanese experience in the 1990s or that of the U.S. during the 1930s Great Depression. We might do well to remember Charles Kindleberger's insight that real estate speculators (specifically the banks and other lending institutions and not the specs to whom they loan money to make a real estate purchase) who end up in trouble "initially feel no such compunction" to take their losses.[51] Because their loans are backed by real estate assets, they presume these can't fall very far on the fallacious basis that home prices rarely if ever decline. The real trouble begins as and when these assumptions about assumptions continue to be invalidated by market forces.

Generally, the consensus view is that if and when home prices and other real estate values do fall, they will never fall very far; hence, the long-standing expectation is that any and all retrenchments would be brief and shallow, and therefore allow for a "soft-landing" scenario. But as we have seen already on the Case-Schiller Home Price index, home prices have been declining for over three years now, and substantially so. At this point in Q4 08 and three years into the housing recession, a prolonged and deep recession in the broad economy has been largely priced into the stock market, but this is not yet being fully reflected in the real estate market.

Asset valuations on the balance sheets of the banks have not been fully discounted. Nor will these assets be fully discounted when they are perpetually being swept under the TARP rug or onto the Fed's balance sheet at mark-to-make-believe valuations. When the economic recovery comes, however, many years in the future that proves to be, the myth is that these asset valuations will recover to their "hold-to-maturity" valuations. The Fed, U.S. Treasury and government are now clinging to the myth or fallacy that real estate values will eventually fully. But that belief assumes that either home prices were not over-inflated at the time of loan origination or that the next reflationary wave will push home prices above the peak home price valuations in 2005-2006. There are many flaws following that line of reasoning. But, for now, they are determined to cling to their expressions of hope that in the long run all will pan out.

That is a speculative risk they are taking and a bet the deflation spiral in the U.S. economy will not wind up like Japan's "Lost Decade" in the 1990s or the Great Depression of the 1930s. Not taking the write-down on these assets "only delays the day of reckoning"[52] says The Big Picture's Barry Ritholtz. The U.S. banks and the U.S. Treasury have been playing a version of the coin flip game. Every month home prices have fallen for the past three years: they all flip the coin and bet again that one month, maybe next month, home prices will stop falling. One month, they will eventually be right. Even a broken clock is right twice a day. But how much more home price deflation will be incurred before says FASB member Tom Linsmeier then?

## HOUSING CRISIS UNDERMINES BELIEF IN SOFT-LANDING SCENARIOS AND SUFFICIENT CAPITAL

The mistake they make is not recognizing that the cause of the recession was not a downturn in the economic cycle, but a downturn in the real estate cycle itself. When the downturn in real estate is accompanied by a rising glut of housing supply on the market, spiraling declines in home values and ever-rising foreclosures (estimated to be north of 5 million homes for 2008-2009 alone, according to Moody's Economy.com) and millions of people losing their jobs, the hoped-for recovery never comes.

"Slowly but inexorably" as Homer Hoyt put it so long ago, the banks are ground down and eventually suffer the consequences. Downturns in real estate cycles tend to be prolonged events. And because more folks own real estate than they do stocks, downturns tend to be so much more wicked than stock market downturns. Bankruptcies are quite obviously not limited to banks and other financial corporations, but extend to the homeowners as well during a real estate downturn.

In part, one function of an economic recession is to dismantle and discredit the belief systems of the previous boom cycle. By and large, financial firms are finding their distress levels to be much higher than they have ever anticipated during this financial crisis. This holds true from Countrywide Financial on down to all the other financial firms whose survival has been too heavily tied to the fate of the U.S. real estate and asset-backed markets. It's all part of the powerful boom-bust cycle that Keynesian market interventionists have strived so hard to avoid, but nevertheless have finally and utterly succumbed to. And worse yet, the dismantling of the boom cycle in the U.S. has spread completely beyond our borders to the entire rest of the world. Richard Kline elaborates on the ongoing economic failure of "unchecked" Keynesian stimulus:

> Every major economy caught the "American disease": the feverish delusion that unchecked macroeconomic stimulus would if "properly managed" make for endless prosperity with no side effects. The world has tried to collectively lift itself up by its Rolex bands, and now the global citizenry is in the downswing of a poorly executed back-flip headed face first into the pavement...
>
> And the worst part, to me, is that public financial authorities in most large economies still do not get it that they cannot collectively

> stimulate their way out of pain. There is too much of the belief that we don't need to clean up the mess, or redesign our macroeconomic strategies but that we can presumably just give ourselves a "methadone level" of stimulus and pull through with no more than night sweats and occasional asset vomiting. That's not gonna happen.[53]

Kline touches directly on one of the primary risks investors and consumers must bear going forward. How does one hedge against the policy risks of massive, unchecked, completely out-of-control economic reflationary policies? If unchecked, I am presuming this path will ultimately lead to massive inflation and possibly even hyperinflation in pockets of the world.

Globally, financial firms' distress levels were so high in October 2008, and mistrust amongst each was so high, they stopped lending entirely to each other in the LIBOR market. They also stopped lending to businesses in the commercial paper market because their own capital needs were so high. And to meet their short-term borrowing needs, they all sought the much cheaper Fed's alphabet soup of new lending facilities they created specifically for this liquidity and insolvency crisis.

## REASSURING INVESTORS UNTIL BLUE IN THE FACE

Market reassurances come from all angles, from the Federal Reserve, the U.S. Treasury, Washington, the White House, company CEOs, *ad infinitum*. Two of the more striking examples of this behavior during this crisis came from the U.S. Secretary Hank Paulson and Merrill Lynch's new CEO John Thain, who took over from the reckless risk-taking Stan O'Neal. The widespread predisposition to offer profuse reassurances in the face of disaster leads me to believe that these executives and policymakers are just doing what comes naturally to them.

## REASSURANCES FROM HANK PAULSON:

July 12, 2007: Just before the stock market peaked, Hank Paulson said, "This is far and away the strongest global economy I've seen in my business lifetime."

August 1, 2007: Paulson added, "I see the underlying economy as being very healthy."

March 16, 2008: On the eve of Bear Stearns' failure, Paulson remarked: "We've got strong financial institutions... Our markets are the envy of the world. They're resilient, they're...innovative, they're flexible. I think we move very quickly to address situations in this country, and, as I said, our financial institutions are strong."

May 7, 2008: Just a month or so before the worst of the financial crisis hit the U.S. economy and stock market, Paulson said: "The worst is likely to be behind us...There's no doubt that things feel better today, by a lot, than they did in March."

July 20, 2008: Just after the GSEs Fannie and Freddie became insolvent, Paulson said: "Of course the list [of difficulties] is going to grow longer given the stresses in the marketplace...but again, it's a safe banking system, a sound banking system. Our regulators are on top of it. This is a very manageable situation."

September 19, 2008: After the domino-like failure of our entirely safe-and-sound banking system, Paulson finally admits to Congress and to the American public that there has been a big gaping hole in the balance sheet of the world, saying: "We're talking hundreds of billions of dollars—this needs to be big enough to make a real difference and get at the heart of the problem. This is the way we stabilize the system. If these efforts result in a net cost to the taxpayer, it's a better bet than the alternative."[54]

"It's a better bet than the alternative"? As we have seen, Paulson's bet—the TARP plan—did not pan out very well at all, as it was originally intended and implemented. To many market observers, Paulson made a rotten bet on behalf of the taxpayers. Speaking of costs to the taxpayers, analyst estimates of the total outlays of Paulson's TARP plan along with the conservatorships of the GSEs, and loans to AIG have risen to a few trillion dollars since September 19, 2008. Although other analysts would have us believe that in the end, the costs to the taxpayer will be much smaller and we might actually make a profit: to these rose-colored optimists, I would like to remind them of John Maynard Keynes' dictum that "in the long run, we are all dead!"

The short run is going to be a bear and damn near kill us. There's no doubt that things felt worse at the end of 2008, "by a lot," than they did in March 2008 when the Fed and Treasury first cranked up their bailout and rescue machinery. The problem is always the same: how to get there from here, when we are so buried under trillions of debt? Or as Barron's Alan Abelson said it:

> If you are one of those trusting souls who think
> the taxpayers will come through unscathed
> and with something to show for having put
> their money at risk besides grudging gratitude,
> we have a piece of property with killer views
> and no neighbors that you can have for a song.
> Did we neglect to mention it's in lovely down
> town Chernobyl?[55]

Had the unfortunate situation with the GSEs and Lehman Brothers arisen in September 2008, the safety and soundness of the banking system might not have been completely compromised. What looked like a manageable situation to Paulson on July 20, 2008, clearly got out of control months later in September. And so here we are mired deep in a severe recession!

By Q4 08, banks and other financial institutions clearly could not handle the financial distress brought about by the credit crisis that devolved into a solvency crisis. Yet, even while their capital needs have been skyrocketing, financial firms had been extremely loathe to acknowledge their increasing capital requirements all throughout the latter half of 2007 and through 2008.

## JOHN THAIN: THE BLAME FALLS MAINLY ON THE PLAIN

A case in point is Merrill Lynch. After Merrill Lynch fired their CEO Stan "The Man" O'Neal and hired John Thain to replace him in the fourth quarter of 2007, Merrill began a series of capital raises beginning in December 2007 and ending in July 2008. The capital raises in December and January were slightly more than $5 billion. By the end of July 2008, the capital raises exceeded $30 billion. There were seven total capital raises in eight months, one for almost every month, with two of the seven capital raises coming in July 2008.

After every capital raise, CEO John Thain offered reassurances to shareholders. On each capital raise, Mr. Thain would promise investors that this will be the last dollar they will ever need to raise. To be sure, it would be a bit of a non-starter if Thain had told new investors that Merrill Lynch would need tens of billions more in capital in the near future. This would be tantamount to guaranteeing your new investors that their new investments would be substantially diluted in the near future.

What investor would ever lend money on those premises? So, Thain did the sensible thing and promised new investors at each capital raise that would be the last bit of capital Merrill Lynch would require. There was another reason Thain would take this approach. Merrill Lynch, after all, was an investment bank, and banks simply never run the risk of letting other banks know they have a big black hole in their balance sheets that will require tens of billions of dollars to patch it up. Whether banks need the money or not, banks will never appear as needing help—until it is too late, of course.

Between March 16 and June 17, 2008, Merrill Lynch's CEO John Thain was quoted at various junctures stating:

> We have more capital than we need so we can say to the market that we don't need more injections. We can confirm that we have tackled the problem... Today I can say that we will not need additional funds. These problems are behind us...
>
> In 2007, we lost $8.6 billion, but we raised $12.8 billion in new capital... We deliberately raised more capital than we lost last year... And we did that on purpose so that we could say to the marketplace that we raised more than enough capital...
>
> We believe that will allow us to not have to go back to the equity market in the foreseeable future... We have plenty of capital going forward, and we don't need to come back into the equity market. No more capital raising, I'm sure we have enough capital...
>
> Our philosophy about this is that we are well-capitalized. We're comfortable with our

capital position. We, like everyone else, are deleveraging our balance sheet.[56]

Stan O'Neal had dealt Merrill a huge black hole for a balance sheet.
Arguably, so blackened was that balance sheet by the opaque waste
residing on it, Thain's visibility was near zero. Much like being in a
thick fog at sea you can't penetrate; you only hope it lifts soon. The
fog thickened instead, requiring Merrill to raise capital from private
investors repeatedly. Even ceding Thain this possibility, the mere fre-
quency of the capital raises should have raised eyebrows and called
into question the merits of Thain's reassurances to shareholders
whom he was diluting into oblivion. On January 22, 2009, it was
revealed that the capital raises exceeding $30 billion were more than
offset by the $21.5 billion losses and the $15 billion of bonuses Merrill executives paid themselves in 2008. The next day Thain was fired.

Reassurances during this credit crisis proved to be as tainted as
the subprime toxic waste that brought on the crisis to begin with.

## DELEVERING BALANCE SHEETS PROVES COSTLY

Delevering the toxic waste on the balance sheets of financial firms
were proving costly. Even though they were later bought out by Bank
of America, Merrill Lynch offers us an excellent case in point. Prior
to the legislation of the TARP program, Merrill had sold $30.6 bil-
lion (the notional value on its books) of its "super senior" asset-
backed CDOs (collateralized debt obligations) on its balance sheet
to an affiliate of Lone Star Funds for $6.7 billion on July 28, 2008.
This translates into a return on investment (ROI) for Merrill of 22
cents on the dollar. However, to do so, Merrill had to provide the
Lone Star affiliate with 75% of the financing, or $5.8 billion, to get
the deal done and the toxic waste off its balance sheet.

Essentially, the notional value of these securities jumped from

$30.6 billion to $36.4 billion. The out of pocket cost to the Lone Star affiliate was less than $1 billion. Put another way, Lone Star picked up these securities for less than 3 cents to the dollar on the notional value of these securities.

Essentially, Merrill could not even give the toxic waste away to get it off its balance sheet. They actually had to pay a waste hauler to come and take it away. Commenting on the high costs of transacting business on Wall Street these days, Federated Investors' Joseph Balestrino remarked "This is almost self-induced balance-sheet destruction. This is far beyond your basic slowdown."[57] This fire sale of CDOs serves as a good illustration of what would happen to all the other financial firms if they de-levered their illiquid and troubled assets from their balance sheets.

To Thain and Merrill's credit, the CDOs remaining on their books only totaled about $8.8 billion. In a statement made on July 28, 2008, Thain commented, "the sale of the substantial majority of our CDO positions represents a significant milestone in our risk-reduction efforts."[58] The cost of doing so, however, was still quite high, and unfortunately, they lost control of their own destiny in September when they were forced into a shotgun wedding with Bank of America.

Other Wall Street firms have been delevering as well in 2008. According to company reports, Goldman Sachs, Morgan Stanley, and Lehman Brothers "cut their combined assets by $97.5 billion or 3.4% in the first half of 2008. The average leverage ratio for the three firms fell to 26.1 from 30.1." [59]

## BORROWING FROM PETER TO PAY PAUL

For Merrill Lynch, this was a very expensive way to transact business. Not only were they forced to pay Lone Star to haul their garbage away, but they have had to raise over $30 billion in capital thus far in 2008 to tackle their deteriorating balance sheet problems. On account of this Lone Star transaction to unload the CDOs, it became necessary for Merrill to raise more capital by selling $8.55 billion in stock in July 2008.

Not surprisingly, Merrill's borrowing costs in 2008, along with other Wall Street firms, have skyrocketed. Merrill's CFO Nelson Chai told analysts on July 17, 2008, that the company had issued $37 billion in long-term debt during the first half of 2008 "and plans to look for opportunities to issue more debt in the market as necessary." [60]

Merrill's debt maturing in April 2018 yielded 8.15% and debt maturing in April 2038 yielded 8.76% on July 25, 2008, reported *Bloomberg News*. The 10-year Treasury note on July 25, 2008, yielded 4.11%. In short, Merrill's credit spread has widened to more than 400 bps over the 10-year Treasury note.

"It's going to be harder and harder for them to borrow long term in this environment, to pay the spreads that investors are going to want," said David Hendler, an analyst at CreditSights Inc.[61] Low borrowing costs have become a thing of the past for these distressed Wall Street firms. The days of buying assets with cheap levered money are long gone. As long as foreclosures remain elevated, borrowing costs will likely remain high for these firms for the foreseeable future.

Even though MER merged with BAC in a forced wedding for $29 per share, they will still retain their name. I am sure this was not done out of the kindness of CEO Ken Lewis' heart, but rather, a recognition that you can't buy the kind of "thundering herd, bullish on America" branding that Merrill Lynch has accomplished as an investment bank. But MER still has financial troubles that have yet to be addressed. Yes, Merrill's CDO risks are diminished, the cost of capital will be higher and UBS analyst Glenn Schorr notes further downside risks for Merrill Lynch will be coming from their commercial RE and other holdings.

It has been a rough ride for Merrill Lynch shareholders. In less than two years, the price declined from almost $99 to roughly $12. This bear market move represents a reversion to its long-term (log-scaled chart not shown) trendline from 1974-1990, suffering the worst bear market since 1974, when its share price last fell 87%.

Banks and financial firms like Merrill Lynch caught in the fire of the Subprime Devil have all been burnt to the ground. Damnation and hellfire is what they received in the end for all their egregious risk-taking. The only silver lining for the banking industry as a whole has been the kindness of taxpayers, not only in the U.S., but really to taxpayers around the world.

## APPLYING THE "HERMENEUTICS OF SUSPICION" METHODOLOGY TO INVESTING

Back in my pre-seminary days, the feminist theologian Elizabeth Schussler Fiorenza introduced me to a new concept "Hermeneutics of Suspicion." Say what? In short, it means to interpret everything with an element of suspicion. The hermeneutics of suspicion is:

> ...a method of interpretation which assumes that the literal or surface-level meaning of a text is an effort to conceal the political interests which are served by the text. The purpose of interpretation is to strip off the concealment, unmasking those interests. It unmasks and unveils untenable claims. It suspects the credibility of the superficial text and explores what is underneath the surface to reveal a more authentic dimension of meaning.[62]

The hermeneutics of suspicion teaches us to question the credibility of the data, the reassurances, the assumptions about assumptions, and the answers provided by company executives. Despite the efforts of regulators, the legislation of Sarbanes-Oxley, and the FASB to date, what companies actually report versus what is actually going on in the company are not necessarily one and the same thing. The same holds true even for the products in the unregulated credit and credit derivative markets.

For purposes of safety and soundness, this makes it imperative for investors of all ilk to always question both the credibility and validity of securities they are investing in. Investors must separate the facts from the fluff in their due diligence—insofar as that is even possible. That is not always an easy task, let alone always possible, but one the investor must nevertheless be up for it, if he/she ever hopes to achieve any measure of success in the stock and credit markets.

In the final analysis, whenever any publicly traded company (financial or otherwise) cries uncle at a shareholder meeting or conference call and then proceeds to offer shareholders and analysts reassurances of any sort, investors should be very wary and consider running for the exits. It is one thing for a company to acknowledge their troubles, but entirely another thing when they begin offering parental reassurances to their investors as if their child had only scraped their knee.

# Northern Rock Standing in a Dry Creek and Waving a Stick

*Never did a ship founder with a captain and crew
more ignorant of the reason for its misfortune
or more impotent to do anything about it[1].*

— E.J. Hobsbawm 1968

ON JULY 25, 2007, Northern Rock's CEO Adam Applegarth wrote an in-house memo to fellow employees stating "It is likely to take the outside world a little time to understand our developing strategy, but you can be assured the outlook for Northern Rock remains very positive."[2] It didn't take the Rest of the World (ROW) too much longer to catch on to Northern Rock's strategy. In fact their strategy was laid bare for the ROW in the immediate weeks that followed this in-house memo.

## No One to Lend Them Any Money

Applegarth said on a conference call for analysts on September 14, 2007 that Northern Rock failed because on August 9, 2007, the bank couldn't find anyone, anywhere in the world who would lend it money. "Life changed on August 9 virtually like snapping a finger," adding that nobody could have predicted a total shutdown of global credit markets.[3]

## LIFE CHANGED AT THE SNAP OF A FINGER FOR THE KNICKERBOCKER TRUST IN 1907

In many ways Applegarth's experience on August 9, 2007, mirrored the experience of Charles Barney, president of the Knickerbocker Trust on October 22, 1907, exactly 100 years earlier. Bank Trusts, at the turn of the century, made huge amounts of loans backed by a very shaky foundation for collateral—securities in the extremely volatile stock market. Stock valuations can go from zero to infinity and back to zero again in a New York minute. Banks can never ever issue loans on a shaky foundation without eventually wreaking havoc upon themselves. Every time in the history of banking that loans are issued on some shaky foundation, it eventually leads to both crisis and panic and sometimes recessions and depressions.

Back in the Rich Man's Panic of 1907, the Knickerbocker Trust, along with many speculators had been attempting to corner the market of United Copper. On Monday October 21, 1907, fears of a copper glut followed rumors that the Morgans and Guggenheims were interested in developing new copper mines in Alaska. The shares in United Copper's stock immediately plummeted at the prospect, "spreading ruin and dragging stocks to levels unseen since the 1893 depression."[4]

The foundation for all those outstanding loans at Knickerbocker Trust collapsed in virtually one day—over a rumor no less! Knickerbocker's business model, based almost entirely on the direction of United Copper's share price, caused the failure of the entire trust company. Risk management at the Knickerbocker Trust was not a strong point. To not see the risk or flaw in their business model or to protect against that flaw was a huge mistake.

The fall in United Copper's share price greatly alarmed the Knickerbocker Trust's 18,000 depositors and the panic among Knickerbocker's depositors quickly spread like wildfire to depositors at other trusts around town.

Pierpont Morgan of JP Morgan sent the future Fed Chairman, Benjamin Strong of Bankers Trust, to audit Knickerbocker's books. During the audit, Benjamin Strong is reported to have caught a glimpse of the grim faces of the Knickerbocker depositors from the back room: "The consternation of the faces of the people in line, many of whom I knew, I shall never forget."

After the audit was conducted, Ben Strong reported back to Pierpont. Upon hearing the gloom and doom results, Pierpont wrote off Knickerbocker Trust as hopeless. Put out to pasture, the trust failed the very next day on the afternoon on Tuesday, October 22, 1907. The bellicose Pierpont Morgan said at the time, "I can't go on being everybody's goat. I have got to stop somewhere."[5]

The next day Pierpont put together a rescue pool comprised of Morgan, George Baker of 1st National Bank, and James Stillman of National City Bank. In an audit of another trust company (the Trust Company of America) conducted by Ben Strong, the results were far more favorable. Upon hearing this good cheer, Pierpont exclaimed, "This is the place to stop the trouble then," and the three bankers pooled $3 million to save the Trust Company of America.[6] Evidently, the Trust Company of America had much less exposure to United Copper's share price than the Knickerbocker trust.

Financially wiped out, a few weeks later the president of the Knickerbocker Trust, Charles Barney, shot himself to death. This supposedly set off a chain reaction of other suicides among the Knickerbocker Trust depositors.

Applegarth was far more fortunate than Charles Barney of the Knickerbocker Trust 100 years earlier, as he was not at risk of ruin when the bank collapsed. Nine months before the collapse, on January 26, 2007, he sold 64% of all his shares. Rather than offing himself, Applegarth has opted for privacy: "I've no desire to talk to the press: OK, bye-bye," he replied when contacted by *Bloomberg Markets*.[7]

It should be noted that Angelo Mozilo of Countrywide Financial also avoided financial ruin by selling almost all his shares early in 2007 as well. Oddly enough, neither Mozilo nor Applegarth needed a "superior spirit" to tell them when to sell yet neither of these CEO's could see the Subprime Devil coming. Or so they told the public. Actions, in these two instances, spoke louder than words. Unlike Mozilo, who received a huge bonus (golden parachute) for the take-over of CFC by BAC, there was no windfall golden parachute for Applegarth when the Bank of England had to perform a "rescue" of the collapsed Northern Rock bank. Golden parachutes could be more of an American thing.

## BANK OF ENGLAND'S RELUCTANT BAILOUT OF NORTHERN ROCK

Fortunately for depositors of Northern Rock, the Bank of England did not write off the failed bank of Northern Rock as hopeless—as Pierpont Morgan did 100 years ago with the Knickerbocker Trust. But only reluctantly did the Bank of England rescue Northern Rock. This reluctance was primarily a function of Mervyn King, the Bank of England's governor, who was philosophically predisposed not to raise the safety nets and thereby create moral hazards.

In the days and weeks prior to the September 14, 2007, insolvency of Northern Rock, Bank of England Governor Mervyn King had been roiling against the moral hazards of other central banks like the Federal Reserve and ECB, willy-nilly injecting liquidity into the money markets on the grounds that it would encourage "risky behavior" among lenders and poor decision-making.

But, in the end, the risky behaviors of Applegarth's strategy had already taken place. The collateral damage wreaked upon depositors of Northern Rock was now too big to be ignored by the Bank of England. The question of whether proper regulation and financial oversight of Northern Rock could have avoided the whole entangle-ment from ever happening in the first place is a subject for another debate.

As a result of Northern Rock's inability to find anyone anywhere in the world willing to lend them any money since that fateful day on August 9, 2007, they were no longer solvent by September 14, 2007.

On the day of Northern Rock's insolvency, Bank of England Governor King found religion and provided the necessary emergency funds to Northern Rock. In a statement that day, King said: "this measure is being taken to alleviate the strains in longer-maturity money markets. The bank will accept 'mortgage collateral' at the auction of 10 billion pounds ($20 billion) in loans next week, which will have a penalty rate of 6.75%."[8] By imposing a penalty rate, King adhered to Walter Bagehot's rule to "lend freely" during a credit crisis, but at a higher rate.

Chancellor of the Exchequer Alistair Darling's assurances that Northern Rock's deposits are "backed by the Bank of England" went largely ignored by Northern Rock's customers. Within a few days following the revelation that Northern Rock was insolvent, custom-ers withdrew more than $4 billion in deposits. Northern Rock CEO Adam Applegarth admitted that he probably would have "done the same thing if I was in their shoes."[9]

Fully apprised of the shortcomings of Applegarth's strategy for Northern Rock, the locals have since been colorfully calling the bank "Northern Wreck", noted *Bloomberg Markets*.

## STANDING IN THE PIT OF THE S&P 500, WAVING A STICK

Fly-fisherman extraordinaire, and author John Gierach, who waxes philosophic about life and fly fishing in his books, once wrote a hu-morous tome called *Standing in a River Waving a Stick*. Gierach's fly-fishing title is an appropriate metaphor for market liquidity. Liquidity serves an extremely important function for market participants. Without liquidity, it is akin to standing in a dry creek trying to catch trout. Without adequate water to bring the fish upstream, there will be nothing to catch. Oh, you can go fishing in a dry creek, to be sure, but don't plan on catching any trout.

As a case in point, the loss of market liquidity affected my own career and that of many others whose careers depended on the order flow that went through the "open outcry" at the Chicago Mercantile Exchange trading pits. Had we failed to adapt to the changing environment and make appropriate adjustments, we could have potentially suffered the same outcome as Mr. Applegarth.

The advent of a global electronic exchange in 1998-1999 called Globex ushered in a new reality for our trading group. Suddenly we had competition. Admittedly, the competition was insubstantial in the early years. But as Globex caught on and its popularity grew, the liquidity of the S&P 500 trading pit was diverted to this new exchange.

Over time, the popularity of the S&P 500 e-mini contract grew and eventually displaced more than 80% of the daily trading volume. The order flow in the S&P 500 futures pit was reduced to a trickle by this displacement. Liquidity on the primary "open outcry" exchange literally dried up as order flow on the Globex electronic exchange for S&P 500 futures burgeoned. The long-standing, time-honored value of the "real estate" of where one stood in the pit, which was once estimated to be worth $1 million a year, had been rendered worth next to nothing by the dominance of the e-mini trading volumes. Open outcry was no longer a viable business model for market makers.

In essence, our trading group found itself standing in a dry creek trying to catch fish. How you gonna manage a day's catch in a dry creek? You can't! Liquidity had simply dried up, and with it the robust profits we were accustomed to. Just how profitable do you think a business model based on liquidity will be if the liquidity is no longer there? Without it, our business model was broken. In acknowledgement that the open outcry business model had lost its robustness and viability, one by one, many of the local market makers in the S&P 500 pit had left the business by 2005.

In the same respect, this is exactly what had happened to Northern Rock. Life changed on August 9, 2007, for Applegarth and the company. Their business model based on liquidity provided by loans from "other people's money" failed them, but in a far more cataclysmic way. It happened virtually overnight, "at the snap of a finger," as CEO Applegarth declared.

## AN EXTRAORDINARY ERROR IN JUDGMENT

Commenting on Northern Rock's overnight fate, MF Global Credit market analyst Simon Maughan said:

> Northern Rock's fatal mistake was that it didn't adequately hedge against the possibility of a steep rise in the cost of borrowing in international credit markets. It was an extraordinary error. They were running a balance sheet that exposed them massively to sudden sharp moves in short-term interest rates.[10]

## UNPREDICTABLE AND UNPRECEDENTED—OR JUST AN EXTREME BUSINESS MODEL

Testifying to UK lawmakers in October, Northern Rock CEO Adam Applegarth said nobody could have predicted the shutdown of credit availability in August.

David Lascelles, at the Centre for the Study of Financial Innovation, took offense at Applegarth's claims, saying "Applegarth was being totally disingenuous. It is no accident that it was Northern Rock rather than another bank that crashed, because he was running an extreme business model."[11]

In a January 2008 report, UK lawmakers investigating the bank's collapse concluded "regulators were negligent, and NR was reckless."[12]

Testifying before lawmakers in October 2007, the Chairman of Northern Rock's risk management committee, Sir Derek Wanless, said the bank's hedging and risks controls were adequate but that "There was an unprecedented and unpredictable change in the market."[13]

The "unprecedented and unpredictable" refrain exploited by Applegarth was soon to become quite the fashionable parlance for Wall Street firms among CEO's and other executives caught in the snares of the evolving subprime meltdown and credit crisis. Describing events as "unprecedented and unpredictable" was meant to imply that unfolding events were along the lines of one of Nassim Taleb's highly improbable "Black Swans." This gave these market participants a convenient excuse to hide behind, that there was no way they could have ever seen this coming, thereby disowning their own personal responsibility and accountability.

## PUSHING RISK MANAGEMENT MODELS TOO HARD

Northern Rock's new chairman, Bryan Sanderson, noted the bank was securitizing mortgage securities from "NY to Sydney. They pushed the model too hard, too aggressively. They were just not sufficiently risk averse."[14]

Sanderson's point is well taken, and should not be overlooked by either investors or risk managers. It is of paramount importance that risk managers acknowledge that there are finite limits to all risk management models, and it behooves them to know precisely where those boundary limits are. This is a discussion our trading group had repeatedly over the past decade. No matter what black box system or mouse trap you build, at some point an adverse shift in the economic climate will come along to threaten it, undermine its foundation, and eradicate its viability. No one describes this phenomenon better in the abstract than the Maestro Alan Greenspan and *The Black Swan* author Nassim Taleb.

## *"YOUR MODELS DON'T WORK"* — NASSIM TALEB

Just months prior to the insolvency of Northern Rock, in March 2007, Nassim Taleb, author of now famous *The Black Swan* walked into Morgan Stanley to give the firm's risk management department a message: "Your models don't work."

> If markets are governed by extreme movements and unexpected events, we shouldn't be fooled into believing worst case scenarios. If you're in banking and lending, surprise outcomes are likely to be negative for you. Put yourself in situations where favorable consequences are much larger than unfavorable ones.[15]

## STRESS TESTING

When it comes to "stress testing" risk management models, Taleb believes they should be tested not to verify that they work, but through efforts to prove the models don't work. Taleb's risk management proposition is much like the philosopher Karl Popper, who argued scientific theories (conjectures) are abstract in nature and can be tested only indirectly, by reference to their implications. Logically, no number of positive outcomes can confirm a scientific theory or conjecture, but a single counterexample can show the theory to be false.

Scientific theories that survive Popper's "process of refutation" or error elimination (EE) are not any more scientifically valid, they are just deemed more "fit" or relevant to the problem at hand. So it should be with risk management models.

## "WE WILL NEVER HAVE A PERFECT MODEL OF RISK" — GREENSPAN, FT, MARCH 16, 2008

Recapping the credit crunch on August 9, 2007, Greenspan noted in a March 16, 2008, *Financial Times* article that

> Market systems and their degree of leverage and liquidity are rooted in trust in the solvency of counterparties. That trust was badly shaken on August 9, 2007, when BNP Paribas revealed large unanticipated losses on U.S. subprime securities
>
> The essential problem is that our models—both risk models and econometric models—as complex as they have become, are still too simple to capture the full array of governing variables that drive global economic reality. A model, of necessity, is an abstraction from the full detail of the real world. In line with the time-honored observation that diversification lowers risk, computers crunched reams of historical data in quest of negative correlations between prices of tradable assets; correlations that could help insulate investment portfolios from the broad swings in an economy. When such asset prices, rather than offsetting each other's movements, fell in unison on and following August 9 last year, huge losses across virtually all risk-asset classes ensued...

Risk management [models seek] to maximise risk-adjusted rates of return on equity; often, in the process, underused capital is considered "waste." [Maximizing return on equity during expansion phases badly under-prices risks when a contraction comes along.]

The contraction phase of credit and business cycles, driven by fear, have historically been far... more abrupt than the expansion phase, which is driven by a slow but cumulative build-up of euphoria. Over the past half-century, the American economy was in contraction only one-seventh of the time. But it is the onset of that one-seventh for which risk management must be most prepared. Negative correlations among asset classes, so evident during an expansion, can collapse as all asset prices fall together, undermining the strategy of improving risk/reward trade-offs through diversification...

These models do not fully capture what I believe has been, to date, only a peripheral addendum to business-cycle and financial modelling—the innate human responses that result in swings between euphoria and fear that repeat themselves generation after generation with little evidence of a learning curve.

We will never be able to anticipate all discontinuities in financial markets. Discontinuities are, of necessity, a surprise. Anticipated events are arbitraged away. But if, as I strongly suspect, periods of euphoria are very difficult to suppress as they build, they will not collapse until the speculative fever breaks on its own. Paradoxically, to the extent risk management succeeds in identifying such episodes, it can prolong and enlarge the period of euphoria. But risk management can never reach perfection. It will eventually fail and a disturbing reality will be laid bare, prompting an unexpected and sharp discontinuous response.

In the current crisis, as in past crises, we can learn much, and policy in the future will be informed by these lessons. But we cannot hope to anticipate the specifics of future crises with any degree of confidence...[16]

## IT'S THOSE PESKY BUSINESS CYCLE CONTRACTIONS RISK MODELS MUST PREPARE FOR

Metaphorically, contractions in the business cycle bring out the "bunker mentality" among risk managers. This is when they are supposed to shut down their little black boxes and seek safe harbor instruments such as those the U.S. Treasuries have historically provided.

That is why when the credit crunch came along in August, Glen Capelo at RBS Capital noted that the high-yield funds that had been buying all that asset-backed-commercial-paper "have all switched to the safe side. I'm sure their managers have all given them a Treasury-only mandate, at least until the dust settles."[17]

As Greenspan so eloquently related to us above, there never has been and never will be a perfect risk management model to fit all occasions. There is no "one-size-fits-all" model out there. As Taleb put it, some models are just more "fit" or more relevant for the situation at hand. There are limits to all risk management systems designed to maximize return on equity (ROE). When systemic risks introduced into the global financial system become too large to ignore, models based on the expansionary phase of the business cycle will fail. This has been deftly proven to Countrywide, Northern Rock, Bear Stearns, and to so many other largely unknown companies during the credit crisis of 2007-2008.

## THE BUNKER MENTALITY

Systemic risks in the financial world, described above by Greenspan in the abstract, are no different than the inherent risks of Mother Nature. For the most part, Mother Nature smiles benevolently and bestows upon us generally fair to excellent weather. Still, there are those times when her malevolent nature takes over, forcing planes to be grounded, boats to batten down their hatches, and cars to pull over onto the side of the road during a really good blow.

There are times when the risks to piloting a plane or boat or driving a car are too great, and the risk of ruin is simply not worth taking. We intuitively know that these vehicles are not safe in a big storm and we appropriately seek safe harbor. For some reason however, that safe harbor response is not always triggered in the animal spirits of the financial community-at-large whose *raison d'etre* is to maximize ROE.

Not all spirits inhabiting the financial world, however, are strictly driven to maximize ROE at any cost. Fund managers like Bruce Monrad at Northeast Investment Management clearly recognized the financial storm on the horizon in mid-2007 when he unequivocally stated "It's time to be pretty cautions in the credit markets" and that "many of these things are beyond our risk desires."[18] Not all risk managers and CEOs are cut from the same cloth as the Applegarths, Mozilos, and O'Neals who failed to recognize that their business models and investment strategies would one day fail them.

There are times of adversity during which fund managers and CEOs should deploy good old common sense and override their risk management and business models that typically, during the liquid expansionary phases of a business cycle, run on autopilot—until the storm passes.

Market participants need to embrace the sound wisdom of Bryan Sanderson to not push our risk management models too hard, and that of Glen Capelo to know when to give a "treasury-only mandate to risk managers," and that of Bruce Monrad to know when a product no longer meets one's risk parameters.

In short, investors must know how to "revulse" the risk—to puke it back up and no longer seek those maximized risk-adjusted rates of return. This implies foregoing the "Alpha" and chasing yields at any cost. We don't have to adopt a kill-or-be-killed mindset. We must learn that we ought not be as "financially ambitious" as Northern Rock! We don't have to be "hurricane or tornado chasers" and kill ourselves in the process of trying to squeeze a few extra pennies out of each quarterly earnings report.

We need to understand that under-used capital is not always "waste," as Greenspan relates. In fact, under-used "waste" capital can be considered one of the best kinds of capital there is during times of financial turmoil. Consider, if you will, the value investors who are intimately aware of the principle that "Cash is King" in certain environments.

To remind ourselves of this fact, all we have to do is glance over at the cash Warren Buffet was sitting in 2007-2008. What was he doing in the first half of 2008? Simply, Buffett was trying to buy at firesale prices the financially distressed bond insurance companies—Ambac and MBIA. Had he been able to get his arms around the Bear Stearns deal in time, he intimated that he would have possibly liked to have done that deal. Having some readily available "cash on the sidelines" is the only way for market participants and investors to take advantage of the inevitable market inefficiencies that crop up every year.

## BANK RUNS, RESERVE REQUIREMENTS AND THE FRACTIONAL RESERVE SYSTEM

It was taken as a "virtual article of faith" the late Murray Rothbard tells us in *Making Economic Sense* that bank runs were supposed to be a thing of the past in the U.S. once the FDIC was established in 1933. Up until the savings and loans failures came to pass in 1985, commercial banking had become regarded as "super-safe." But since the S&L's collapsed in the mid 1980s, all those old assurances went by the wayside. Happily for Rothbard, the failure of the S&L's gave some credibility to his repeated warnings that our banking system is "inherently unsound and even insolvent."

Rothbard notes the reason our financial institutions are "inherently unsound" is because they are built upon a "Fractional Reserve Banking System" and somewhat outlandishly argues for a return to the "non-inflationary policy of a 100% reserves" banking system to make his point. The Federal Reserve Bank today sets a reserve requirement of about 10% of the total deposits made at commercial banks. This means a typical bank taking in deposits can make loans up to ten times that of the total deposits made at its bank.

Rothbard argues that the present reserve requirements in the fractional reserve system are both fraudulent and too low. After all, we are finding banks and other financial institutions were far too undercapitalized for both the S&L crisis and the housing crisis. Lucky for us in the current environment, most of our financial institutions, by hook or by crook, have been able to raise badly needed capital to repair their deteriorating balance sheets in 2008.

## PUBLIC CONFIDENCE

The fascinating thing about bank runs, when they occur, whether they take place in 1907 or 2007, is that when one unsound bank or financial institution collapses or otherwise fails, it tends to have a huge domino effect on other financial institutions. Of course, this can not be tolerated to any great degree or length of time within our financial system.

Because the money is not actually "in the bank," the fractional reserve banking system rests entirely on "public confidence." Rothbard complains that this type of banking system is "not a legitimate industry," no more than "a house of cards...so long as it continues to be a system of...fraudulent making of contracts that it is impossible to honor."[19]

## POLITICAL AND FINANCIAL EXPEDIENCY

Rothbard bristled about the structure of our current banking system and the number of bailouts that have had to take place under it. Moral hazards resulting from easy money had to be cast aside lest everyone discover that the whole banking system was being "held together by smoke and mirrors" without which "the financial system would collapse."

Likewise, First Pacific Advisors complained two weeks after the bailout of Bear Stearns that each time the government performs another bailout, the country unduly raises the safety net,

> so that the market's discipline in a capitalistic
> system has been truncated. [We are witness
> to] a growing level of decisions that are based
> upon expediency rather than sound long-term
> decision making. Each time these expedient
> decisions are made, the level of risk within the
> U.S. economy has been increased.[20]

First Pacific is rightly concerned that the safety nets are far too high, and that one of these days, if the government does not take care, it will find itself under water and unable to service its debts. In effect, the default risk in the U.S. is rising with each and every new bailout of our major financial institutions, be it Bear Stearns or our government-sponsored enterprises (GSE's) Fannie Mae and Freddie Mac.

Before the creation of the FDIC in 1933, and before the ever-increasing bailouts by the Federal Reserve, other central banks and Sovereign Wealth Funds, it was bank runs "severe as they were that kept the banking system under check and prevented any substantial amount of inflation," contends Rothbard.[21]

Rothbard's insights are also instructive with regard to inflation. It is impossible to ignore the inflationary pressures that have resulted inside the first year of this credit crisis, as central banks try to keep the financial system liquefied and keep the economy from sinking into a recession or worse. The concerted efforts of various central banks around the world to prop up the credit markets has resulted in the prices of all commodities virtually doubling across the board. The global inflation in 2008 has led to hoarding of foods and a great deal of social unrest, and even caused the known deaths of three people in China who were trampled in a stampede to buy cooking oils.

To avert the hyperinflation that Rothbard fears could easily result under our fractional reserve banking system, central bankers will have to make an equally concerted effort to mop up the excess liquidity they have injected into the system.

Banking reserve requirements can be set higher or lower depending on the central bank. Central banks determine the reserve requirements that commercial banks must meet for purposes of lending. For instance, in the 1930s, when the Fed feared there might be another stock market bubble in the making that would lead to another 1929-style crash, the Federal Reserve doubled the reserve requirements from 12% to 24% in 1936-1937.

I have suggested over the years that the Fed would at some point be required to increase the reserve requirements to increase the safety and soundness of our banking system. To date, however, all the regulators have asked and required is that these under-capitalized financial firms raise more capital. These firms, like Merrill Lynch cited above, have been successfully raising capital more or less up until this point, but not all banks will be so lucky in the final analysis.

More Countrywide Financials and Northern Rocks lie waiting in the wings to fail. In fact, our GSEs, Fannie Mae and Freddie Mac, would have failed by the middle of 2008 had it not been for the "explicit guarantee" of the U.S. Government and Treasury backed by the full faith and credit of the U.S. taxpayers. If the taxpayers' ability to fund the GSEs becomes compromised (for whatever reason) while foreclosures are still rising and as home values are still plunging, the housing crisis will morph or otherwise evolve into a full-blown epidemic in the U.S.

# NO SIR, THE FIRST THING IS CHARACTER: LENDING PRACTICES OVER THE PAST HUNDRED YEARS

> **Untermyer:** Is not commercial credit based primarily upon money or property?
>
> **Pierpont Morgan:** No Sir, the first thing is character.
>
> **Untermyer:** Before money or property?
>
> **Morgan:** Before money or anything else. Money cannot buy it... Because a man I do not trust could not get money from me on all the bonds in Christendom.
>
> — JP Morgan's testimony during his cross-examination at the Pujo hearings May 1912 to Jan 1913[1]

DURING THE HEYDAY of "relationship banking" before the corrupting influence of the roaring 1920s began, JP Morgan exemplified the personification of both banking and bank lending practices. As Pierpont Morgan explained at the Pujo hearings, lending was based first and foremost on a man's character rather than his collateral or his money. The KYC "Know Your Client" rule ensured that a banker from the House of Morgan would know something about his client's ability to repay the loan before lending money.

## BANKSTERS AND HUCKSTERS—AN OVERVIEW OF BANKING PRACTICES IN THE 1920S AND 1930S

That all changed in the 1920s and early 1930s when the "Banks" by and large morphed into "Hucksters" and began issuing loans based on all sorts of shaky foundations and then repackaging them as "gilt-edged" guaranteed mortgage bonds, real estate bonds and foreign bonds that they sold to virtually anyone they could find to hustle on Main Street. Far from being gilt-edged, these loans that they made were not even close to being safe and sound loans. Actually, these so-called gilt-edged investments turned out to be no more than a pigs-in-a-poke. "Pig-in-a-poke" refers to a confidence trick originating in the Late Middle Ages, when meat was scarce but apparently rats were not. The scheme entailed the sale of a "suckling pig" in a "poke" (bag). The wriggling bag actually contained a rat that was sold unopened to the victim.

According to Bernard Reis and John Flynn, authors of *False Security: The Betrayal of the American Investor*, in 1937 there were billions of dollars of securities in default that were "sold to the public by reputable banking houses" during the 1920s and early 1930s. The staggering amount of credit defaults outstanding in 1937 stood at:

- Investment Trusts      $3 billion
- Foreign Bonds          $1.9 billion
- Real Estate Bonds      $6 billion
- Guaranteed Mortgages   $1.09 billion2

The impact of these defaults on the bondholders, namely the American public, left millions of investors destitute and at the mercy of family, friends and charities. The Congressional Committee to Investigate Real Estate Bond Reorganizations chaired by Congressman Adolph Sabath reported in their findings that the typical investors fleeced by Wall Street firms were:

> thrifty, hard-working citizens of the nation and not the Wall Street speculating class. Many placed their life savings in real estate securities so that in the evening of life, they might live pridefully independent of gratuities...only to be destitute today.[3]

## "PREMIER INVESTMENTS IN AMERICA" AND "SHARE IN AMERICA'S GROWTH"

These were the popular slogans during the Roaring 20s and Great Depression. The question arises: How did the American public come to be so badly fleeced by the banksters and hucksters of that era? Deception, fraud, deregulation and lack of government supervision generally ruled the day.

Unfortunately for the American investor back then, some of the seeds had been sown in Congress. Legislation to deregulate the industry began to be introduced bit by bit in 1917 and 1918, and yet again in 1928, that were contrary to public interest. A bill introduced in 1927 and then reintroduced in both 1928 and 1929 to protect investor interests "both died in committee."[4] Legislation and accounting regulations failed investors at every turn. In 1929, the 1885 Guarantee Fund Provision law was repealed altogether.

Even self-regulation within the industry was absent. Mortgages were allowed to be marked at make-believe valuations and no reserve requirements were required. Consider the following—it should sound like a very familiar refrain to the mess we are in today:

Insurance Department permitted companies to carry the mortgages [they] owned at [face value] no matter...even if the mortgage was in default...The department never required any reserve to be set up for probability of loss or outstanding guarantees...The department never investigated the nature or extent of mortgages being sold to the public that were in default as to interest and taxes. Nor did they require any loan loss reserves be set up for the probability of loss.[5]

## INFLATED APPRAISALS OF THE 1930S WERE MERE "EXPRESSIONS OF HOPE"

Any sane person would have told the Insurance Department that those companies can't be allowed to carry the mortgages they owned at face value if the mortgage was in default! It was criminal of the Insurance Department to permit that. The modern day equivalent to these mortgages of yesteryear might be what we call Level 3 assets, i.e. assets marked to make-believe. And back in the 1930s, there is evidence that market appraisals were being inflated as high as 70% over what should reflect the true value of the real estate bonds and guaranteed mortgages during that era.

By 1931, the strain on appraisal departments became so severe that mortgage companies had "adopted a long-range view of real estate values which permitted the expression of hope for the future...properties were always worth 1.5 times the amount of the loan."[6] Mortgages that fell into default "for many years" were bundled or repackaged into group securities, in a way not unlike today's subprime mortgages at risk of default were bundled and repackaged in structured investment vehicles (SIVs), collateralized debt obligations (CDOs) and the like.

## SAFEGUARDING INVESTOR FUNDS THROUGH A TRUSTEE

The aforementioned underwriters of bonds in the 1920s boasted about the safety and soundness of the securities they issued. Assertions were made at some bond houses that no investor ever lost a penny. Advertisements from bond houses as late as 1933, in the darkest moments in American banking history, made claims like "The most secure of securities known to man" or "depression-proof securities" or "At a time when many sources of income have been seriously impaired, you enjoy a guaranteed return." Or even "peculiarly excellent for women investors, bringing the peace of mind that comes from certainty."[7]

According to authors Bernard Reis and John Flynn, one of the greatest contributing agents to the injuries inflicted upon the American public was the absence of trustees to protect the bondholders' interest.

It is not that there were no trustees to protect bondholders' interests. It was that the trustees were simply set up to act as puppets for the underwriters. They were trustees in name only. Yet underwriters used these trustees as selling points to guarantee the public's safety. In an excerpt circulating in that day from a booklet entitled "Safeguarding Investors Funds through a Trustee," the following was submitted:

> Our interest as trustee is identical to the bond-
> holders' interest... Underwriters are jealous of
> their reputation. They exercise a ceaseless vigil
> to keep inexperienced individuals away from
> this work... No sane underwriter will violate
> his trust. Underwriters do not guarantee their
> bonds, but in every bond issue that is written,
> there is a moral guarantee that is implied and
> religiously protected. The reputation of the un-

derwriter's institution depends upon the underwriter's honesty. No disinterested trustee
could ever hope to lend the competent and
interested loyalty, which is demanded by the
underwriter in his relation to the bond buyer
and borrower.[8]

As Reis and Flynn drilled further down through this promotional
document, they found a section entitled "Liabilities, Duties, Powers,
and Rights of the Trustee." To their astonishment, they found the
trustee was stripped of all duties and powers, and had no liability
exposure.

## LIABILITIES, DUTIES, POWER, AND RIGHTS OF THE TRUSTEE

- The trustee shall have no responsibility for the validity of
  the lien...

- The trustee shall not be liable for the consequence of any
  breach of covenants...

- The trustee shall be under no obligation to take any action towards the enforcement of this trust. [9]

- Etc, etc, etc...

## CONTRARY TO THE PUBLIC INTEREST

Underwriters of loans during that era fraudulently neglected their
fiduciary responsibilities to the investing American public. In 1932-
1934, The Pecora Committee found the flotation of foreign securities by bankers (of which almost $2 billion were in default as of 1937)
as one of the most scandalous chapters in the history of American
banking. No consideration was given to the creditworthiness of for-

eign borrowers and their abilities to repay the loans; much like little consideration was given to the subprime borrowers' creditworthiness and ability to repay the loans in 2003-2006.

> Far from exercising discrimination...bankers failed to check information furnished by foreign officials: ignored bad debt records, disregarded political disturbances, failed to examine or examined only perfunctorily economic conditions in foreign countries, failed to ascertain whether the proceeds of the loans were applied towards the purposes specified in the loan contracts, and generally indulged in practices of doubtful propriety in the promotion of foreign loans and in the sale of foreign securities to the American public.[10]

The Pecora Committee also found that banks underwriting these foreign loans maintained "fictitious" market prices "during the distribution period of a new issue."[11] This is an illegal and fraudulent practice known artificial price fixing. A similar practice of over-inflating the value of the home at loan origination occurred during the subprime spree a few years back.

Wall Street's fleecing and re-fleecing (yes, they were fleeced again when those bonds in default were eventually restructured under the cover of bankruptcy reorganization laws—much to the detriment of the investor) of Main Street widows and orphans led federal regulators to resurrect a variety of "Chinese Walls" between investors and banks in the 1930s—such as the Glass-Stegall Act and the SEC Act. After the testimonies of some of the most influential bankers were heard before the Pecora Committee during the Great Depression in 1932-1934, banks were rightly vilified and popularly came to be known as the "Banksters."

The public confidence in Wall Street fell to an all-time low. In his 1939 memoirs, titled *Wall Street Under Oath*, Ferdinand Pecora wrote

> Bitterly hostile was Wall Street to the enactment of the regulatory legislation... Had there been full disclosure of what was being done in furtherance of these schemes, they could not long have survived the fierce light of public city and criticism. Legal chicanery and pitch darkness were the banker's stoutest allies.[12]

Now stripped of the yesteryear integrity and character, the once revered banking gods of Wall Street during Pierpont Morgan's day became denounced as today's greedy little devils.

## NEVER AGAIN

Ostensibly, the Glass-Steagall Act of 1933 was enacted to prevent such misleading and fraudulent scams as occurred in the 1920s from ever recurring in the U.S. Much like the Great Wall of China was intended to protect them from foreign barbarians, the Glass-Steagall Act resurrected Chinese walls in the financial banking system that were intended to protect U.S. investors from the Hucksters in the banking industry. But the Gramm-Leach-Bliley Act repealed the Glass-Steagall Act of 1933 on November 12, 1999, to open up competition among commercial and investment banks as well as insurance companies.

The Chinese walls were torn down, allowing conflicts of interest to arise again. A case in point mentioned in chapter one is Goldman Sachs' underwriting and selling general obligation notes for states and local municipalities to one group of investors to buy on one hand, while advising other investors to sell short those general obligations. They get paid fees on both sides of the trade. "Are you really surprised? It's dealers talking out of both sides of their mouths," said Florida's director of bond finance Ben Watkins.[13]

As regulatory measures, those Chinese walls worked to some degree for a great many years. However, by the 1970s through the financial innovation, the staid financial topography had already begun shifting again in ways that would entirely undermine the measures intended to regulate the financial markets back in the 1930s. "Wall Street is famous for devising new-fangled derivatives to circumvent regulations," notes Caroline Baum.[14]

If we fast forward to the new millennium, we find that much of this financial innovation led to the deregulation of the financial markets, specifically the credit markets. As Martin Mayer decried in a June 12, 2008, interview with Chris Whalen:

> A lot of what is called innovative is simply a way to find new technology to do what has been forbidden with the old technology. Innovation allows you to go back to some scam that was prohibited under the old regime. The fact that the whole purpose of the innovation is to get around the existing regulation never seems to occur to regulators or members of Congress... What got forgotten was the reason why we separated commercial banking and investment banking in the 1930s.[15]

Equally astounding is that the regulators and members of Congress would find nothing wrong with the innovative lending practices that evolved in the new millennium. The government even began legislating bad lending practices based on extremely shaky foundations. On March 27, 2004, President Bush introduced a new bill called the Zero Down Payment Act of 2004. It was intended to be the final blueprint to enable all Americans to live the Great American Dream. The American Dream has since flip-flopped into a nightmare for many subprime homeowners in 2008. Not surprisingly, the National Association of Home Builders had expressed their support for this legislation.

Lending practices devolved so badly that popular loan originations in the new millennium had catchy little acronyms and names:

- No Income, no job and no assets loans (NINJA and NO-NO loans)
- 100% Loan-to-Value Mortgages
- Piggyback Mortgages—simultaneous first & second mortgages
- No Documentation, No Income Verification (LIAR loans)
- 0% down payments
- Adjustable Rate Mortgages (ARMs) with high resets
- Negative Amortization Mortgages
- Interest Only, No Principal Repayment Mortgages

These various types of loan originations in the new millennium were repackaged into a variety of different types of bonds/investment vehicles that could then be resold to investors. There were a few qualitative differences between the structured investment vehicles (SIVs) of today and the bonds of the 1920s. One qualitative difference can be found in the promotional labeling of them—but beyond that there is very little contrast. Back in the 1920s, these bond investments were often called "gilt-edged, whereas in the new millennium, they were assigned a "Triple A" credit rating—the highest credit rating that can be sold. "Triple A" and "gilt-edged" were designations given to indicate these investments were safe and secure with a very low risk of default so that even pension funds and other institutions could buy them.

By various market mechanisms in the new millennium, Wall Street firms were able to bundle these loans and repackage them as highly safe and secure "Triple A" investment vehicles. The practice seemed to border on being both misleading and disingenuous to investors. And, in fact, that is in part what the SEC indictments of Bear Stearns hedge fund managers Ray Cioffi and Matt Tannin, whom we met in chapter two, are all about.

Under the Zero Down Payment Act of 2004 and other wildly lax lending practices, it was made possible for loans to be made out to people with no income, no job, no down payment and no documentation, and ARMS with high reset. These were extremely risky loans to make and would inevitably lead to high rates of default, which ultimately helped trigger the collapse of our financial system and economy.

By August 2007, confidence in the credit markets disappeared altogether. Trust was nowhere to be found. The weeks and months to follow on Wall Street and elsewhere were exceedingly glum. Central bankers, economists and financial institutions all faced a grim road ahead. Nowhere was the glum mood among these men better captured than in Morgan Stanley's Richard Berner's recounting of the annual Jackson Hole Economic Symposium at the end of August 2007:

> After a day of clouds and sprinkles, this year's weather was nothing short of spectacular, with the temperature ideal and hardly a cloud marring the intensely blue sky by day or the starry firmament at night. But the tone of the conference went in the opposite direction. Discussions over meals, in the halls, and on the mountains centered on the threat to housing

wealth, to housing activity and to consumer spending from even moderate home price declines. Most fundamentally, of course, observers are concerned that the economic fallout from these developments will be greater than what the Fed anticipates, and that the time for action has come.

Even the Grand Tetons' majestic beauty could not temper concerns about the state of the U.S. economy and financial markets at the Kansas City Federal Reserve's annual Monetary Policy Symposium this weekend in Jackson Hole, Wyoming. This venue has unfailingly provided a relaxed backdrop in which to debate and reflect on sweeping issues with the best of the best. This time, however, the atmosphere was stressed, echoing market conditions. Concerns that the one-two punch of a budding liquidity crunch on top of the ongoing housing downturn could trigger a U.S. recession, with broader implications for the global economy and markets, hung heavily over the discussions.

Fed Chairman Bernanke wasted no time cataloguing the downside risks to economic activity. As he described it, an ongoing repricing of risk has abruptly morphed into a broad-based liquidity squeeze that is both scaling back the availability of credit and increasing its price, threatening significant collateral damage to the economy.

The dislocations in money markets continue to intensify, and Chairman Bernanke

himself argued that past data wouldn't be useful in assessing the future fallout from those
dislocations... Additional money-market dislocations could promote using unconventional
tools or a more aggressive response.

...importantly, responses lacked the con-
viction of the past, and as I see it, that's no bad
thing..., triggering a rethinking of both regulation and how monetary policy should deal
with suspected asset price bubbles.

The new logic is pragmatic, perhaps best expressed at Jackson Hole by the Governor of the
Swedish Riksbank, Stefan Ingves. In effect, he
said that our models don't adequately capture
the influence of asset prices on growth and inflation. But our experience tells us that they none-
theless matter for economic behavior, and policy
should consider them in a forward-looking way.

And it's critical to do that when asset
prices rise, not just when they decline. "In my
view it is well worth keeping an eye on house
prices and other asset prices and passing judgment on the risks that their developments may
give rise to. If the probability of very negative
outcomes can be reduced *ex ante*, I believe this
to be a good thing and a better solution compared to picking up the pieces *ex post*." Not only
does that sound right to me, but I also think
that's just what other central bankers will do.
It simply requires good pedagogy; in Governor
Ingves' words: "We must explain that we do

not target house prices but that we do not ignore risks associated with them."

The last line of criticism at Jackson Hole was
leveled at the Fed's response to current market
conditions. Many market participants think that
the Fed's discount-window strategy is not working, and are pressing officials to do more to avoid
a credit crunch and a recession. Many believe that
their discount window strategy should be viewed
as a backstop for markets, so that market conditions rather than the volume of borrowing should
be the metric for judging its success or failure.

...there was no sign of improvement while
officials were at Jackson Hole. Money-market
turmoil persists; manifest most prominently in
interbank lending and asset-backed commercial paper rates.

At work is a forced re-intermediation of the
banking system, as issuers unable to roll over maturing ABCP are calling on their bank sponsors
to absorb the commitments they made to back
up CP in just such circumstances. Inherently, that
reduces leverage in the financial system, as lenders shift from a funding source that requires no
capital to one that does, and tightens credit.

...So they will honor existing commitments, but funding new ones involves tapping
the markets—markets that are still in varying
degrees dislocated. And that means tightening
financial conditions, with collateral implications for economic activity.[16]

## Axel Weber at Jackson Hole Symposium

Axel Weber, president of the Bundesbank, in Jackson Hole, Wyoming, said, "The current turmoil in the financial markets has all the characteristics of a classic banking crisis, but one that is taking place outside the traditional banking sector... What we are seeing is basically what we see underlying all banking crises..."[17]

Weber's comments highlighted the fact that what we were experiencing was an old-fashioned run in the "non-bank financial system." Paul McCulley coined the non-bank financial system as the "Shadow Banking System." To the participants of the symposium, Mr. Weber conveyed the point of view that the only difference between a classic banking crisis and the turmoil under way in the credit markets was that the institutions most affected at the moment were the conduits and structured investment vehicles raising funds in the commercial paper markets, rather than at regulated banks.

Unfortunately, Weber added, "most of the conduits are owned by the banks."[18] In many cases, sponsoring banks are being forced to take these risky, opaque assets back onto their balance sheets, which in turn were causing banks to keep hold of their own cash, putting even further pressure on heightened tensions in the short-term money markets.

## Shadow Banking Requires Far Fewer Reserves Than Jimmy Stewart's Bank

By way of simple illustration, Pimco's director Bill Gross contrasted the reserve requirements of the Shadow Banking System of today to the banking system of yesteryear as portrayed in the 1946 American film classic *It's a Wonderful Life*. The reserve requirements of banks in the 1940's were far more stringent than of today's shadow banks.

# Into the Shadows

Source:Pimco

## PAUL MCCULLEY AND THE RUN ON THE SHADOW BANKING SYSTEM

There was a "run on the shadow banking system," McCulley said. And so the term "shadow-banking" was coined. McCulley noted that at its peak, the shadow banking system held $1.3 trillion of assets, which was now going to have to be put back onto the balance sheets of the banks. The issue is "how it is done and at what price," said McCulley back in September 2007.[19] McCulley got his answer to how it would get done a year later in September 2008. After Lehman Brothers went bankrupt, all that uninsured commercial paper disappeared. (See "death of the commercial paper chart" back in chapter two)

## No Funding Backstops in the Shadow Banking System

"Unlike regulated real banks that are backstopped by access to the Fed's discount window," McCulley explained, "unregulated shadow banks fund themselves with uninsured commercial paper (CP), which may or may not be backstopped by liquidity lines from real banks."[20]

Thus, because the shadow banking system is not backstopped by the Fed, it is inherently more vulnerable to runs than traditional banks. This happened in August 2007 when the issuers of uninsured commercial paper could not rollover their CP. That is, when the high-yield investors refuse to ante up again, these unregulated financial institutions were confronted with a liquidity crisis.

This required them to tap their back-up lines of credit with the regulated commercial banks. Unfortunately for many of these firms, the commercial banks were not there to backstop them, and thus they were forced to liquidate their assets at fire sale prices. "And make no mistake," said McCulley, a liquidation is "precisely what has been happening in recent weeks. The only material difference from a traditional bank run is that you do not have depositors standing in lines outside their banks day and night."

McCulley noted that the participants at the Jackson Hole Symposium referred to this as the Fed's "plumbing problem," meaning that the entire global financial system had suddenly become "clogged up" with securities that nobody wanted anymore. This led to institutions like Northern Rock unable to "find anyone, anywhere in the world, who would lend it money."

Despite all the cash injections of hundreds of billions of dollars provided by central bankers since the crisis began on August 9, 2007, "these injections [got] stopped up in the real banking system, which [was] reluctant to lend them on to the shadow banking system."[21]

## A (SO FAR) IMPOTENT ROTO ROOTER

McCulley had been hopeful that those injections would begin to provide the much-needed liquidity to the shadow banking system when they first began. But by the time of the symposium, he could see that those injections "were not effectively roto rootering the plumbing—getting Fed-created liquidity from its discount window to the shadow banking system."[22] The reason for this, quite simply, is that not one commercial bank with access to the Fed windows could trust the character that Pimco's Bill Gross had christened with the name of Waldo.

## FINDING WALDO IN THE
## SHADOW BANKING SYSTEM

Waldo, in the global financial system circa 2007-08, is this opaque "anytime, anywhere" character who kept popping up during the on-going credit crisis. Waldo is a toxic waste loan. When he first arrived on the scene in August 2007, there was not one banker in the crowd of bankers that wanted anything to do with this little fellow any longer. They had all morphed into tight-fisted JP Morgans. Not all the bonds in Christendom could get money out of these bankers for that shadowy character who could not be trusted.

Typically, Waldo could be spotted residing in some type of asset-backed security—often having to do with subprime mortgages. Waldo and subprime loans could be said to be synonymous, except Waldo could very well be found in other types of loans. By definition, Waldo could be any type of toxic loan, but typically subprime or a variation thereof. The problem with Waldo is no one knows how many billions of dollars of toxic waste he will actually represent over the next couple years, and worse, "no one really knows where [these Waldos] are hidden," mentioned Bill Gross.[23]

The first known Waldos to pop up were the Bear Stearns hedge funds back in June and July 2007. At first, it was hoped that Waldos would be contained to these two Bear Stearns' hedge funds. That is, everyone hoped against hope that there would be no "spillover risks" to the rest of the financial community. Unfortunately, noted Gross in early September 2007, these Waldos had "been popping up with regularity in seemingly staid institutions such as German and French Banks that have necessitated state-sanctioned bailouts reminiscent of the LTCM Crisis."[24]

## "THE SIGNIFICANCE OF PROPER DISCLOSURE IS, IN EFFECT, THE KEY TO THE CURRENT CRISIS"

This is what Bill Gross said in his September 2007 missive. Of course, unregulated markets are permitted to *not* make full and proper disclosure as required by the Truth in Securities Act of 1933.

We would do well to recall Ferdinand Pecora's dictum that Wall Street in the 1920s and early 1930s "could not long have survived the fierce light of publicity." Legal chicanery and successful lobbying on the part of Wall Street firms tore down the Chinese walls, making it possible for them to once again sell unregulated products to investors by the time the new millennium arrived. Elaborating on proper disclosure, Gross added:

> Financial institutions lend trillions of dollars, eu-
> ros, pounds, and yen to and amongst each other.
> In the U.S., for instance, the Fed lends to banks,
> which lend to prime brokers such as Goldman
> Sachs and Morgan Stanley which lend to hedge
> funds, and so on. The food chain in this case is a
> symbiotic credit extension, always for profit, but
> never without trust and belief that their money
> will be repaid upon contractual demand.

> When no one really knows where and how
> many Waldos there are, the trust breaks down,
> and money is figuratively stuffed in Wall Street
> and London mattresses as opposed to ex-
> tended into the increasingly desperate hands
> of hedge funds and similarly levered financial
> conduits.
>
> These structures in turn are experiencing
> runs from depositors and lenders exposed to
> asset price declines of unexpected proportions.
> In such an environment, markets become in-
> credibly volatile as more and more financial
> institutions reach their risk limits at the same
> time. Waldo morphs and becomes a man with
> a thousand faces. All assets with the exception
> of U.S. Treasuries look suspiciously like every
> other. They're all Waldos now.[25]

Most often, Waldo turned out to be none other than a subprime
loan that morphed into a foreclosure of a thousand faces—oops,
make that millions of foreclosed faces. First, mortgage loan defaults
spiraled above 1.5 million in the first quarter of 2007. As 2008 draws
to a close, foreclosure revisions indicate in 2008 they may be as high
as 2.5 million homes and rising to roughly 4 million in 2009—barring
some radical new legislation to keep people in their homes, of course.

While all that doom and gloom was going on in Jackson Hole in
late August 2007, Countrywide CEO Angelo Mozilo, in one of his more
accurate assessments, was bemoaning that "this is one of the greatest
financial panics I've seen in 55 years in financial services."[26] Many of
us who have lived through the various financial crises since the 1970s
would concur that this housing crisis is much more nefarious.

In Bill Gross' January 2008 missive, he expressed his increasing alarm at the tensions in the credit markets spiraling ever higher and downside risks to the economy in 2008. We find him reflecting further on the shadow banking system of our day:

> What we are witnessing is essentially the breakdown of our modern day banking system, a complex of levered lending so hard to understand that Fed Chairman Ben Bernanke required a face-to-face refresher course from hedge fund managers in mid-August. My PIMCO colleague, Paul McCulley, has labeled it the "Shadow Banking System" because it has lain hidden for years—untouched by regulation—yet free to magically and mystically create and then package subprime mortgages into a host of three-letter [later to be dubbed Alphabet Soup] conduits that only Wall Street wizards could explain.
>
> As I've noted before, it is certainly true that this shadow system with its derivatives circling the globe has democratized credit. And as the benefits of cheaper financing became available to the many, as opposed to the few... Yet, as is humanity's wont, we overdid a good thing and the subprime skim milk has soured.
>
> Financial conduits supported by a trillion dollars of asset-backed commercial paper were constructed on the basis of AAA ratings that whispered—nay shouted—that these investments could never fail: no skim, just crème

de la crème. Now, as the subprimes undermine these structures and the confidence in
them...the commercial paper market shrinks
by hundreds of billions a month, central banks
worldwide are facing a giant stress test of the
modern-day shadow banking system. The pub-
licized and photographed overnight "runs" on
Countrywide and the UK's Northern Rock in
mid-August were nothing compared to what's
taking place in the shadows of the real banking
system.

Credit contraction...is spreading with the
speed of an infectious bacterial disease. Even
Agencies, the step-sisters to Cinderella Treasuries, have been avoided due to billion dollar
write-offs at Freddie and FNMA... Fed ease has
lowered Treasury yields, but for the rest of the
market—the segment that influences the bottom line of U.S. corporations, homeowners,
and consumers—not much has changed.

The ultimate destination of Fed Funds
is dependent on the state of the domestic
economy which, in turn, will be influenced by
the direction and level of U.S. housing prices.
Chairman Bernanke and his governors will
have to feel their way along this treacherous
path with canes in hand—not totally blind, but
significantly hampered by a lack of historical
context which might point the way to the ideal
rate via precedent as opposed to feel.[27]

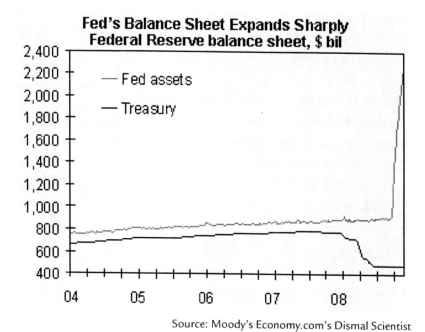

**Fed's Balance Sheet Expands Sharply**

Federal Reserve balance sheet, $ bil

— Fed assets

— Treasury

04    05    06    07    08

Source: Moody's Economy.com's Dismal Scientist

## SHADOW BANKS ARE STRESS-TESTING CENTRAL BANKS ROUND THE WORLD

It would not be exaggerated hyperbole to suggest that the subprime explosion has taken on dimensions that could be likened to Paul Revere's "Shot Heard Round the World." Responding to the subprime explosion, the European Central Bank (ECB), Bank of England (BOE) and Federal Reserve (FED) have instituted the dangerous practice of taking onto their balance sheets as collateral these dubious and unsound mortgage loans. According to the *Financial Times*, Jim Grant of *Grant's Observer* wrote "investment bankers the world over are bundling up mortgages to deposit in the special liquidty facilities created by the [central banks]."[28] Within the first 12 months of the 2007-2008 credit crisis, the balance sheets of the ECB and

BOE had been inflated by 21% and 19.4% respectively. In the fourth quarter of 2008, the assets on the Federal Reserve's balance sheet exploded from $800 million to more than $2.2 trillion and rising.

## Fed's Balance Sheet Explodes with Purchases of Mortgage-Backed Securities

Commenting on the art of banking in England back in the 1860s, C. Poulett Thomson intimated that it wasn't very hard at all, provided that the banker "only learn the difference between a Mortgage and a Bill of Exchange." Elaborating, Jim Grant penned that "central banks are lending government securities against the inherently illiquid mortgage collateral that never had a place on the balance sheet of a properly run monetary institution in the first place."[29]

Central banks should play no role in monetizing illiquid mortgages. "Insofar as a currency derives its strength from the balance sheet of the issuing bank," Grant argues that the worldwide mortgage mess has created a situation in which the national currencies are now "unsound and becoming [even] more so."[30] Yet, *Financial Times'* John Dizard reports that the folks in Washington and Wall Street are:

> ...trying to figure out how to get yet more liquidity for housing-related paper... As Merrill Lynch's David Rosenberg told clients in December 2008, "the outright purchase of illiquid mortgage-backed securities is probably required...but the Fed alone cannot unclog the congestion in the capital markets."[31]

A nation's currency is only as sound as the collateral that backs it. Assets and collateral backed by subprime and other types of risky loans and mortgages have thus far proven to be nothing more than wasting assets. So, the Fed has a growing problem on its hands to say the least!

Much like the tomato is a wasting commodity—assets tied to these loans began rotting almost immediately after their origination. And these mortgage-backed assets have continued to waste away since the time the Fed first placed them onto their balance sheets. When it comes time for the Fed to mop up the excesses, and purchase back all the dollars they have issued during this liquidity and insolvency crisis, they will have to sell these mortgage-backed securities to the market. These mortgage securities will probably be worth less than when than when the Fed bought them, causing the Fed to show a significant capital loss. "So long as the Treasury [keeps] issuing colossal guarantees and debt levels of their own, the Fed is doomed no matter what it does," said Richard Kline, after the Fed had asked permission from Congress to issue their own debt on December 10, 2008.[32]

Nationally, median home prices have already declined more than 15% since their peak valuations in 2005. But what is on the Fed's balance sheet is the toxic stuff, the stuff that is 30% or more off its origination value. Near term, these assets will, of course, continue to decline further in value through much of 2009. This collateral will further degrade the balance sheets of the Federal Reserve. As John Dizard and David Rosenberg point out, with the situation as dire as it is as we enter 2009, there is a mad scramble to create a facility that can take onto its balance sheets even more of these illiquid mortgage-backed assets, because the Fed is not going to be able to go it alone. In the meantime, the risks to the Federal Reserve Bank are escalating parabolically, given the explosion of its balance sheet (shown above).

In his latest book *The New Paradigm for Financial Markets*, billionaire speculator George Soros contends, "This is the worst financial crisis since the 1930s."[33] According to Soros, there have been several times in the past 25 years that the global monetary system has undergone stress tests and the financial system has come out of it to live another day.

Usually, one or more central banks are involved in performing some sort of rescue or bailout when a shock is introduced to the financial system. Each time they succeed, the central banks raise their nets a little bit higher. And each time the central bank's tolerance for potential collapse in the financial system becomes lower and lower—much like the zero tolerance policy of the U.S. Forest Service with respect to forest fires. But each time the financial system somehow manages to live to see another day, Soros posits, we are thus emboldened to take even bigger risks.

Eventually, if the risks are too over-levered, we risk a catastrophic collapse of the financial markets, which has already occurred with the crash in the fall of 2008. But perversely, the great unwind of these overleveraged risks has yet to take place at all. Rather than being shed through liquidation and firesales, these risks have simply transferred been transferred onto the balance sheet of the Federal Reserve. One day, the Federal Reserve will have to figure out a way to unwind its balance sheet of toxic assets. How they will extricate themselves from those risks, I haven't a clue. But market observers, including me, will all be watching closely how they manage these risks. In a Wall Street interview, Mr. Soros elaborates:

> Each time the authorities saved us, that reinforced the belief that markets are self-correcting. Each time when you bail out the economy, you need to find a new source of credit, and a new instrument that allows for the expansion of credit. It's difficult to imagine what you can do when you are already lending effectively on 100% inflated house prices.
>
> I have a record of crying wolf at these times. I did it first...in 1987, then in...1998 and

now. So, it's three [times] predicting disaster.
After the boy cried wolf three times...the wolf
really came.[34]

Mr. Soros is on record for believing that we have reached the culmination of a super-credit cycle expansion that began at the end of WWII. In Mr. Soros' view, we have just embarked on a credit contraction, an unwind of a 60-year credit expansion cycle, but central bankers and policymakers are doing everything in their power to prevent that contraction. Central bankers around the world are vigorously fighting the escalating headwinds of this credit contraction and providing much-needed liquidity to the global financial markets.

Can the credit expansion game continue without shrinking and without a significant contraction first? And more importantly, can the Federal Reserve ride out the asset deflation spiral without destroying its own balance sheet now that they have begun taking on the rotting collateral on inflated home prices and adopted "a long range view of real estate values [permitting] the expression of hope for the future?"[Å] The hope for the Fed is that the tide of rising defaults will soon crest and subside without too much more asset deflation. It's a gamble and roll of the die for the Fed.

## DE-LEVERING THE OVER-LEVERED AND THE PARADOX OF THE AGGREGATE

Home prices have been declining since they peaked in 2005. Harvard economist Martin Feldstein commented on August 12, 2008, that "The downward spiral in house prices is an ongoing process that is doing a lot of damage. Things have gone from bad to worse."[36] At the moment, there is no end in sight to the asset deflation of home values.

Paul McCulley notes that a major contributing factor is the fact that when everyone decides to de-lever, that is, to sell their home and get out from under their mortgage debts at the same time, it inevitably drives down home values even further.

At the collective level, however, it has given us the paradox of deleveraging: when we all try to do it at the same time, we actually do less of it, because we collectively create deflation in the assets from which leverage is being removed.

In other words, we can't all shed our assets at the same time. But that is precisely what homeowners who have lost their jobs and their ability to service their mortgages are being forced to do. The solution to the problem as McCulley sees it is simple: have Uncle Sam step up and buy all these homes that everyone is trying to sell. In his view, the situation demands a "fiscal policy response, not just a monetary one."[37] The appropriate course of action is for Uncle Sam to lever up his balance sheet and:

> ...take on the assets being shed by those deleveraging so as to avoid pernicious asset deflation... Levering Uncle Sam's balance sheet to buy or guarantee assets to temper asset deflation will put the taxpayer at risk – but will do so for their own *collective* good![38]

Getting Uncle Sam from point A to point B, however, is another matter entirely. Even though the original TARP program was intended to buy up those toxic assets on the banks balance sheets, most of them wound up on the Fed's balance sheet instead. McCulley's proposed solution to buy up deflating homes is apt to be a non-starter. That said, Uncle Sam is levering up his balance sheet to create jobs, rebuild infrastructure and the like. But these programs do nothing to stop the deflating home values and the delevering process that is taking place.

## AAA: Just Give Me
## La Crème de la Crème, Baby

The seeds for over-levering in the shadow banking system were sown not just by the availability of cheap credit, lax regulation and oversight, but also in part by the credit rating agencies. Credit rating agencies have been given the fiduciary responsibility of assigning a credit rating to securities, and played a significant role in greatly enlarging the risks taken within the shadow banking system.

Abundantly cheap credit was levered up precisely because the bundled products of the shadow banking system were supposed to be supported by asset-backed securities "constructed on the basis of AAA ratings which shouted that these investments could never fail, just crème de la crème."[39] The Triple A rating meant that these investments were supposed to be the "gilt-edged" investments.

This over-leveraging is particularly true when we look at collateralized debt obligations or the CDO market in recent years, which became ever-so-popular among our banks and shadow banks. Unfortunately, these CDOs were about as safe as those gilt-edged investments of the 1920s and 1930s. Over-levering in them became a huge problem. As a case in point, UBS's chief financial officer Marco Suter owned up that its risk management team had:

> ...never capped the size of their CDO positions partly because most of them were rated AAA and didn't throw up any red flags... People should have respect for big numbers. Sometimes people start to fall in love with models, and they forget to look at notional values.[40]

So, with that kind of thinking that there was no risk involved with those CDOs, why should UBS have set any reserve requirements?

Ousted UBS Chairman Marcel Ospel was blamed by shareholders for building up "enormous risks" and "intentionally pushed it with his expansion goals," said Herbert Brandli, president of Profond, a Swiss pension fund. UBS's balance sheet ballooned 21% between 2005-2007, and by the end of 2007 UBS had become "the most leveraged major bank in the world with assets amounting to 53 times its total equity." Konrad Hummler, managing director of another Swiss bank, Wegelin & Co., described UBS's assets to equity ratio as a "nuclear bomb."[41]

Another in-house UBS report alleges Ospel only became aware of the full extent of UBS's subprime exposure on August 6, 2007. But even then UBS's own controllers viewed their burgeoning CDO positions as low risk because of the designated AAA ratings. "We couldn't see the forest for the trees," explained the new UBS chairman and CEO Marcel Rohrer in April 2008.[42] As if as late in the game as August 2007, after a full blown credit crisis hit Wall Street, senior management thought their CDO trees would grow to the moon, in spite of the subprime fire devouring the forest behind them.

In a twist of irony, the folks on Main Street could see the raging fires emerging in the subprime forest. Main Street could see the risks and writing on the wall. The burgeoning subprime game was just a ticking time bomb, and was advertised on financial real estate blog sites everywhere. So it quite escapes me how Ospel, Rohrer, Mozilo, Applegarth and so many other bright minds on Wall Street could not see the forest for the trees.

If we were to take these executives at their word that they had no foresight other than to know it would be fortuitous to sell their shares before the music stopped, what are we to conclude? That they were perhaps blinded by and a victim of their own successes, I don't think so. It is difficult to fathom just what these executives were thinking other than to maximize their own personal gains when they took on these reckless and enormous risks that could not be fully decomposed in the levered world of structured finance.

One can, however, easily imagine these senior executives' rationales. Historically, default rates were extremely low in mortgage-backed securities as an asset class, after all. And I imagine that they could easily extrapolate from there, that as long as people are holding their jobs and still working, they could assume those mortgages will continue to be paid. And so they continued to push their models too hard and too far, beyond their limits when the rules of the game had changed once subprime entered the fray.

## NEVER SEEN ANYTHING LIKE IT

Still, it is extremely difficult to buy into Rohrer's "couldn't see the forest for the trees" rational when so many individuals both inside and outside of the industry could see the catastrophic CDO forest burning for miles around. As a case in point, Paul Singer, founder of the hedge fund Elliott Associates LP, saw the enveloping CDO forest fire as early as 2005. In Singer's mind, the investment-grade ratings given to many CDOs by the credit-rating agencies bordered on the absurd.

> What we found was an extraordinary level of mispricing of risk. The ratings of the securities were extremely erroneous...never seen anything like it in years. Financial institutions did not check, and the rating agencies let them down.[43]

Singer's research showed that a 4% decline in home values could wipe out 84% of a typical CDO's value, and that a 7% decline in home prices could "destroy its value completely," reported Evan Kafka from *Bloomberg Markets*. The question arises: How did CDOs get an investment grade rating of AAA in the first place if a simple little stress test such as Mr. Singer's could wipe out the entire value of a CDO? It is hard to imagine that the credit rating agencies would overlook that stress test on their CDO models and assume home prices would never modestly decline.

So perhaps something else was afoot. *Bloomberg Markets* editor Ronald Henkoff alleges that banks like UBS were putting "the pursuit of revenue ahead of basic risk management."[44] Chiming in on Mr. Henkoff's allegation, *Bloomberg Markets* editor Lisa Kassenaar adds:

> The banks' craving for ever-higher fees helped lead them to disaster. They underwrote and invested in billions of dollars of CDOs [because the securities carrying] top ratings and higher yields earned banks bigger fees.[45]

This is just one of the many instances of financial institutions losing site of their fiduciary obligations leading up to this financial crisis. These allegations of fiduciary neglect, if proved true, could lead to several SEC violations for conflicts of interest and misleading investors. But don't hold your breath!

## TODAY'S CREDIT RATING AGENCIES AND REGULATORS ARE ALMOST AKIN TO YESTERYEAR'S TRUSTEES OF THE 1920S

Credit rating agencies such as Moody's, Fitch and Standard & Poor's have been entrusted with the responsibility of providing credit ratings to CDOs and various other structured investment vehicles (SIVs). To the extent that these credit ratings are intended to protect investor interests, these agencies are the modern-day counterpart to the trustees protecting bondholder interests back in the 1920s and 1930s albeit with a great deal more fiduciary responsibility. The potential for "conflicts of interest" and misleading investors that existed at the credit rating agencies was quite high.

Bloomberg's Richard Tomlinson and David Evans noted that our credit rating agencies have played a critical and little-understood role in "assessing risk and acting as de facto regulators in a market that has no official watchdogs." The actual regulators beg off responsibility, complaining, "We don't have the resources to get our arms around it. As regulators, we just have to trust that rating agencies are going to monitor CDOs and find the subprime," said Kevin Fry, chairman of the U.S. National Association of Insurance Commissioners.[46] It is striking that the folks entrusted with regulating the credit rating agencies tell us that they "just have to trust the rating agencies...to find the subprime." Another safeguard for the investor had thus been removed.

The credit rating agencies surely should have recognized the qualitative difference between prime and subprime loans. As subprime loan growth exploded, these security products were increasingly repackaged into the CDOs into which they were being bundled. How did these CDOs, carrying so much more subprime wastepaper, still garner the AAA ratings? This begs the question of the credit rating agencies' complicity in the whole subprime mess. Were the rating agencies misleading investors, pension funds and the like?

The credit rating agencies such as Moody's, Standard & Poor's and Fitch shirk their fiduciary responsibilities and accountability with the flimsy disclaimer that they have just been offering their "educated opinions." Joe Mason, former economist at the U.S. Treasury Department, laughs at the disclaimers provided by Moody's and Standard & Poor's. "The ratings giveth and the disclaimer takes it away. Once you're through with the disclaimers, you're left with very little new information."[47]

Senior management and the compliance departments at UBS and other financial firms that were underwriting these CDOs certainly understood the pitfalls of these disclaimers. They also knew that they were at the same time hiring the credit rating agencies to take part in the construction of the CDOs that they would later sell to investors. Somewhere in this fine arrangement, one might suspect a conflict of interest might exist for both parties; that is, the credit rating agency doing the ratings and the investment bank doing the underwriting.

Typically, each CDO is comprised of 100 or so bonds and securities, some of which also happen to be debt investments backed by those dreaded subprime home loans. It is the bank's job to put these 100 or so bonds into a CDO. Then it is the credit rating agencies' job to subdivide that CDO into sections or what they call "tranches." Each one of these tranches gets assigned a grade. The highest-rated tranches are called "super seniors" or AAA and the lowest tranches are called "toxic waste."

Rating agencies actually "participate in every level of packaging a CDO... Rating agencies run the show," says Charles Calomiris.[48] The head of Fitch's structured finance, Gloria Aviotti, offers a slightly more balanced view than Calomiris, observing that rating agencies act as consultants to the banks in determining the composition of the CDO, but that the banks make the "final decisions."[49]

## WITH A WINK AND A NOD

As consultants in the field of these structured investments, along with the underwriters, these credit rating agencies are extremely well paid for their services. Ultimately, however, the onus and accountability falls back upon the banks like UBS. Still, there is plenty of room for complicity on behalf of the credit rating agencies who assigned the investment grade ratings of AAA or Aaa to approximately 90% of all CDOs, according to *Bloomberg News*.

Interestingly, it should be noted that Michael Milken, the king of junk bonds who was indicted on 98 counts of securities fraud, actually created the first CDO in 1987, according to Satyajit Das, author of *Credit Derivatives: CDOs & Structured Credit Products*. That should have been a big clue to the banks as to the merits of a CDO packaged in any shape or form, no matter how you slice or "tranche" it. At Milken's sentencing, Judge Kimba Wood told him:

> You were willing to commit only crimes that were unlikely to be detected... When a man of your power in the financial world...repeatedly conspires to violate, and violates, securities and tax business in order to achieve more power and wealth for himself...a significant prison term is required.[50]

Rating agencies use a simulation software program called "Monte Carlo" to calculate a CDO's probability of default. Unfortunately, notes Arturo Cifuentes, a former Moody's vice president who helped develop the company's original method of rating CDOs, the simulation program has an "input problem." The assumptions the program makes "about default and recovery rates may be incorrect. They could be wrong, and the ratings could be misleading."[51] Do you suppose that it is just possible that the credit rating agencies' employees might have known there was an input problem?

When all is said and done, these ratings are based on a fairly sophisticated model, but a model nevertheless that is "not an exact science. This is very much our opinion as to the creditworthiness," says Kimberly Slawek, managing director at Derivative Fitch that rates CDO's. Because it is not an exact science, Slawek's colleague Kevin Kendra teaches recruits "how not to believe the outputs of these models...I want them to understand why the model may or may not apply to the assets they're trying to analyze."[52]

It is a wonder that banks and other financial institutions would lean on these credit ratings at all. Satyajit Das saw the CDO market as fraught with dangers for investors, adding that the "regulators seem to be fairly sanguine about all of this. The thing that I find quite bewildering is the lack of urgency and focus. The fuse has been lit, somebody should be trying to find where this wire is running to."[53]

Perhaps the reason the regulators had been so sanguine about this subject stemmed from the fact that they know so little about the problem. As Kevin Fry put it, the regulators didn't have the resources to get their arms around the problems so they just had to trust the credit rating agencies to find the toxic assets. The credit rating agencies, however, did not have to find the toxic subprime assets embedded in the CDOs. They were the ones bundling them into the CDOs they were grading so that the banks could market and sell them to investors as being "investment-grade."

## REGULATE THE CREDIT RATING AGENCIES MODELS

Chris Whalen, in his June 24, 2008, missive titled *It's the Models, Stupid*, makes a valid argument that it falls under the jurisdiction of the SEC to actually regulate the models as well as regulating the markets as they were commissioned to do in the Truth in Securities Act of 1933. This 1933 act was two-fold. First, it mandated that investors receive material information regarding the securities being offered. Secondly, it prohibited deceit, misrepresentations and other fraud in the sale of securities to the public.

> If the model is used for pricing a security, rating a security and, in a larger sense, for all of the asset allocation decisions made by Buy Side investors, then the SEC has a statutory responsibility to supervise the use of models. This just

shows, yet again, that the SEC does not fully understand the markets that they are required by law to supervise.[54]

## STATE AND LOCAL GOVERNMENTS FACE RISKS OF A DECLINING TAX BASE AND BUDGET DEFICITS

Strikingly, state and local governments have successfully lobbied the credit rating agencies to upgrade their credit ratings, on the basis of their low default rate and overall creditworthiness. This comes just at a time when their creditworthiness is about to measurably erode as the fallout from the 2007-08 credit crisis rolls into 2009 and beyond.

State and local governments depend on property taxes for the majority of their revenues. Property taxes are determined largely by either their assessed or market trending values. In the face of falling home values and rising foreclosures, their tax base (revenue) is set to decline in 2009 and beyond. They could offset this in part by raising property tax rates. This was the long-term bailout solution to the savings and loans scam in the 1980s. It is estimated the total cost of that scam to taxpayers was $124 billion. But "passing through" additional taxes to distressed homeowners (if they aren't already upside-down and negatively amortized) will be very difficult to do anytime soon. The other choice would be to cut spending and eliminate jobs, causing even more woes to more homeowners and local communities. Tough decisions to be made lie ahead—to be sure.

## "ZAITECH" WORMS ITS WAY INTO THE AMERICAN PUBLIC SCHOOL SYSTEMS AND STATE AND LOCAL MUNICIPALITIES

Zaitech is a word taken from the Japanese and English languages to describe the financial engineering techniques that have been employed over the 25 years since the U.S.-Japan accord in 1984. In that accord, the U.S. and Japan "reached an agreement on a wide range of liber-alization measures," rapidly advancing the deregulation of financial markets ever since.[55] Financial engineering flourished as deregulation of the financial markets evolved. New financial technologies allowed for the securitization of products like CDOs—the bundling of real estate loans offering higher and higher yields. Zaitech derogatorily now means speculative-levered investments and "imprudent financial dabbling."

## IMPRUDENT FINANCIAL DABBLING BY PUBLIC SCHOOL AND SEWER SYSTEMS

Unfortunately, imprudent financial dabbling has penetrated deep into the heart of America, not just on Wall Street. This is a worri-some trend and should be of concern to all U.S. citizens if the infec-tion has gone viral, which it appears to have already done.

Over the past several years, many local communities have found themselves unable to afford tax increases to meet their budgetary needs in the past decade. So they turned to solutions that could only be provided by Wall Street's salesmen. Attempting to help commu-nities close these growing budgetary gaps, investment bankers went about creating custom-made products for them. At the same time, these investment banks were lobbying state legislators to relax statu-tory constraints and pass laws sanctioning these financial products for the various communities they were trying to market to.

A case in point occurred back in September 2003. Back then, the Erie City School District in Pennsylvania was confronted with the prospect of having to condemn its crumbling 81-year-old middle school. A local JP Morgan banker, David DiCarlo, offered up a solu-tion to the cash-strapped school board. All the school board had to do was sign some papers that would all them to participate in interest-rate swaps. The swaps, DiCarlo speculated, "would benefit them if interest rates increased in the future."[56]

Initially, DiCarlo was right. Interest rates did indeed increase for a few years and presumably this did benefit the Erie School District. However, interest rates are closely tied to the short-term borrowing rates, which are set by the Federal Reserve's monetary cycle and are cyclical in nature. The Federal Reserve tightens short-term interest rates when the economy and inflationary pressures heat up. Conversely, they cut rates to stimulate job growth and the economy.

Eventually interest rates went the wrong way in 2007, and the school board ended up paying JP Morgan $2.9 million "to get out of the deal." Complaining about the deal, Erie school board superintendent James Barker said: "That was like a sucker punch. It's about resources being sucked out of the classroom. If it's happening here, it's happening in other places."[57]

James Barker was right. This had been happening throughout the Pennsylvania public schools. According to Martin Braun and William Selway of *Bloomberg Market*, 15 other Pennsylvania school districts entered into interest-rate swap deals worth $28 million since 2003. The schools got $15 million, and the banks selling the swaps took $13 million. Echoing sentiments of the 1930s, "The school districts are getting fleeced," cried an outraged Pennsylvania Governor Ed Rendell.

Chairman of the U.S. Securities and Exchange Commission Christopher Cox said that "It's a serious problem, not only in Pennsylvania but across the country."[58] Through financial alchemy and deregulation, municipalities have begun taking on imprudent risks that would not have even have been possible in years prior—when they typically raised capital through bond sales to meet their budget needs.

Before September 2003, interest rate swap deals "weren't sanctioned in Pennsylvania." After much lobbying by financial advisory firms, the state legislature signed into law that September a provision "allowing schools and towns to use interest-rate swaps to lower borrowing costs and raise cash."[59]

What is more, these same schools are now being forced to pay steep exit fees to unwind their contracts. The financial firms are telling school officials the swap deals should not have lost them money. "They tell me that's never happened before," said Ernie Werstler from the Exeter Township School District.[60] Yes, Ernie, it would appear that another one of those robust financial models must have gone bust again. It is what a financial executive hiding behind his innovative financial product/model would call "totally unprecedented." But, in a win/win for JP Morgan, they got paid a steep entry and exit fee.

And we don't want to overlook SEC Chairman Christopher Cox's very important observation, this is happening to school districts in other states, too. How prolific and widespread this issue becomes over the course of the next few years is unknown, but it carries huge downside risks to the U.S. economy and U.S. taxpayers. With risks like these escalating, it is no wonder Goldman Sachs is advising investors to short municipal credit! Chris Whalen, the institutional risk analyst, reported on June 24, 2008:

> We got a really scary call from a reporter in Wisconsin yesterday. It seems that several of the largest school districts in the state decided to borrow short term and buy CDOs to help finance future health care liabilities—obligations that the state school system cannot fund. Now that the ratings on these CDOs have fallen, along with the market value, the cost of the debt has gone up thanks to an "conflicts of interest" "innovative" trigger provision crafted by a certain large bank we won't mention.

> Why these school districts were even allowed
> to borrow to fund interest rate speculation is
> unclear. The WI Attorney General reportedly is
> investigating both the members of the school
> district boards and the dealers involved.[61]

This is going on all throughout the country! The investment banks who sold these interest-rate products to the school districts with risk factors beyond their tolerances exhibited a great deal of fiduciary negligence. To turn around and fleece the same school districts with steep exit fees when these interest rate products blow up on them is another indication that the banks have lost sight of their role within the communities they are supposedly serving. But when they start shorting municipal credit in communities where they had a role in drowning them in debt—well, that borders on the criminal for the inherent conflict of interest alone!

Elsewhere, Lehman Brothers sold to Florida's state school districts and agencies $842 million of mortgage-backed securities in July and August 2007 through Florida's State Board of Administration (SBA). It was the job of the SBA to invest the pooled monies of these various state agencies. At the onset of the crisis, Florida's state-funded pool exceeded $25 billion.

The fiduciary responsibility as to how and where to invest these monies fell largely to the executive director of the SBA, Coleman Stipanovich. These mortgage-backed securities defaulted four months later, in November 2007. Florida's Alex Sink said she was unaware of these purchases at the time and complained that JPM and LEH were "offloading tainted debt on Florida and other states at a time those assets were plummeting in value."[62]

*Bloomberg Markets* editor David Evans noted that after the credit crisis hit in August 2008, "Wall Street firms were quietly peddling mortgage-backed securities to the states eager for higher returns" they offered.[63] In short, when the credit crisis hit, Wall Street firms then schemed to sell their pig-in-a-poke to the states.

Former U.S. Treasury official Joe Mason noted that when Wall Street "couldn't sell it to more sophisticated investors they found less sophisticated investors like local government pools."[64] If Mason's contention that Wall Street firms actually preyed on and misled unsophisticated investors into this subprime trap, there could well be legal ramifications for plenty of securities fraud violations.

Meanwhile, the burden on Florida and other states will be quite high. In one Florida County, the school board CFO Hal Wilson claimed funds had been "stolen from our local taxpayers because we entrusted their money with the state and our elected officials assured us it was safe."[65] Of course, they had to assure the school boards the products they were peddling were safe or they would never have been able to close these sorts of deals.

As of August 15, 2008, the Florida pool held $830 million of Countrywide mortgage debt. When Countrywide Financial incurred a credit rating downgrade on August 16, 2008, to a step above junk, their debt no longer met the minimum risk profiles of the state fund. The state fund oversight committee held a meeting on August 22, 2008. At that meeting, they "approved a justification memo [stating that] our recommendation is to continue to hold the paper to maturity." Yet, according to David Evans, Stipanovich told Florida state pool trustees on October 15, 2008, that "the pool had no direct exposure to subprime mortgages."[66] This claim appears misleading and could come back to haunt Stipanovich at a later date.

Amidst all the credit rating downgrades of debt that the state had purchased, the state board held a public meeting on November 14, 2007. At this meeting Stipanovich offered the following reassurances:

> Most importantly, I want to emphasize that no
> client has ever lost money in the State Board of
> Administration's short-term fixed income invest-
> ment program and we remain confident that
> our portfolios in this program will meet their
> objectives. I feel very good about our situation.[67]

Mr. Stipanovich's pitch to the state board in November 2007 that "No client has ever lost money" is exactly the same type of sales pitch that the Title Guarantee & Trust company offered investors in a letter on February 6, 1933: "More than $2 billion has been invested with us in over 40 years, and no investor has ever lost a penny."[68] Those assurances in 1933 proved to be unreliable (past performance is no guarantee of future results) and ill founded. Those claims offered little more than false security.

Mr. Stipanovich was admittedly blinded by his optimism of "hear no evil, see no evil." He undoubtedly believed in the interest-rate products he was investing for the State of Florida and simply didn't believe the credit crisis was real or that it would have any lasting ramifications. His optimism was most certainly aided and abetted by his visits to Lehman Brothers in New York.

On that very point, on a visit as late as early November 2008, Stipanovich attended a Lehman presentation titled "Potential Opportunities to Explore" [suggesting] that Florida could buy more structure finance commercial paper for the state pension fund."[69]As late as November 2007, it appears Lehman Brothers was still hawking its toxic wares to unsophisticated investors, and Mr. Stipanovich was still a willing audience.

By November, the school districts and state agencies must have entirely lost faith in Stipanovich as they began to withdraw funds from the state pool and liquidated approximately $10 billion from the pool before the state froze the fund, fired Stipanovich, and turned over the management of the fund to Blackrock (who would take over the management of assets of the failed Bear Stearns in March 2008.) Effectively, the liquidation amounted to a "run" on the state pool.

## FINANCING COSTS DOUBLE TO 9% FOR MANY STATE AND LOCAL MUNICIPALITIES

As if the prospect of a declining tax base and unwinding financially imprudent products from Wall Street banks, state and local municipalities wasn't enough, schools and hospitals have to confront another, perhaps even more nefarious, threat to their financial well-being in the future—their borrowing costs shot up after the auction-rate muni market collapsed. The auction-rate securities market is where issuers of municipal debt go to meet their short-term borrowing needs.

The $2.6 trillion auction-rate market first seized up in February 2008 after traditional investment banks refused to backstop them. Banks implicitly guaranteed the issuers of muni-debt they would backstop them in the event of a failed auction. Nevertheless, when push came to shove they were not there for the municipalities and other issuers of debt. "For 20 years the auction-rate market has met the needs of issuers and investors. The failure of the market was completely unexpected, like a dam break," said the managing director of the Securities Industry and Financial Markets Association, Leslie Norwood.[70]

The collapse of the auction-rate market took the entire industry by surprise. It never even occurred to the SEC that the buyers/investors (the banks themselves were the primary investors bidding on these auctions and would then resell the product to their customers) would disappear. It takes both a buyer and a seller to make a market, and in this case, the buyers simply stopped showing up. "The SEC was so unconcerned about possible failures that its list of material [risk factors] requiring disclosure never included unsuccessful auctions," reported Bloomberg authors Michael Quint and Darrell Preston.[71]

The auction-rate market failed municipalities not because the municipalities had any credit rating problems. The auction-rate market collapsed in part because the muni-bond insurers MBIA and Ambac had credit rating problems. As it turns out, the way municipalities were able to obtain a low interest rate/cheap credit was to buy bond insurance from a bond insurer. Bond insurers had AAA credit ratings but were at risk of losing their AAA rating as the credit markets deteriorated. Bond insurers were in particular trouble and at risk of insolvency at the time because of the escalating subprime mortgage-related losses steamrolling onto their books. The bond insurers, attracted to the fat fees available to them by insuring subprime loans, had made the unfortunate mistake of expanding their business model to include subprime-related products. Bloomberg authors William Selway and Martin Braun noted:

> Losses suffered by bond insurers on securities tied to U.S. home loans have cascaded through financial markets to hurt local governments whose budgets are already being squeezed by the slowest pace of economic growth in five years.[72]

One of the largest advertised failed auctions in February 2008 was the New York Port Authority. Their cost of borrowing jumped to the max limit of 20% when their auction failed. As Caroline Baum quipped at the onset of this credit crisis, "liquidity is never a problem, until it isn't."[73]

In another case, short-term rates on debt issued by California's Housing Finance Agency harrowingly jumped to 9% from 4.5% on June 19, 2008. Interest-rate spikes are taking place in municipalities all around the country. "Even if the auction-rate market survives, we're not going to see the kind of rates we're used to," said Rady Children's Hospital CFO Roger Roux in San Diego.[74]

Neither the buyers nor the sellers in the auction-rate market believe it can survive this shock. Investment banks like Citigroup are saying they believe the "market will never come back." Issuers of debt, like Wisconsin's debt director Frank Hoadley, are asserting "It's a damaged product, and I can't imagine issuers ever using it again. A lot of people will have to die and institutional memory go away before people will come back to it."[75]

## THE PEDDLING OF AUCTION-RATE DEBT TO RETAIL INVESTORS

Long before the auction-rate securities market failed, the executives of the financial firms underwriting auction-rate securities knew that the demand for these securities were falling off a cliff back when the credit crisis first hit in August 2007 and that one day they might be held to be the buyers of last resort if the auctions failed to generate sufficient demand. All would be have been fine if the underwriters lived up to their end of the bargain and acted as the buyers of last resort, but they didn't do that in February.

UBS makes a good case study. Their risk management department only allowed them to hold $2.1 billion in auction-rate securities on their books, but they had $11 billion of auction-rate securities to move. Executives recognizing the hazards of auction-rate securities back in August 2007 began to "mobilize the troops. The pressure is on to move inventory," according to an August 30, 2007 e-mail from David Shulman, the head of UBS's municipal securities group. As the problem worsened and the inventory continued to grow, Shulman added, "This is a huge albatross," in an October 31, 2007, e-mail. The crisis worsened for Schulman, and in a December 11, 2007, e-mail to a UBS colleague, Paul Wozniak, wrote: "We need to move this paper and have to explore all angles possible. We need to do this as quickly as possible."[76]

One of UBS's retail clients, Yanping Cui bought auction rate securities in the New Hampshire student loan agency at the urging of her broker, who told her "it's very safe and as liquid as possible" in

December 2007. Another UBS retail client, Richard Stahl, also bought the same New Hampshire student loan securities in January. At the same time UBS brokers were selling these securities, UBS was telling the New Hampshire student loan agency that their auction was in danger of failing. The auction failed a month later, in February 2008. Cui was told by her broker that she wouldn't be getting her money back until the market recovered. Stahl complained "this is a definite conflict of interest. On the one side they're my financial adviser, and on the other side they're the underwriter and the auction manager."[77]

This credit-crisis story had a rare happy ending seven months later. Investors all across the country filed complaints because they had no access to their money to pay their bills. The collapse of the auction-rate securities market created a Main Street liquidity crisis. In the summer of 2008, Massachusetts Secretary of State William Galvin and New York's Attorney General went after every single one of these firms that sold auction-rate securities to retail clients for committing fraud "by selling the bonds as the equivalent of money market securities."

"The increasing risks that developed in 2007 were known to the financial services firms that sold them, but were not disclosed to investors who bought them," said Atlanta attorney J. Boyd Page, who specializes in securities fraud.

## SO WHERE DOES IT ALL TAKE US?

The ability of state agencies and municipalities to service the higher interest rates at the very same time their tax bases are threatened will be extremely challenging going forward. The usual easy solution for these agencies would be to simply trim the budget and raise the property tax rate. Only thing is, as mentioned above, passing through these increased financing costs to homeowners will be almost impossible. The other, more difficult, choice would be to cut spending, which is probably the inevitable course.

As banks of last resort, "le dernier resort," central bankers had every reason in the world to be glum at the Jackson Hole symposium. The question, of how to unwind this whole quagmire without unduly burdening the hard-working taxpaying citizens in the U.S., England and Europe, remains an unanswered question still seeking a solution. It is hoped that home prices will magically reflate themselves so that the wasting collateral on the balance sheets of the central banks and financial institutions will be eventually be made whole. But it is exceedingly difficult to look beyond the valley we are descending into and still think we can come out on the other side more or less "whole."

Reflating home values will likely only be made possible by further U.S. dollar devaluations. The U.S. dollar devaluations have already put severe inflationary pressures on the global economy once this decade. Inflation, if we are not too careful, can lead to hyperinflation. In the end, the cost of reflating home values may only serve to inflict a very painful bout of inflation on hard-working tax-paying citizens that they did little to bring about.

There are no easy solutions for anyone that I can see, just hard realities to be gutted out. In the end, many hard-working tax-paying citizens will remain at risk for the foreseeable future. In short, it seems inevitable that several more unpleasant Minsky moments will roil our domestic and global economies as adjustments to the global imbalances are made. And there seems to be little our central banks—*le dernier resort*—can do to prevent it. The question as investors and individuals is thus: how do we hedge these unprecedented risks and challenges we have never before had to confront? Are we up for and ready for the challenges?

# THE DEMISE OF THE ONLY
# INVESTMENT MODEL YOU WILL
# EVER NEED

*Because it demands large-scale paradigm destruction
and major shifts in the problems and techniques of science,
the emergence of new theories is preceded by a period of
pronounced professional insecurity... generated by the
persistent failure of the puzzles of normal science to come
out as they should. Failure of existing rules is the
prelude to a search for new ones.*

—Thomas S. Kuhn 1962[1]

AS WE PROCEED throughout this chapter, it will be helpful at the onset to keep in mind Fitch's Kevin Kendra's lesson plan for how to work with models, teaching recruits at the credit rating agencies "how not to believe the outputs of these models... I want them to understand why the model may or may not apply to the assets they're trying to analyze."[2] In other words, Kendra's point is to simply show some common sense, please. Former Fed Governor Alice Rivlin stated this matter a bit more to the point as it relates to the subprime crisis and why we are in the mess we are in:

> We will never have a perfect model of risk in a
> complex economy. But the culprit [of the hous-

> ing crisis] was not imperfect models. It was a
> failure to ask common sense questions, such as
> "will housing prices keep going up forever?"[3]

As analysts and investors we must always examine and question the built-in assumptions behind financial model inputs. When those assumptions lose their validity, the outputs/results will be skewed. We see this happening everywhere around us these days: whereby financial institutions have been issuing loans in recent years that were traditionally backed by once-solid but now very shaky collateral—mortgage-backed securities. As we have shown, mortgage-backed securities are typically stable as long as total mortgage delinquencies remain in very low single digits.

Investors and institutional portfolio managers tend to rely on time-tested models on which to base their investment and asset allocation decisions. For example, growth investors build models that screen for stocks that offer GARP—an acronym for growth-at-a-reasonable price. Famous investors like Jack Dreyfus, Peter Lynch, William O'Neil and David Ryan can be generally said to fall into this camp. Value investors, on the other hand, build models that screen for companies that offer extremely deep value. Typically, they are looking to buy companies undervalued by the market and trading for 50 cents on the dollar—that is, below a company's tangible book value. Famous investors in this camp are Benjamin Graham and Warren Buffett.

Institutional portfolio managers recognize that equities are always a risky asset class—regardless of whether the intelligent investor screens for stocks based on value or growth. They tend to rely on buy-and-hold investment models that offer investors diversification but not necessarily non-correlated holdings. This approach to investing entails a blend of asset classes, typically limited to bonds and stocks.

## Every Model Has an Achilles Heel

There are limits to the logic of any investment approach or model that one uses. As we have seen in the most recent market crash, every investment model that was long-only, buy-and-hold oriented without strict stop loss risk management tools in place was sorely stress tested. As we have learned already from Alan Greenspan, Karl Popper, Nassim Taleb, there is no such thing as a perfect model. Models are abstract in nature. We can test models until we are blue in the face to verify a particular investment model's validity, but they are all false positives. That is, an investment model can show countless numbers of positive outcomes when stress tested, but it only takes a single counterexample to expose a model's Achilles heel.

All models have an Achilles heel. This is one of the most important lessons we can take away from the collapse of our financial system. It was flawed, too! The flaws in the financial system were exposed as the credit markets began shutting down in August 2007. All it took to totally destroy the rest of the financial system was a few additional missteps by our policymakers in September 2008. Even before the financial markets totally collapsed in September 2008, former Fed Chairman Paul Volcker said that the financial system itself had "failed the test of the marketplace" back in April 2008.[4] Paul Volcker's assessment is shared by others. In another interview, Institutional Risk Analyst Chris Whalen had this colorful exchange with Bob Feinberg back in June 2008:

> **The IRA:** So you see the U.S. banking industry going the way of king coal? Obviously the neither the Fed nor the Congress is willing to admit that a big constituency like the banking industry is moribund.

> **Feinberg**: The bottom line is that the system is broken and can't be fixed. The reason the banks keep coming up with opaque products is that they're trying to de-commoditize a business that is mature and adds little or no value to the economy. In fact, over time and on net, the banking system destroys value... I stand by my previous view about the model being broken, but I don't think people realize that this can't be fixed, that industries have life cycles, and the banking industry is about a half century past its best-if-used-by date.[5]

No matter what investment model an investor chooses to follow, he or she should always strive to know the strengths and weaknesses of that particular model and its limitations.

We can never fully know everything that is going on around us and in the financial markets. Even the most plugged-in market participants do not always fully comprehend everything that is going on (even the Federal Reserve Chairman). It is very important to recognize that no one is never so plugged-in that he or she can fully decompose all the risks that threaten their investments. So, while the investor may not entirely understand why his or her investment model is breaking down, he or she can always control the amount of risk exposure they have to the markets. Reducing one's risk exposure to the markets can be as simple a strategy as hedging one's position, diversifying into non-correlated positions or going to cash.

Yes, by moving to cash critics will argue that you are engaging in a game of market timing and that you risk missing some of the upside potential. Likewise, using hedging strategies to protect one's investment would potentially limit some of the upside potential while insuring against some of the downside risks.

While there are plenty of knocks against market timing strategies per se, there are clearly times when staying fully invested in the stock market is strictly fool's play. As a case in point, look at what happened to the dot com bust in 2000. Most of those internet stocks went bust. The broad market lost 50% of its valuation. The tech index lost 85% of its value by 2002, and as 2008 draws to a close, the NASDAQ index remains 75% off its peak valuations. Yet, still the buy-and-hold crowd regurgitates the supposed wisdom of their favorite model, which is merely based on long-term stock index returns. There are so many fallacies in the "buying stocks for the long haul" philosophy that I can not point them all out. Let me simply state one of Keynes observations: "in the long run, we are all dead." What happens to your return on capital can devastate your financial future as all too many of us have been finding out the hard way since 2000.

Furthermore, "buy stocks for the long haul" has only been empirically valid for the indexes themselves and not individual equities. The attrition rate of publicly traded companies that have failed over the past 100 years is appalling. The survival rate is horrible. So pathetic is the survivorship ratio that only one stock in the Dow Jones average has been in the index since before the 1929 crash. That one company is Phillip Morris. And Phillip Morris almost ceased to exist a decade ago because that company's business model, like every other company's, has flaws in it, too. Litigators almost destroyed the company and put it out of its existence back in 1999. Every single other company that was in the Dow in 1929 was put out to pasture and no longer exists. They have all been swept aside.

So, those empirical studies are only valid for measuring the long-run returns of stock indices, not individual stocks. To buy individual stocks, investors must have an exit strategy. And exit strategies are always a function of the entry or buy criteria. When the buy criterion becomes invalidated, your risk management strategy demands that you exit and close out the position. You'd have to be a closet indexer (one who only invests passively in market indexes) to follow this "buy stocks for the long haul" strategy. Closet indexers, by the way, are generally doomed to mediocre performance.

One of the great advantages we have as investors is the ability to not participate in the markets. We only need to participate in the financial markets when we can clearly put the odds greatly in our favor. When the odds in our favor begin disappearing, the catalysts begin to wane; our risk exposure by definition begins to rise. When the cyclical and structural drivers of our financial markets run out of gas, as they did in both the dotcom and housing busts, the only safety left to us is the sidelines or to fully hedge our positions as best we can.

Astute investors will build tools and models that know when it is best to be on the sidelines. One of the most astute investors of our time, who knew when it was time to be in and out of the markets, was Marty Zweig. In fact, he published a book titled *Winning on Wall Street*. In his book, he detailed the tools and models he developed and used to make himself and investors in the Zweig fund a lot of money.

Marty Zweig built a buy-and-sell investment model (as opposed to the buy-and-hold models) that he was able to use quite profitably in normal markets. Being an astute investor, he designed the model to signal to him when to be in the market and when to be out of the market. His model was essentially one of those market timing models that so many portfolio managers and academicians eschew. But his model made a great deal of money, and by Zweig's one counterexample alone, in Karl Popper parlance, he disproved the critics' theories about market timing models. Zweig called it the "Super Model" and "the only investment model you will ever need."

The investment returns far exceeded that of the broad market. In a span of 30 years, from 1966 to 1996, Zweig's model showed annualized returns of 18% versus 4.6% returns for buy-and-hold models. So successful and popular was Zweig, even critics of market timing subscribed to the Zweig newsletter.

While market-timing models can generally be easily discredited, it is worth noting that some of the most vociferous opponents to market-timing models come from institutional portfolio managers. The reason for this is they primarily get paid management fees by their clients to manage money in stocks and bonds. That is, they are paid to invest their clients' money in stocks and bonds and not sit sidelined with it in too much cash. When markets are performing well and are not misbehaving, if cash levels begin to get too high, the portfolio manager risks a phone call from one or several of his clients complaining of being in too much cash. If the portfolio manager is not comfortable putting that cash immediately to work, the client typically threatens to take that money out of the fund and invest it in a condominium or something. A portfolio manager is faced with two choices: sit on cash and risk shrinking the assets of the fund through client redemption, or rebalance the portfolio by buying more stocks and bonds. The difficult position portfolio managers often face is understandable.

Zweig also understood that his market-timing model would work only in normal markets. He understood precisely the limits of his model; he knew its strengths and weaknesses. He identified three specific market conditions when his model would not work. These three conditions have been present throughout the entire first decade of the first millennium.

So, even though his model has given buy signals to be in the stock market this decade, they have not panned out so well. And this is precisely because of the presence of these three conditions. Marty was smart, too. He had even designed risk management tools to tell him when his model was giving a false signal. That is, these tools would invalidate the buy signals generated by the model. In short, he knew his Super Model's Achilles heel. And that is precisely the point. Inherently all models have their flaws. It behooves the investor to know "how not to believe the outputs of these models," as Kevin Kendra informs us.

One of the major premises of Zweig's Super Model was based on monetary policy considerations. Monetary policy is generally considered a cyclical driver of the stock market. That is, "the major direction of the market is dominated by monetary considerations, primarily Federal Reserve policy and the movement of interest rates."[6]

Generally speaking, when the economy is collapsing, the Fed begins to loosen credit in order to stimulate and reflate the economy. As a rule, reflating is a net positive for equities, because the stock market is a discounting mechanism and prices in events before they happen. In short, the stock market itself is a leading economic indicator. Makes sense right? And Zweig built his Super Model around this most basic and simple rule.

> For a raging bull market [in equities], you need falling interest rates, the dollar is "our currency, but your problem." probably an economic recession, lots of cash on the sidelines, good values in the stock market—namely low price/earnings ratios—and a great deal of pessimism. If all these conditions converge, the [equity markets] should rally very, very strongly, and the first rally of the bull market should be the best one.[7]

Investment strategies should never be determined on the basis of one indicator, argues Zweig, "but the results found here strongly argue against the Fighting-the-Fed."[8] Zweig cautions his readers to "remember though, no indicator or model is right all the time."[9] This is a very important disclaimer, and it is good to see he threw it in. Quite frankly, the "only investment model you will ever need" simply won't work in abnormal markets, nasty economies and bear market conditions.

Zweig understood this well, but many of his followers did not. So he outlined three economic or fundamental conditions that are present at or during part of a bear market. These conditions, Zweig states, "have highly negative implications for the market."[10] Since he recognized that his cyclical model would not fare well under these three conditions, he developed three very simple indicators for his model to follow that would signal to him when to be out of the stock market.

These three conditions are: 1) extreme deflation, 2) ultrahigh P/E ratios, and 3) an inverted yield curve. Zweig left off a very important fourth condition that dovetails fairly well with an inverted yield curve and which defined our economic plight throughout much of this decade and the 1970s: namely, negative real interest rates. Negative real interest rate environments are when the Federal Reserve's short-term borrowing rates are below that of the inflation rate. In normal markets, the Fed funds' short-term borrowing rate is generally at or above the stated inflation rate. In abnormal markets, the Fed funds' short-term borrowing rates are well below the stated inflation rate.

If one or more of these negative conditions converge on the scene, we can expect Zweig's Super Model to sputter and choke, if not be downright misleading or wrong altogether. But in normal market conditions, stocks tend to be a superior asset class when the Fed monetary policy is accommodating and interest rates are falling. In sum, Zweig says "Don't Fight the Fed," and in normalized market conditions, this is a very good rule for investors to follow. But this market aphorism has been so bandied about over the years that it is accepted almost *a priori* and without questioning its Achilles heel or fallibility, much like the Fed's infallibility has been presumed by many market participants. Far from being infallible, however, there are indeed economic environments when the Fed is *so behind the curve* that that article of faith borders on the nonsensical.

As a rule, the basis of Zweig's "Don't Fight the Fed" monetary model is solid, and when used in conjunction with a few other indicators, Zweig postulates that one can "make major market timing judgments."[11] As noted earlier, market timing has been badly discredited on Wall Street for umpteen different reasons and due to voluminous research studies. To Zweig's credit, his market-timing models had held up extremely well for over 30 years, despite the Wall Street crowds' general denigration.

## MONEY MAKES THE MARE GO!

In general, the basic assumption behind Zweig's Super Model is that the stock market is largely driven by money, and lots of it. There is absolutely nothing wrong with that premise. Money makes the mare go, as many students of the market have been saying for decades. The first one to have coined and used the "money makes the mare go" phrase was, I believe, a contemporary of Zweig's—Edson Gould. Gould was another one of the great students of the stock market. Both Gould and Zweig emphasized that if the markets are flush with money, and the velocity of money flows are generally elevated, conditions for corporate earnings growth will generally be solid. Money managers tend to place great emphasis on corporate earnings as that which drives individual stocks and the stock market in general. But increases in the money supply and money flows precede rising revenue and earning streams.

The trick is to know when that begins to happen. In normalized markets, simple reductions in the Fed funds borrowing rate would usually do the trick and provide the market signal to go long in the stock market. But that seems so last century, given the abnormal market conditions we have had to deal with this century!

The virtual collapse of our financial system and our economy with the escalating rise in unemployment rate in 2008 signal that the financial distress millions of Americans are facing is very real. The collapse of the financial system and the economy is no sideshow for the majority of Americans. How far and deep that distress ultimately persists in the economy remains a real concern for us all.

A huge and prolonged contraction in consumer spending will slow the velocity of money in a meaningful way. This necessitates a big squeeze on corporate operating margins and earnings recessions for the broad stock market. During periods of earnings recessions and economic conditions with little to no GDP growth outside the government spending and lending, there will be a significant down-shift in earnings expectations for U.S. stocks.

## THE VOODOO ON EARNINGS MULTIPLES

This will necessarily expose the stock market to an earnings multiple compression that can push the earnings multiple into single digits. In normal markets, too high a P/E multiple would be a legitimate risk to stock market investors. But in abnormal markets where the economy is unduly depressed, contrary to Zweig's general supposition, there is a legitimate risk that the earnings multiple goes below investor expectations. In fact, given today's economic backdrop, it is possible for the general market multiple to swing into the single digits. Most investors, I assure you, are not prepared for that type of Armageddon scenario.

And yet, single digit multiple markets were common under prolonged adverse economic conditions, and equities will have to be re-priced accordingly. Zweig notes:

> For the markets as a whole, P/E's in the 10-
> 14 area are roughly normal. Very low P/E's
> in the 6-8 zone tend to be bullish in the long

> run, while P/E's in the twenties reflect excessive
> speculation, gross overvaluations and poor fu-
> ture stock performance.[12]

If in today's world the financial system didn't have a "plumbing problem" and black holes in its balance sheets, and the consumer didn't have a debt problem, everything would be pretty much hunky dory. The velocity of money would be generally strong, and consumer spending growth would be apt to lead to a sustainable recovery. This would likely induce businesses to increase capital expenditures and hiring, which are the prerequisite outlays that would lead to a meaningful increase in revenues and earnings growth rates.

Short of that dreamy outlook, investors should be aware that earnings multiples will likely compress into single digits. This is most easily accomplished by even lower stock prices than we saw in October and November 2008. There is a nagging, persistent plumbing problem and a contraction in both financial lending and consumer spending. The $64,000 question is how bad will those be, and how long will that last, not whether monetary policy is accommodative or not. In today's abnormal markets, analysts are looking at a different set of indicators. For the time being, until the economy and market conditions are normalized, Marty Zweig's Super Model based largely on monetary policy signals must simply be set aside.

Quantifying those risks to both the economy and stock market are paramount. All attention has turned to addressing these concerns among economists, analysts and market participants in general. "We're taking the pulse of the economy a little more frequently," noted Credit Suisse economist Jonathan Basile as early as September 4, 2007.[13]

Confidence was shaken when panic seized the credit markets in August 2007, and fear has remained palpable in the financial markets ever since, even after the freely lending central banks attempted to unclog the plumbing in the financial system and have all engaged in a race towards embracing a zero interest rate policy—ZIRP for short. This occurs when central banks cut interest rates to 1% or lower. ZIRPs ensure a negative real interest rate environment. A ZIRP was employed in the U.S. between 1937 and 1948 and Japan in the past decade. Japan's stock market has been in a bear market since 1989, making new bear market lows even in 2008—19 years after the market peak in 1989. Japan's ZIRP policy is a clear case in point that Zweig's monetary indicators will have great difficulty in abnormal markets.

In the midst of all these uncertainties, the investment community collectively must make risk management decisions. All most of us care about in the investment community is to figure out how to rub two nickels together and make a couple of bucks in the next few quarters or the next few years.

## THE STOCK MARKET RESPONSE TO FED'S POLICY OF MONETARY ACCOMMODATION IN 2007-2008

In August 2007, the stock market was flashing a fairly low risk entry signal, setting up on the long side of the stock market on the morning of August 16, 2007—precisely at the peak of the credit crunch that month. The setup was based largely on some technical models. But the technical model was aided and abetted by Zweig's "Don't Fight the Fed" monetary model." On August 16, 2007, the Fed cut the discount rate 50 basis points. To be sure, that discount rate cut did not elicit a buy signal under Zweig's Super Model.

But keen market observers said to themselves "first a discount rate cut, next a Fed funds rate cut." They made bets in the stock market, speculating the Fed would begin cyclically easing monetary policy.

They were right. And the stock market began to discount the future good news. These same market participants made even bigger bets that the Fed would surely cut rates at their next meeting on Tuesday, September 18, 2007, after the horrible jobs report on Friday, September 7, 2007. They were right again, and when the Fed cut the discount rate and prime rate on September 18, 2007, the stock market rallied almost 3% that day. The breadth of this stock market rally was so strong, even Zweig's momentum indicators kicked in, giving further confirmation to his monetary indicators flashing green buy signals.

By this time the stock market was more than 10% off its intraday lows of August 16, 2007. But the Zweig Super Model does not care about catching market bottoms and tops, it only cares about being in the market when the cyclical drivers for a sustained bull market are present. The S&P 500 closed at 1520 on September 18, 2007. Three weeks later on October 11, 2007, the stock market peaked at 1586, a mere 5% above the closing price of 1520 when Zweig's Super Model first flashed its buy signal.

The Super Model buy signal worked only for a few weeks, and then it didn't. There was no raging bull market; it died with a T.S. whimper. A month after the October stock market peak, Zweig's Super Model generated a stop loss signal. Zweig employed risk management tools to tell him when his Super Model buy signal was generating a false positive. One indicator to signal a false positive happens any week in which the stock market closes down more than 5% in one week after the Super Model buy signal is generated (I am simplifying slightly). The S&P 500 closed down more than 5% the week of November 5, 2007. The risk management tool Zweig's model employs generated a sell signal, invalidating the Super Model's September 18, 2007, buy signal.

No big deal. But why did the Super Model buy signal fail? The models don't care why. But it is important for us as investors to look around and ask why the model signal did not work. What happened that was so significant in Q4 07 to invalidate the signal? Quite simply, the financial sector began to recognize the losses sustained during the credit crunch in Q3 07. Reporting of the Q3 earnings season for financial firms began in the second week of October. As soon as it was learned that the financial sector was slipping into an earnings recession, investors began to lose faith in the "Don't Fight the Fed" mantra. Investor confidence was rattled by the news of the financial sectors earnings recession. And they were right to be a bit more guarded and circumspect in their equity investments. After all, the financial sector was responsible for driving roughly 25% of the S&P 500's total earnings. Investors had lost an important tailwind to driving earnings growth in the S&P 500, regardless of the rate cuts the Fed had just embarked upon.

The new feeling generated by the financial sector's earnings recession was simply: "Oh #!##, the Fed is behind the curve again." Investors hate it when they feel the Fed is behind the curve. And they displayed their displeasure after the next two Fed meetings when they felt the Fed was not cutting rates aggressively enough. This was particularly the case at the October 31, 2007, Fed meeting to cut rates and again on December 11, 2007. They even showed displeasure after the fifth rate cut on January 30, 2008—the second that month, but less vehemently so. The trajectory of declining stock prices indicated two things. First, it indicated the Fed was indeed behind the curve, and secondly that things were indeed getting worse in the financial markets.

In December 2008, one of the many tumors in the financial markets was the structured investment vehicles, or SIVs. Even though U.S. Treasury Secretary Hank Paulson was working vigorously to implement a "SuperSIV" that would buy assets from trouble funds from financial firms and bond insurers, this particular tumorous danger was shrinking on its own as financial firms sought to reorganize them so as to arrange their own rescue and avoid a firesale. Paulson's Su-perSIV never got off the ground, but a form of the SuperSIV was cre-ated in September 2008, known as Paulson's TARP plan.

Another problem cropping up in December 2007 was the call to freeze the resets on the adjustable rate mortgages (ARMs). In the-ory, the plan to potentially help homeowners avoid foreclosure was a good one. In practice, however, the plan faced significant hurdles and would at best help only a very few of the anticipated 1.8 million ARM resets in 2008-2009. Beyond that, government meddling with and modifying contractual loan agreements between private parties was highly frowned upon by the financial industry.

"We do not think it is hyperbolic to say that the sanctity of such contracts, entered into in good faith, is at the cornerstone of capi-talism. And if we are to in any way devalue that sanctity, we face a far greater liquidity crunch than the one in which we currently find ourselves,"[14] said Deutsche Bank Analysts.

"If contracts governing changes to the underlying loans are negated by the U.S. government, are [you as] an investor, ever going to purchase a U.S. mortgage backed security again?" asked John Robbins, 37-year in-dustry veteran and former head of the Mortgage Bankers Association.[15]

The crisis on the foreclosure front was getting desperate. Offi-cials were seeking viable solutions to the subprime crisis and coming up empty-handed. The economic data from December indicated the manufacturing sector of the economy was now contracting, and ini-tial jobs report showed that job creation had abruptly stalled. Worse yet, the unemployment rate suddenly jumped 0.3%. This prompted Bear Stearns' chief economist John Ryding to note: "Since 1949 the unemployment rate has never risen by this magnitude without the economy being in recession."[16]

So there we were at the beginning of a new year and the econ-omy was almost assuredly slipping into a recession. By late November, the Federal Reserve had created and opened up new lending facilities just so that financial firms could meet their year-end lending needs. "This is a much tougher monetary-policy environment than anything I experienced," Greenspan told the *Wall Street Journal* on December 14, 2007.[17]

The stock market continued to decline, notwithstanding three rate cuts in four months going into 2007's year-end. Commenting on the precariousness of the financial markets at year-end, Goldman Sachs Chief Financial Officer David Viniar said, "Just looking at the world's capital markets and looking at the lack of liquidity that we saw in November, it has to make us cautious."[18]

One of the worries expressed by Moody's was that corporate defaults would quadruple in the next year "after the number of companies that lost their investment-grade credit ratings."[19] The risk of a credit rating downgrade for the bond insurers MBIA and Ambac Financial Corp. made financial firms very uncomfortable. At stake: if the bond insurers had their credit ratings cut, it would mean that more than $2 trillion of mortgage-related securities would lose their AAA ratings. Further, if the bond insurers lost their credit ratings, then so too would all the firms and municipalities that borrowed the bond insurers AAA credit ratings to borrow cheaply. The credit rating agencies, Moody's, Standard & Poor's and Fitch placed all the bond insurers on credit watch for a potential downgrade.

This situation was getting uglier, and more short hedges piled into the S&P 500. Moreover, industry-wide downgrades "would lead to losses of $200 billion on securities being insured as some holders [like pension funds] would be forced to sell their bonds in a depressed market because of their investment guidelines," according to Bloomberg.[20] The damage from subprime securities was widening, and could not be ring-fenced.

The stock prices of the bond insurers were heading into the low single digits. According to the credit default markets, MBIA and Ambac Financial had a more than 70% chance of going bankrupt by mid-January. Reassurances from the CEOs of the bond insurers had little to no effect. Rumors of a rescue of the bond insurers began to circulate to keep them afloat. But New York State Insurance Regulator Eric Dinalo, who was fighting to prevent bond insurer credit rating downgrades, said a rescue of the bond insurers would take time. A week later, on January 24, 2008, credit strategist John Tierney at Deutsche Bank said, "Everyone has considerable exposure to the monolines and everybody is just very worried about what happens if they get downgraded to even AA."[21]

In December 2007, the broad stock market had fallen to its lowest level relative to bonds since 1970, according to the Fed's valuation model. The stock market began the New Year quite poorly out of the gate, and stocks would get a whole lot cheaper based on the Fed's valuation model as the year 2008 progressed. So much for that valuation model offering investors any signal but a flawed one!

Recognizing the financial crisis was worsening, the minutes from the December 11, 2007, Federal Reserve meeting showed many policymakers had argued for aggressive easing of the Fed funds rate to safeguard against a substantial downturn in the economy. A month later, on January 10, 2008, indicating aggressive rate cuts by the Fed would be forthcoming, the Federal Reserve Board Chairman Ben S. Bernanke stepped out and said:

> We stand ready to take substantive additional action as needed to support growth and to provide adequate insurance against downside risks... Incoming information has suggested that the baseline outlook for real activity in 2008 has worsened and the downside risks to growth

have become more pronounced. A number of
factors, including higher oil prices, lower equity
prices, and softening home values, seem likely
to weigh on consumer spending as we move
into 2008. The committee must remain exceptionally alert and flexible, prepared to act in a
decisive and timely manner and, in particular,
to counter any adverse dynamics that might
threaten economic or financial stability.[22]

Another indicator of when it might be time to buy the stock market
began to flash on the same day that Bernanke indicated aggressive
rate cuts were imminent. This time it was the "cash-on-thee-sidelines"
model. The chief investment officer at AG Asset Management, Elizabeth
Dater, noted: "It's telling you everybody's very nervous, but it's also telling you there's a huge amount of cash on the sidelines which if you can
take a long-term view, even a medium-term view, is very positive."[23]

Generally, there is a grain of truth to the cash-on-the-sidelines
indicator. Unfortunately, the S&P 500 was still trading in the 1300s
in January 2008. Less than a year later, the S&P 500 began carving
out a trading range in the 800s, roughly 35-40% lower. In both the
medium and long-term view, this indicator was flashing the wrong
signal to investors. While no one could know definitively that the
market would lose so much value with almost record levels of cash
on the sidelines, the point here is that market indicators can and do
flash false signals and that investors need to implement both buy
and sell signals in their risk management strategies. Again, an exit
strategy is a function of the entry. If the entry criterion is invalidated,
an exit is demanded of the investor.

Still another indicator was flashing another false signal to investors that day as well. This time it was a contrarian indicator.

"The number of investors bearish on U.S. equities [exceeded] those who are bullish by the most since November 1990," cited *Bloomberg News*.[24] Bullish indicators were falling by the wayside in this nefarious bear market. And all the while, the Zweig model had been sidelined as early as the week ending November 5, 2007.

By the end of January, the Fed had cut the Fed funds rate from 5.25% in September 2007 to 3%, about where the inflation rate stood at the time. Market observer Robert Schiller, who created the Case-Schiller Home Price Index, began to worry the Fed would have to cut rates probably below the rate of inflation, creating a negative real interest rate environment. "We are starting to see a change in consumer psychology," Schiller said. Behind that shift in consumer psychology was the fact that the consumer was losing all his props. The value of the consumer's real estate and stock holdings were simultaneously in decline, and the only prop left was what little real income growth he could muster. As job losses mounted and the unemployment rate accelerated, the consumer would be deprived of even that remaining prop as 2008 unfolded.

By February, the January jobs report would show U.S. business had begun to shed jobs. It is rare that payrolls would fall outside of a recession. So here, too, was another indicator the economy was entering a recession, and the Fed remained behind the curve with respect to its monetary policy even though they had already cut rates 2.25% in less than five months, one of the most aggressive Fed easing cycles in history. Simply put, the Fed was fighting a decline in the economy, and the economic decline was winning hands down.

## DON'T FIGHT THE FED, YOU JUST MIGHT WIN

Suddenly the axiom "Don't Fight the Fed," was losing its punch. This was the second time this decade that Zweig's "Don't Fight the Fed" monetary model broke down. Back in June 2001, when I first noted that the Fed's accommodative monetary policies were pushing on a string, I published an article relating the observation in *Futures* magazine. Sportingly, my editor, Howard Simons, dubbed the monetary model in 2001 as "Don't Fight the Fed, You Just Might Win." Just as happened in 2001, the economic headwinds were whipping the Fed's aggressive policies of monetary accommodation to prop up the economy and indirectly the stock market. Under abnormal market conditions, investors simply can not expect Fed monetary policies to be the cyclical driver it is known to be under normal market conditions.

In early 2008, home prices began falling at the fastest pace since the Great Depression. At the World Economic Forum in Davos, Switzerland, Lehman Bothers Vice Chairman Thomas Russo told attendees that he feared that declining home values would "prompt people to snap their wallets shut, choking the 70% of the economy driven by consumer spending"[25] And Russo's fears didn't even touch upon the fact that new foreclosures in the fourth quarter averaged almost 3,000 a day. More than 250,000 homes had been foreclosed in Q4 07, and that rate would be rising throughout 2008. "This has reached the point of being catastrophic," said William McCarthy, a Colorado mortgage broker who declared bankruptcy in July when his business failed after 18 years. "I had a client who called me sobbing because his wife committed suicide rather than face eviction. Something's got to be done to help people. My wife goes to bed crying every night, and there's nothing I can do. The bank won't even return my calls."[26] It looked as if the stars were aligned for no growth in the U.S. economy. Had it not been for U.S. exports still strong in the first half of 2008, the entire economy would have hit a brick wall.

In February, the auction-rate securities market began to fail. On February 13, 2008, the auction-rate securities market collapsed. On that fateful day, the underwriters of these securities, who were expected to be buyers of last resort if there wasn't enough institutional and retail demand for them, failed to fulfill their role and buy the auction-rate securities they were underwriting. UBS, Goldman Sachs, Lehman and Citigroup all allowed auctions to fail. The mounting losses from the collapse of their subprime securities prevented them from fulfilling their traditional obligations. Bank of America reported that "80% of all auction bonds sold by cities, hospitals and student loan agencies were unsuccessful" that day.[27] The failure of the auction-rate securities market further indicated that the widening impact of the housing crisis simply could not be ring-fenced. On February 28, 2008, Ben Bernanke told the Senate that "it's fair to say the central bank has a tougher time responding to the current slowdown compared with the recession of 2001."[28] There was certainly no shortage of negative news in the financial markets, and it would soon get worse.

The roots of the housing crisis extend back to evolving government policies since post WWII. By 1994, the Clinton administration would set a 67.5% homeownership target by 2000. President Bush followed the protocol of his predecessors on December 16, 2003:

> This Administration will constantly strive to promote an ownership society in America. We want more people owning their own home. It is in our national interest that more people own their own home. After all, if you own your own home, you have a vital stake in the future of our country.[29]

President Bush signed a $200 million-per-year American Dream Downpayment Act which would help approximately 40,000 families each year with their downpayment and closing costs. The Administration proposed the Zero Down Payment Initiative to allow the Federal Housing Administration to insure mortgages for first-time homebuyers without a down payment. HUD's Acting Secretary Alphonso Jackson said:

> Offering FHA mortgages with no down payment will unlock the door to homeownership for hundreds of thousands of American families, particularly minorities. President Bush has pledged to create 5.5 million new minority homeowners this decade, and this historic initiative will help meet this goal.[30]

More than 40% of first time home buyers financed their purchases with no-down-payment loans, according to a study done the National Association of Realtors. On March 4$^r$, 2008, complaining about the escalating foreclosure rates, Bernanke said, "more can and should be done" advocating loan modifications would be helpful. "Principal reductions that restore some equity for the homeowner may be a relatively more effective means of avoiding delinquency and foreclosure."[31]

The crisis was so palpable in March 2008 that RBC's Thomas Tucci said, "Every day is like the 1987 stock market crash. There isn't a day when you're not at the edge of your seat. The system is at daily risk."[32] But the 1987 crash was short lived, lasting less than two months. We were into our seventh month of stress-testing the financial system, with no relief in sight!

About this time, Janet Tavakoli, president of Tavakoli Structured Finance, observed yet another model breaking in the financial sector. This time it was the correlation models the financial engineers used. "The banks that have been using correlation to calculate their risk will have to go back to scratch. By using correlation models as the main means of risk management, the engineers threw out sound banking practices," said Ms. Tavakoli.[33]

At the heart of the heightened tensions in the financial markets was the subprime mortgage crisis. Yet in a bizarre disconnect from reality, Thornburg Mortgage's CEO Larry Goldstone said "Quite simply the panic that has gripped the mortgage financing market is irrational and has no basis in investment reality." Goldstone made his comments on March 7, 2008, just a week before the collapse of the housing market would devour Bear Stearns. Over half of their business model comprised securities from the housing market. On the same day Goldstone said there was no basis for the panic in the mortgage financing market, Freidman, Billings and Ramsey said the U.S. mortgage markets needed "about $1 trillion in new investment to halt a slide in prices that began last year."[34]

In mid-March, in response to the mushrooming mortgage financing crisis, the Fed began creating a new lending facility. This one would be called the new Term Securities Lending Facility, or TSLF. Under TSLF, the Fed could offer treasuries in exchange for acceptable collateral to primary dealers that included AAA-rated mortgage securities sold by Fannie, Freddie and other banks. Critical of the Fed's new facility, Barclay's Ajay Rajadhyaksha said:

> At the end of the day, people will realize it's not a silver bullet. The Fed's move doesn't completely resolve the effects of tighter bond-secured lending... One of the problems the mortgage market faces right now is that no one has the capital to go out and buy more.[35]

## TWO DOLLARS IS BETTER THAN NOTHING

The new TSLF could have been very helpful to saving Bear Stearns, but oddly enough, the Fed did not implement this facility in time to help Bear. A week after Bear Stearns died, the Fed held the first Term

Securities auction that could have provided Bear the liquidity they would have needed to be saved. Rather odd, isn't it?

The Achilles heel to Bear Stearns' business model was its huge inventory of mortgage-backed securities. During the week of March 10, 2008, Bear Stearns had been the subject of rumors that it was no longer liquid. All week long company spokesmen adamantly reassured the investment community that the company's "liquidity cushion" was sufficient to weather the crisis in the credit markets. Nobody cared to listen to such reassurances. Preferring to listen to the market signals and rumors, clients and investors left the company in droves.

By the end of the week, on Friday, March 14, 2008, it became evident to Treasury Secretary Paulson that Bear Stearns was not going to survive and would need a bailout requiring government intervention to avoid bankruptcy. Alan Schwarz got a call from Mr. Paulson, who told him, "You need to have a deal by Sunday night," before the Asian markets opened, or his firm would be facing bankruptcy on Monday morning. On Sunday, Mr. Paulson placed a call to JP Morgan's CEO, Jamie Dimon. Dimon told Paulson that the bank was considering making an offer of $4 a share for Bear Stearns. Paulson said, "That sounds high to me. I think it should be done at a lower price."[36]

Apparently, Treasury Secretary Paulson was concerned about appearances and did not want the government to be perceived as bailing out Wall Street investors. On Sunday afternoon, Bear Stearns received a call from a JP Morgan rep who said, "The number's $2." Mr. Schwarz took the JP Morgan offer back to his board of directors and said, "Two dollars is better than nothing!"[37] While none of the directors dissented with Mr. Schwarz and JP Morgan later announced the $2 deal, the lowball offer of $2 failed to go through as Mr. Paulson had hoped. Because of the lightning speed of the first major weekend- warrior deal, they had overlooked an important clause that gave Bear Stearns a great deal of leverage. That leverage allowed the deal to be renegotiated up to $10 the following week.

To secure the financing for the deal, the Federal Reserve said it would provide $30 billion to JP Morgan for Bear Stearns' assets. Again, we ask why could the Fed not have just provided Bear Stearns with the $30 billion directly? The Fed justified its role in the Bear Stearns so-called rescue as necessary to prevent a broader financial panic: "With financial conditions fragile, the sudden failure of Bear Stearns likely would have led to a chaotic unwinding of positions" and "could have severely shaken confidence," said Fed Chairman Ben Bernanke.[38]

Economist Joe Mason complained "The Fed is so far outside the traditional bounds...it is taking a step back in time to a system of direct credit where the government decided who gets funding [JP Morgan] and who doesn't [Bear Stearns]."[39]

More problematic than who gets what and who doesn't is: who pays for it? The so-called rescue/bailout had also placed taxpayer funds potentially at risk. "History suggests the Fed may not recover some of the almost $30 billion investment in illiquid mortgage securities it received from Bear Stearns," said Joe Mason.[40] According to Mason, the average recovery on failed bank assets is 40 cents on the dollar. On some loans "you are going to be lucky to get 40%," added Janet Tavakoli of Tavakoli Structured Finance.[41] On the other hand, Federal Reserve Chairman Bernanke said he was "reasonably confident" taxpayers would not lose money on their Bear Stearns investment. Now, who is one supposed to believe—Mr. Historical Precedent or Mr. Reasonably Confident?

Fed historian and Carnegie Mellon economics professor Allen Meltzer added, "Officials are playing with fire. With good luck, none of these liabilities will come due. We can't expect that good luck, and we haven't had it."[42] What Meltzer and Mason were implying is that the government began placing taxpayer dollars at risk with the Bear Stearns operation, long before they placed the GSEs into a conservatorship and long before lawmakers authorized $700 billion to rescue the rest of the banking system facing its own insolvency issues six months later.

In an interview, JP Morgan's CEO Jamie Dimon admitted that the firm could not possibly have bought Bear Stearns without funding from the Federal Reserve—that is, funding with taxpayer dollars.

> To me, it was much more about the downside, the risk. We are in the business of risk, and we don't mind taking it. The real point for me when you take risk is that you always talk about risk-return and whether you can handle all the potential outcomes. We would not and could not have done it on any basis without the Fed's help... I do believe this, though, that it was an obligation to our country that JP Morgan had.[43]

Goldman Sachs CFO David Viniar was asked two days after the Bear Stearns rescue if the credit crisis would have any "permanent implications" for Wall Street's appetite for leverage. His answer: "No, I don't."[44] And if you stop and think about it for a minute, his answer was absolutely correct when one realizes that the appetite for leverage is perpetually being funded by the regulators at the Federal Reserve and U.S. Treasury. All at the taxpayers' expense, I might add. Rather than discourage the moral hazard of excessive risk-taking on Wall Street, safety nets/bailouts and rescues actually encourage more of the same behavior.

The financial markets will perpetually lever up if allowed to. Markets will never self-correct as the deregulator proponents insist they should do as long as they always have the taxpayers around for a safety net. Markets are only capable of self-correcting if there are no safety nets underneath them to rescue them. The taxpayer safety net must be pulled so the risk-taking on Wall Street can become more prudent than folly! Will reducing leverage reduce Wall Street's profitability? Absolutely it will. But it will also reduce their losses, and that will be for the greater good. It's either we remove the safety nets or we better regulate the industry so Wall Street does not lose sight of its role serving the public interest! As a proponent of more oversight than we have had this past decade, Institutional Risk Analyst Chris Whalen states:

> In our view, the mortal sin of [former Fed Chairman] Alan Greenspan and other U.S. regulators over the past two decades was not irresponsible monetary policy, but rather dropping the ball on bank supervision and market structure.
>
> In particular, in the two decades of Greenspan's tenure, the Fed's Washington staff, other regulators and the Congress allowed and enabled Wall Street to migrate more and more of the investment world off exchange and into the opaque world of over-the-counter [OTC] derivative instruments and structured assets. This change is described by people like Greenspan and Treasury Secretary Hank Paulson as "innovation," but our old friend Martin Mayer rightly calls it "retrograde."
>
> Greenspan and the quaint economists who dominate the Fed's Washington staff have created vast systemic risk that need not exist at all and that now threatens our entire financial system.

BSC failed not because it had too little capital or too little liquidity, but because the thousands upon thousands of OTC trades which flow through the firm's books are bilateral rather than exchange traded. It was the understandable fear of counterparty risk, not a lack of capital or liquidity, which killed BSC. The irony is that the "financial innovation" of OTC derivatives and structured assets takes us backward in time to the chaotic situation that existed in the U.S. prior to the crash of 1929.

Would that the Congress and the Fed had the courage to confront Paulson and the other banksters who have turned America's financial markets into an increasingly unstable, derivative house of cards. If all federally insured commercial banks, mutual and pension funds were required by law to invest only in SEC-registered, exchange-traded instruments, the threat of further systemic risk could be eliminated tomorrow. What a shame that neither Chairman Bernanke nor FRBNY President Timothy Geithner said that when they appeared before the Senate Banking Committee [to answer questions regarding their role in the Bear Stearns rescue operations].[45]

Somewhere in here, the taxpayer needs to put his foot down and just say no! If that entails a taxpayer revolt with pitchforks on Capitol Hill to enact reform, so be it. By the time the U.S. Treasury begins to say that they are trying to "protect taxpayer interest" we are already in trouble. By the time the Fed tells us they are only protecting us from the consequences of the messy unwinds in the financial markets, the taxpayer has already been screwed. Taxpayers must demand pre-emptive measures and reforms so that the U.S. Treasury, Federal Reserve and Jamie Dimon never again have to feel obligated to reach into the taxpayer's pocket while simultaneously telling us they must do this thing for our own good and that "they have our back!" The dollars that have been expropriated and continue to be expropriated from the taxpayer under the guise of only doing it "for our own good" is obscene! "You can't have the Fed in a 'trust-me' mode," said Todd Petzel from Offit Capital Advisors.[46]

Anna Schwarz, who co-authored *A Monetary History of the United States*,' called the Bear Stearns operation "a rogue operation...to me, it is an open and shut case. The Fed had no business intervening there."[47]

"We have to start now to recognize the strategic instability of the path we are on. The Fed needs to prepare markets for how it won't intervene, which it didn't do before the Bear Stearns meltdown," said Carnegie Mellon professor Marvin Goodfriend back in May 2008.[48] But the trajectory of events and moral hazards that have transpired since Goodfriend's comments has only prepared us for far greater market interventions, not less.

## THE WORST IS OVER, NOW GET YOUR SMILES ON, BOYS!

Insofar as the Bear Stearns so-called rescue put out one of the major fires in the financial market crisis, the Fed bailout placed a punctuation mark in the broad stock market. The stock market put in an intermediate-term low on Monday, March 17, 2008, the morning after JP Morgan's $2 offer was announced. Because the Q1 07 earnings season would upside surprise market participants due to exports, the stock market rallied through the earnings season up until May 19, 2008. Investors enjoyed a brief two-month 15% relief rally.

Back in the crash of 1929, the worst day of the 1929 market crash, October 29, 1929, later became known as "Tragic Tuesday." That day, the buying didn't just dry up, "it disappeared." When workers left downtown New York that evening for home, the evening newspaper boys in Grand Central Station were shouting "Read 'em and weep!" In the weeks that followed, "clandestine meetings" were held in the basement of the New York Stock Exchange. At the close of each of these meetings, the president of the New York Stock Exchange would prompt his colleagues "Now get your smiles on, boys!"[49] In a similar manner, after the crash of Bear Stearns, a sense of renewed optimism was publicly expressed on Wall Street. Their optimism may not have been disingenuous so much as it was misplaced.

After the Fed and JP Morgan buried Bear Stearns on March 17, 2008, the market angst began to diminish in the weeks that followed. The credit markets managed to function in somewhat of a hobbled fashion, thanks to the Fed opening up lending facilities to take the toxic waste off the balance sheets of other financial firms and place it onto its off-balance-sheet lending facilities. It did not take to long for hope to creep back into the markets and hear that Wall Street firms and Fed officials had begun to proclaim the worst was over. In early June, Federal Reserve chairman Bernanke said that the risk of a "substantial downturn" in the economy had receded in the past month. Fund manager BlackRock bought shares of Lehman Brothers during the second week of June with BlackRock's president saying at the time, "We have confidence in the firm. They have a history of being a team, a place of focus, of working out their situations, of having confidence in the marketplace."[50]

Echoing BlackRock's expression of optimism three days later, Lehman Brothers CEO Dick Fuld declared, "Our core business and our strategy are sound, even after the firm's mortgage business shrank. With this franchise's strength and power, we can go it alone. I believe in the model." Three months after this expression of confidence, Lehman's business model would cease to exist. Another model bit the dust!

## A CONSPIRACY OF OPTIMISM

Of course, the worst was not yet over. Far from it, and as Marc Faber, author of *Tomorrow's Gold*, related in one of his commentaries a few months after Bear Stearns had been nixed:

> We have seen the heads of virtually all financial institutions stand up over the last few months and claim the worst is behind us. Why would anyone listen to these people? They didn't see the disaster coming, and yet somehow they are qualified to tell us it is all alright! Perhaps I am just unduly skeptical, but this reeks of a conspiracy of optimism. The recession has barely started, let alone reached its nadir. The market moves of late have all the hallmarks of a classic sucker's rally. This isn't discounting the recovery, this is denial! Far from being behind us, the worst may well still be ahead![51]

Indeed, Faber was prescient; the worst in fact did lie ahead. At the end of April 2008, as the Q1 08 earnings season drew to a close Michael Farr, president of Farr, Miller & Washington, said, "At the end of every quarter, Wall Street CEOs say that was the worst quarter. None of them has suggested a catalyst that will grow their profit margins. Why would I buy financials believing in their 'we're at the end' propaganda?"[52] Still, sell-side Wall Street firms persisted in the claims that the worst was over and that it was safe to reenter the stock market. And for a few months, they were right.

## NIGHTMARE SCENARIO FOR THE BOND INSURERS

But the post Bear Stearns bear market rally ran out of gas on May 19, 2008. In the following month, the credit-rating agencies would reduce the credit ratings of the bond insurers. Losing their AAA stamp would create a ripple effect within the financial system simply because their credit rating downgrade would also mean a downgrade on roughly $2 trillion worth of securities that they guaranteed. By June 18, 2008, investor Bill Ackman, who had been short the bond insurers MBIA and Ambac Financial for the whole ride down, indicated to other investors in NY that losses posted by the bond insurers might prompt a breach of "the capital limits allowed by regulators, making them insolvent."[53] Countering Bill Ackman's solvency concerns for the bond insurers was MBIA's spokesman Kevin Brown, who said that because MBIA had a capital surplus of $3.9 billion, the issue of solvency was "both highly theoretical and extremely unlikely." That was rather dismissive of Bill Ackman's concerns by the MBIA spokesman. But consider this: who are you going to believe? Bill Ackman, who had been right all along, or a company spokesman whose business model had been failing for a year and a half due to the fact because the company took on risks that the business model was not prepared to handle? Confirming Ackman's concerns, CreditSights analyst Robert Haines wrote in a June 8, 2008, report that:

> Statutory surplus levels at some of the monoline financial guarantors are extremely alarming. MBIA may be forced to pay a total $7.9 billion in claims on a present-value basis and Ambac may be forced to pay $6.2 billion. That's what puts these companies into the nightmare scenario.[54]

It was tit for tat all month long for MBIA. On the one hand, investors and analysts had reason for grave concern, and on the other hand you had MBIA dismissing these outside concerns. Moody's credit-rating agency cut MBIA's credit rating five levels in late June. In response, Fitch's analyst Thomas Abruzzo said MBIA was facing a "tenuous situation" as the company sought to "cover payments and collateral calls triggered by the Moody's downgrade." To which MBIA's CFO replied, "MBIA is not in a tenuous situation."[55]

## JUNE SWOON

But a far worse development than the bond insurers was that our GSEs, Fannie Mae and Freddie Mac, were beginning to succumb to the housing crisis. The Achilles heel to their business model had been found! And by June 25, 2008, Goldman Sachs reversed its May 5, 2008, call to buy bank stocks, saying the recommendation was "clearly wrong." Goldman said the industry's woes appeared "to be far worse than originally anticipated."[56] Most other Wall Street firms joined Goldman Sachs in their flip-flop on the credit crisis and financial stocks in Q2 08. Amidst all the flying debris in the financial markets, the stock market swooned to its worst June performance since the Great Depression, according to *Bloomberg News*.

## CROSSING THE RUBICON

By July 13, 2008, the battered Fannie Mae and Freddie Mac enterprises were in talks with the U.S. Treasury, Federal Reserve and White House officials to come up with a plan, any plan, but hopefully a plan that would work. On July 14, 2008, Paulson was asking Congress for authority to buy unlimited stakes and lend to the companies. Translated, Paulson was asking for unlimited access to taxpayer monies.

Sean Egan, president of Egan-Jones Credit Ratings Co., called the Secretary of the Treasury's request for unlimited authority to save Fannie and Freddie with unlimited taxpayer dollars "crossing the Rubicon"—a phrase abstracted from the history books denoting the point of no return when Julius Caesar crossed the Rubicon River in Italy with his army in 49 BC to make his way to Rome. The act of crossing the river boundary broke the Roman law, making war inevitable. Today the phrase is commonly used to indicate a risky and revolutionary course of action being taken.

Institutional Risk Analyst Chris Whalen was far more melodramatic in his assessment: "It is time to recognize that the GSEs were always dependent upon government support and now we must make the implicit explicit."[57] And Whalen was exactly right, there was always an implicit government guarantee, Paulson was just asking lawmakers to legislate what was already factually known to be true. Paulson also made reference to taxpayer protections once again saying that any stock purchases or lending to the companies "would carry terms and conditions necessary to protect the taxpayer."

To Paulson's credit, he never seems to forget the taxpayer. Still, some lawmakers were not very comfortable with the Treasury Secretary's request. Senator Richard Shelby pointedly said, "we are potentially layering taxpayer resources on top of massive systemic risk." Senator Jim Bunning took a bigger swing at the Treasury Secretary's proposal.

> The taxpayers have reacted and the market has reacted to your plan by driving down Fannie Mae shares 26 percent today, right now. Freddie Mac's are down 29 percent at this moment, just in case you are interested in how the markets are reacting to your wonderful plan.[58]

Other lawmakers' sense of permissiveness knows no bounds, like Democratic Representative Barney Frank, who feign and just rollover: "I trust him. This is not some irresponsible teenager." Frankly, we could do with fewer pushovers on Capitol Hill when the new Obama administration takes over; they will be of little help to either Obama or the rest of America.

Unfortunately, as always seems to be the case, there was good reason to be uncomfortable, for as we have seen in hindsight with AIG, TARP, Bear Stearns and all the others, when these statements of remembrance to the taxpayer are made, they have not gone so well for the taxpayer thus far, so they do not hold much water.

The usual round of reassurances by company CEOs ensued. "Given the market turmoil, having options to access provisional sources of liquidity if needed will help to strengthen overall confidence in the market. We continue to hold more than adequate capital reserves," said Fannie Mae's CEO Daniel Mudd. And Freddie Mac's CEO Richard Syron added:

> We are heartened by yesterday's announce-
> ment, [which should] go a long way toward re-
> assuring world markets that Freddie Mac and
> Fannie Mae will continue to support America's
> homebuyers and renters.[59]

In other news that same day, some doom-and-gloom rumblings rippled through the newswire in Citigroup, because the toxic assets on their off-balance sheets were gargantuan. Short of just hiding the monstrous waste, Citigroup's off-balance sheet was and still is a huge black hole. "You will rapidly realize what a farce these off-balance-sheet things are. You could pick up a lot of loan losses with the stuff you're putting back on," said Ladenburg Thalmann analyst Dick Bove in reference to Citigroup's off-balance-sheet assets.[60]

"If you start adding up all the potential exposures, it's a huge number. The banks will say that it was disclosed. Investors are saying, 'Yeah, but it was cryptic. We really didn't know what you were telling us,'" added Sam Golden, former ombudsman for the U.S. Office of the Comptroller of the Currency. To avoid an all-out horrific earnings report that quarter, Citigroup's new CEO Vikram Pandit decided to spread out the unloading of $400 billion of on-balance-sheet assets over the next three years. Presumably, when Pandit moved these assets onto the balance sheets, he did so by introducing them as Level Three assets that he could mark them at mark-to-make-believe prices.

It was further disclosed by *Bloomberg News* that Citigroup's deputy controller, Robert Traficanti, wrote a letter to the FASB on June 9, 2008, complaining that a rule requiring banks to evaluate their off-balance-sheet assets and liabilities every quarter was too onerous. "We believe that this model is impractical from an operational standpoint. We would not be able to perform this analysis given the resources we currently have. We would need to hire many more accountants."[61] An outside observer like myself might simply suggest to Traficanti that if they haven't the resources to manage their asset base, they might consider shrinking their asset base to a more manageable size—a size that is appropriate for the resources that they have. Think Shrink!

## FINANCIAL CRISIS STRIKES DEEP, INTO THE REAL ECONOMY IT CREEPS

Looking over the collateral damage at the beginning of the third quarter, billionaire investor George Soros said, "This is a very serious financial crisis and it is the most serious financial crisis of our lifetime. It is an idle dream to think that you could have this kind of crisis without the real economy being affected."[62] Of course, Soros was absolutely right. The escalating woes were not limited to the financial sector; risks to the broad economy were readily apparent as well, particularly in the housing sector, where it was most acute.

"As long as housing values continue to drop from month to month, it's impossible to know when the end of the credit crisis will be. I want to see housing prices stabilize and increase before I put a stake in the ground and say our problems are behind us," said Jack Ablin, Chief Investment Officer at Harris Bank.[63]

Jack Ablin offers up a key insight that investors should heed. As bad as things are in our economy today, there have to be ways to measure them, and measuring home prices is one way to do just that. Home prices can be used as a coincident or leading indicator for the state of the economy. And these measurements of the economy can be very useful indicators for the investor. To which I might add, as investors, we want to see the unemployment rate stabilize as well! Until these events come to pass, you can rest assured the economy will remain mired in a severe recession. This also assumes corporate earnings will on balance be contracting and stock market rallies will be suspect.

## P/E MULTIPLES—TOO HIGH, TOO LOW OR JUST RIGHT?

No one can or rightly should trust a stock market rally's sustainability in an economy that is recessionary or trending below growth potential. The fact is that that is the future we face, and this could go on for a period of several years or longer. In a recessionary or low-growth economic outlook, it is perhaps best to view the stock market as having a definitive valuation ceiling over its head. One of the better historical models to determine where that valuation ceiling might be is through the use of the historical P/E ratio, or price to earnings ratio. The P/E model is not perfect, but it can still be used as an excellent tool for both investors and professional money managers alike.

The basic concept is easy to understand: price/earnings multiple can only expand so far before price becomes overvalued. Conversely, the price/earnings multiple can only compress so far before price becomes undervalued. The simplicity of the model makes it a widely used conventional tool.

## VALUATION MODELS SUPERIOR TO ZWEIG'S SUPER MODEL IN ABNORMAL ECONOMIES

The stock market is an asset class. During periods of extreme optimism, stocks tend to become overvalued and more risky. During periods of excessive pessimism, stocks tend to be undervalued and less risky. The intelligent investor will want to reduce risk exposure during periods of extreme optimism and increase risk exposure during periods of excessive pessimism. In this sense, the intelligent "value" investor takes on shades of market timing, but based on valuations and not Marty Zweig's Super Model based on cyclical monetary and momentum indicators. In the abnormal economic conditions in which we find ourselves today, it is more appropriate to adopt tools from the value investor's model than Zweig's more cyclical Super Model during normal market conditions. But one of the conditions under which Marty Zweig knew his Super Model would not do well was when price/earnings multiples were "ultrahigh," as he liked to call it.

It is helpful to have an idea of what the S&P 500 earned in the previous year, what it is expected to earn in the current year, and the estimates of what the earnings will be in the following year. Because earnings are notoriously unpredictable, and analysts undershoot and overshoot all the time, the most reliable earnings multiple is the trailing 12-month multiple. But for our purposes, we just want to make several observations that can be quite useful to both the investor and professional equity/money manager.

## YESTERYEAR—OUR RECENT PAST

First, we must use the P/E valuation model contextually. By that I mean, we need to understand the economic backdrop in which the stock market exists. For example, consider the chart above over the past 20 years, after the 1987 crash. Take into consideration all the financial innovation, engineering and alchemy, the excessive leverage

## S&P 500 12-MONTH P/E

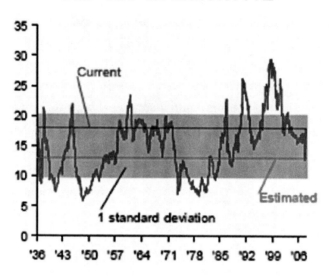

Source: http://www.birinyi.com/

and risk-taking, Greenspan's so-called miracle of productivity, along with all the pro-forma and various other fudged earnings reports. In that world we see that the P/E multiple enjoyed a meaningful expansion above 20 for the first time since the Roaring 20s (1928-1930). In this world, a market multiple below 15 would be considered cheap.

Relative to the past 20 years, now that the stock market multiple is under 15 again, we could say stocks are cheap. But as Bill Gross points out, we do not live in that world anymore. The era of deregulation, low borrowing costs and tax cuts is over. That world will not be our future! Therefore, as the year 2008 draws to a close, stocks are not really cheap—quite yet!

> Stocks are [only] cheap when valued within the
> context of a financed-based economy once dom-
> inated by leverage, cheap financing and even

lower corporate tax rates. That world, however, is in our past not our future. More regulation, lower leverage, higher taxes and a lack of entrepreneurial testosterone are what we must get used to—that and a government checkbook that allows for healing, but crowds the private sector into an awkward and less productive corner.

We are now morphing towards a world where the government fist is being substituted for the invisible hand, where regulation trumps Wild West capitalism, and where corporate profits are no longer a function of leverage, cheap financing and the rather mindless ability to make a deal with other people's money. Welcome to a new universe stock market investors![64]

## BACK TO THE FUTURE

Wow! What Gross said!

But we do live in a relative world. And contextually, we just have to ask ourselves: relative to what? In economic terms, the economic outlook for the U.S. economy post 2008 will probably be most akin to Great Britain in the 1930s. But, we don't have a long-term historical P/E model of Great Britain dating back to the 1930s to work with. Making do with these limitations and what we have, the economic outlook for the post-2008 era will probably most resemble the 1930s or 1970s, and contain shades of both.

And if we say we are going back to the future that means the S&P 500 long-term historical P/E model is likely to return to its "oscillating" norms from 1936 to 1987. A P/E over 20 is most certainly overvalued and a P/E under 10 is most certainly undervalued. And this is the significant point. When I last checked the S&P 500 multiple in October 2008, it was roughly 15. Given that the multiple of 15 is smack dab in the middle of 10 and 20, we can say that the S&P 500 was roughly "fairly valued" in October 2008. That is neither overvalued nor undervalued, it is just right. Risks can be said to be roughly equal, if this were the only tool at our disposal upon which to make judgment calls as to risk factors (it is not). But on that P/E valuation basis, investors in Q4 08 should probably stay the course and not make any large adjustments until the market becomes overvalued. Especially after a 53% decline in little more than a year—the S&P 500 and Dow Jones tend to do fairly well after "Half-Off Sales," even if it is a bumpy ride.

The intelligent investor will likely adjust his portfolio and seek to reduce his risk exposure to the equity market when the S&P 500 P/E ratio approaches 20. Conversely, the intelligent investor will likely seek to increase his risk exposure when the S&P 500 P/E ratio is at or under 10. When the S&P 500 is neither overvalued nor undervalued, your job as a prudent investor or money manager is to stick your finger in the wind to see which way the economic wind blows—ill or fair—and adjust your risk tolerance level accordingly!

## EXTREME DEFLATION

Another red flag for Marty Zweig's Super Model is "extreme deflation." Marty Zweig measured and defined extreme deflation as occurring when the Producer Price Index declines by 10% on a six-month annualized basis. Using Zweig's extreme deflation model at the close of 2008, the U.S. economy is on the verge of slipping into a condition Zweig considers extreme deflation. On a four-month annualized basis through November 2008, U.S. producer prices are declining at a 15.75% rate. And on a five-month annualized basis, producer prices are declining at a 12.2% rate.

As an economy, we are on the verge of entering extreme deflation (perhaps needing only one more data point) by Zweig's measurement, and this has corresponded with an extreme drop in the stock market, as Zweig would expect. Lately, everybody living in the U.S. has been aggressively schooled by the lessons of deflationary forces present in both the stock and real estate markets. By Zweig's measurement, periods of extreme deflation were only present in the U.S. economy during the past 100 years in 1919-1921, 1929-33, and 1937-1938.

The only problem with using extreme deflation as an indicator is that it is not a leading indicator. Rather it is a coincident indicator, which is not very useful for the stock market to say the least! But it is interesting to note that the U.S. economy is but a data point away from a deflationary headwind not experienced since 1938. Deflation has pros and cons. While our home values and equity portfolios are being crushed, at least gasoline at the pump is half the price it was in the first half of 2008. That alone can put a couple hundred extra dollars in the consumer's disposable income pocket a month.

## THE YEAR AHEAD: 2009

Directly ahead for the stock market, the beginning of the year ought to do quite well, and people's expectations will be surprised on the upside. The reason for that is two-fold. First, the obvious catalyst is Obama hitting the ground running. Secondly, Federal Reserve Chairman Bernanke has targeted 30-year mortgage rates. He intends to see that the 30-year mortgage yields decline to 4.5% roughly in the first half of 2009.

To that end, Bernanke has issued a statement of intent to buy 30-year treasuries on December 1, 2008, an historic day to be sure. The upside to this story is that 4.5% long-term mortgage yields will attract a lot of refi-activity and some home buying. The downside is that 4.5% mortgage rates will not do much to stir aggressive home buying to take up the glut of excess supply on the market due to the extremely high foreclosure rates we expect to see in 2009. Moreover, the 4.5% rates do little for those folks already delinquent or upside down on their mortgages. Even 4.5% won't be a silver bullet that arrests the extremely high foreclosure rate we must still somehow muddle through.

At some point, the honeymoon with the Obama administration will end. And the full brunt of new challenges and economic realities will hit us full force. The Forgotten Man must wake up to the idea that it is not a healthy thing to be overly reliant and dependent on the government. No matter how big the government grows, they will never become a permanent solution; they will never be a perfect form of government. Just as we learned there are no perfect models of risk, there are no perfect models of government. Each has its own Achilles heel. In the words of Vito Tanzi, former director of fiscal affairs at the IMF:

> We will end a financial crisis with a fiscal crisis.
> We will get out with a very large public debt
> and very large public spending. That, for sure,
> will slow down the rate of growth for the next
> 10 years or so.[65]

One day we will have to wake up to the reality that we can't become too dependent on the government. Already, we are overly dependent. "We're seeing a more statist world economy. That is not good for growth in the longer run,"[66] says Ken Rogoff, former chief economist at the International Monetary Fund. A large socialist/ welfare government is not good for the economy in the long run. The Forgotten Man must push-back on the ever-burgeoning size of the government and find the resolve to move the economy forward. The Forgotten Man will have to remember the long-ago forgotten virtues of being self-reliant and thrifty. He will have to remember the government is not enough, and that he must become a real force to push the economy forward, not the government. Let us hope the Forgotten Man does not forget his role.

In his January 2009 missive, Paul McCulley once again addressed the need for the U.S. government to expand its role during this economic crisis to protect capitalism from its own Schumpeterian "creative destruction" or its own "inherent debt-deflationary tendencies" as McCulley likes to call it. And he calls on the government to employ the "Minsky Policy Solution" to reflate our way out of debt! Yes, the government and the Federal Reserve have fully adopted the Minsky Policy Solution to reflate the economy, but will it work? Many, including myself, have well-founded reservations. McCulley elaborates on both the problem and the policy solution to the crisis:

> The TARP, which Congress fought intensely about, and is still fighting about, given how the Treasury has used it to date, does indeed fill a gap in the federal safety net against systemic risk. It allows the Treasury to go where the Fed can't, literally lending to anybody against anything, or simply injecting equity into anybody against nothing...to maintain the capitalist financial system as a going concern... Whatever you call it, the TARP is a huge new tool for the visible fist of Treasury to support the invisible hand of capitalism...
>
> If there was a positive externality of Lehman's demise, it is that policymakers finally found their socialist mojo, putting in place the necessary laws for the government to lever up and risk up its balance sheet *"more than proportionate"* to the private sector's new-found proclivity to do just the opposite...

That is indeed what is needed to save capitalism from its inherent debt-deflation pathologies. The paradox of deleveraging and the paradox of thrift are beasts of burden that capitalism simply can't bear alone. Only the Minsky Solution can lift that load...

This Minsky Solution thing is that *"more than proportionate"* socialist response [whereby] the government not only steps up to the risk-taking and spending that the private sector is shirking, but goes further... providing a meaningful reflationary thrust to both private sector risk assets and aggregate demand for goods and services...

The Fed does presently stand ready to print as much money as necessary to accommodate the financing of an all-in reflationary fiscal policy thrust, as promised by President-elect Obama. Through holes in the floor of heaven, Hyman Minsky weeps tears of joy... And call me cautiously optimistic that Reflation will get traction... But prudence demands that I at least acknowledge that even the best laid reflationary plans might go awry, at least in the short run.[67]

Should the government manage to pull off the feat of saving capitalism from itself with a "more than proportionate" socialist policy solution, once the government is done stamping out the fires of capitalism's own creative destruction, it will then have to retrench and rely on businesses and consumers to step up and restart a new cycle

## Journeying with Minsky

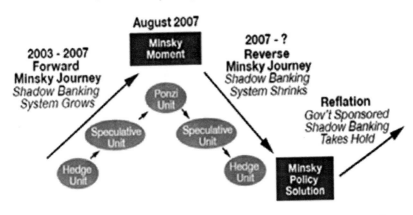

Source: Pimco

of risk-taking and spending. The easy-to-comprehend primary risks ahead are two-fold. First, there is the risk that the reflationary policy solution does not mop up its excesses in time to prevent an out-of-control inflationary or hyperinflationary cycle.

The second major risk is that the government will forget and exceed its own role within a capitalist system once it turns socialist on us—there may be no looking back at the capitalist system under which this country operated for the first 200 years of its history. Adopting a socialist model may be akin to crossing the Rubicon or the point of no return.

Richard Kline, who for one was happy to see an end to the final chapter of capitalism's abuses under an unregulated financial system, had this to say about the recent demise of America's capitalist society and economy:

> It's impolitic to say so, but I for one and [sic] damned glad that the financial system we know it is dead. The last fifteen years have been excru-

ciating. There is no guarantee that we get a better society out of crisis, and our transit through
fascism may be more prolonged and injurious
than a best case scenario, but the...Economy [in
the past decade] has sucked anything of lasting
value in this country and this world. If we can't
turn the page, then burn the page, and write a
new one. The sun still comes up; children still
get made and mostly fed; the blackbird whistles,
the crows cart off the carrion. It's illusions which
have died more than anything—so far.[68]

Unfortunately, there is no guarantee that we get a better financial
system than the one we have known for the past 30 years. I doubt,
given the trajectory of the bail-and-rescue policies in 2008, that it
will differ much from the financial model that utterly collapsed in
2008. As Yves Smith put it as 2008 drew to a close:

We have worried out loud that the policy rem-
edies being pursued by the U.S. amount to trying to restore the status quo ante to as great
a degree as possible... Although it may be difficult to work two agendas, crisis response and
addressing the root causes of our economic
mess in parallel, focusing solely on the former
runs the considerable risk of that we will see
only a shallow recovery, with many of the elements of the crisis soon reasserting themselves
in more virulent form.[69]

But from this point forward, America certainly will be writing a new
chapter in its history. What that shall exactly bring we don't quite

yet know. "Future policymakers must confront the reality that is, not the one that should have been. And investors must do likewise, casting aside personal philosophies for a clear-headed view of the future horizon," says Bill Gross. We must recognize that we face myriad unforeseen risks and consequences to the socialist and reflationary policy solutions being adopted. As the new Obama administration takes center stage, we can hope they sever the status quo and purge the root causes of our economic mess. This will entail a great deal of hardship for the private banks that got us into this mess, but that will certainly be more than offset by the benefits provided to the real economy. To this end, Chris Whalen, hoping that the new administration will seek to put an end to the ongoing opaque bank bailouts said,

> But hope remains if we return to first prin-
> ciples. Transparency and accountability lead
> to credibility, the short version of why bank-
> ruptcy is better than bailouts. That may be the
> chief lesson of the past year. Hopefully our new
> President and his government will take the les-
> son as well.[70]

The risks are high and the political and economic outcomes remain uncertain precisely because the situation is so very unstable. Collectively, however, we can join McCulley's cautious optimism that things will "get better if you give them time," as Jesse H. Jones said 60 years ago in his memoirs of the Great Depression. But, by the same token, we can assume nothing, and given the missteps thus far, we must absolutely challenge our policymakers every step of the way to adopt sensible solutions rather than "dys-solutions on the path to dissolution."[71]

The government will also soon begin aggressively regulating the financial markets. This is a responsibility that they have for the most part shirked over the past 30 years. However, the investor must not sink back into some imagined or false security that the government will have "fixed the system" with their ever-tightening protections. They will most certainly not have fixed the system. All systems and models have flaws, as I have gone to some pains to point out in this book—even capitalism!

We must understand that the new regulations themselves will be riddled with their own set of flaws and weaknesses. Since there is no such thing as a perfect model, neither can there be a perfect regulatory model that provides full protection to the investor. Risks can never be fully decomposed as our financial engineers have recently discovered—the loop can not be fully closed. There is no such thing as a risk-free lunch!

For that reason, and as far as investing in the stock market goes, remember the P/E model that shows risks historically increase measurably above a 20 P/E and decrease measurably below 10. The intelligent investor must at all times be exceptionally practical, self-reliant, capable of looking out for himself and never presupposing the government can or should protect him in his investments. Be prudent and mindful of risks both foreseen and unforeseen. Do your own "due diligence" and recognize that on balance we may have to embrace a world of lower expectations with respect to investment returns and economic growth over the next decade.

Cheers!

# BIBLIOGRAPHY

## CHAPTER ONE

1. Jesse H. Jones, *Fifty Billion Dollars, My 13 Years with the RFC*, 1951
2. Scott Lanman, *Central Bankers See More Credit Losses, Fischer Says,* Bloomberg News August 23 2008,
3. Caroline Binham, *Britain Faces Worst Slump in 60 Years, Darling Tells Guardian,* Bloomberg News, August 30, 2008
4. Bob Willis, and Rich Miller, *US Economy Employers Eliminate 533000 Jobs Most Since 1974,* Bloomberg News, December 5 2008
5. Jesse H. Jones, *Fifty Billion Dollars, My 13 Years with the RFC*, 1951
6. Mark Zandi, Economy.com
7. Mark Zandi, *The Homeownership Vesting Plan*, December 18 2008
8. Val Zavala and Lisa Ling, *Foreclosure Alley,* KCET.org, Socal Connected, Sept 29 2008
9. Mr. Mortgage, *My Case FOR Mortgage Principal Reduction,* December 14 2008
10. Anonymous
11. Fred Shwed, *Where are the Customers Yachts?*, 1940
12. Liz Capo McCormick and Gavin Finch, *Libor Signals Seizing as Banks Balk at Lending,* Bloomberg News, August 25 2008
13. Chris Whalen, *Whalen Interview with Joseph Mason: No True Sale,* March 3, 2008
14. Chris Whalen, *Fear and Leverage on Wall Street, A GSE Roundtable Discussion,* Institutional Risk Analyst, July 21 2008
15. Chris Whalen, *Fear and Leverage on Wall Street, A GSE Roundtable Discussion,* Institutional Risk Analyst, July 21 2008
16. John Helyar, Alison Fitzgerald, Mark Pittman and Serena Saitto, *Ten Days Changed Wall Street as Bernanke Saw Massive Failures,* Bloomberg News, September 22, 2008
17. Christopher Donvill and Chris Berritt, Wall Street Woes May Be Wall Street's Fault US Chiefs Say, Sept 22, 2008

18.  Alison Fitzgerald and John Brinsley, *Treasury Seeks Authority to Buy $700 Billion in Mortgage Assets,* Bloomberg News, September 20 2008

19.  John Helyar, Alison Fitzgerald, Mark Pittman and Serena Saitto, *Ten Days Changed Wall Street as Bernanke Saw Massive Failures,* Bloomberg News, September 22, 2008

20.  Henry Goldman and David Mildenberg, *Wall Street Losses Cut Tax Bill, Sap New York Revenue,* Bloomberg News, August 12 2008

21.  Mike Shedlock, *Tyrone Georgia Finance Director: "We're Broke,"* Global Economic Trend Analysis, August 25 2008

22.  Mike Shedlock, *Jefferson County Alabama Considering Bankruptcy,* Global Economic Trend Analysis, August 25 2008

23.  Moody's Economy.com

24.  Jennifer SteinHauer, States' Funds for Jobless Are Drying Up, NY Times, December, 14 2008

25.  Yves Smith, New IMF Study of Banking Crises Contradicts Bailout Bill Premise and Details, Naked Capitalism.com, September 27, 2008

26.  Martin Hennecke, *Bailouts will Push US into Depression,* CNBC.com September 11 2008

27.  Joe Mysak, *Goldman Draws Ire for Advising Default Swaps Against New Jersey,* Bloomberg News, December 10 2008

28.  Jesse H. Jones, *Fifty Billion Dollars, My 13 Years with the RFC,* 1951

29.  Joe Kernen and Becky Quick, CNBC

30.  Alison Vekshin and Jim Rowley, *Paulson, Bernanke Seek Support for an Agency to Buy Bad Debt,* Bloomberg News, September 18 2008

31.  Jesse H. Jones, *Fifty Billion Dollars, My 13 Years with the RFC,* 1951

32.  Ibid.

33.  Amity Sclaes, *The Forgotten Man: A New History of the Great Depression,* 2007

34.  Edwin Chen, *Obama Says He Will Enlist Campaign Supporters to Move Agenda,* Bloomberg News, December 2, 2008

35.  Julianna Goldman, *Obama Says He'll Ask Governors to Help Craft Stimulus,* Bloomberg News, December 2 2008

36.  Jesse H. Jones, *Fifty Billion Dollars, My 13 Years with the RFC,* 1951

37.  Ibid.

38.  Anatole Kaletsky, , Tiimesonline.com, Sept 12 2008

39.  Chris Whalen, *A Workable Private Bank Assistance Plan or Why President Bush Should Fire Ben Bernanke and Hank Paulson,* September 26 2008

40.  John Helyar, Alison Fitzgerald, Mark Pittman and Serena Saitto, *Ten Days Changed Wall Street as Bernanke Saw Massive Failures,* Bloomberg News, September 22, 2008

41.  Hugh Son and Craig Torres, *AIG Gets 85 Billion Fed Loan Cedes Control to Avert Collapse,* Bloomberg News, September 16 2008

42.  Ibid.

43.  Chris Whalen, *FDIC Won't Run Out of Money, But WaMu May Be Toast,* Institutional Risk Analysis, September 19, 2008

44. Chris Whalen, *Who Should Be the Next President of the Fed of New York?*, Institutional Risk Analysis, December 9 2008

45. Craig Torres, Fed Allows Goldman Morgan Stanley to Become Banks

46. Paul McCulley, *The Paradox of Deleveraging*, Pimco.com, July 2008

47. Peter Cook, Bloomberg TV September 20 2008

48. Gary Shilling, Bloomberg TV, September 20 2008

49. Alison Vekshin and Jim Rowley, *Paulson, Bernanke Seek Support for an Agency to Buy Bad Debt*, Bloomberg News, September 18 2008

50. John Helyar, Alison Fitzgerald, Mark Pittman and Serena Saitto, *Ten Days Changed Wall Street as Bernanke Saw Massive Failures*, Bloomberg News, September 22, 2008

51. Peter Cook, *Interview with Senator Jim Bunning*, September 19 2008

52. Chris Whalen, On *the Prime Solution: Interview with Eric Hovde*, Institutional Risk Analyst, December 11 2008

53. Kathleen Hays, *Interview with Josh Rosner*, Bloomberg TV

54. Matthew Benjamin and Brian Faler, *Backlash Over Bailouts Grows in Congress, Wall Street*, Bloomberg News, September 19 2008

55. Dawn Kopecki, *Shelby Says Treasury Plan May Not Work, Calls for Alternatives*, Bloomberg News, Sept 22 2008

56. Chris Whalen, *On the Economy: For Barack Obama, It's All About Credibility*, Institutional Risk Analysis, December 17 2008

57. Chris Whalen, *More Bank Less Bucks A Four Point Plan for the Rescue*, October 6 2008

58. Michael Tsang and Eric Martin, *SP500 Drop Makes Decade Worst, Granville Sees Crash*, Bloomberg News, Oct 7, 2008

59. Warren Buffett

60. Mark Buchanan, *Ubiquity, 2000*

61. Chris Whalen, *FDIC Won't Run Out of Money, But WaMu May be Toast,* Institutional Risk Analyst, September 19, 2008

## CHAPTER TWO

1. Mark Buchanan, *Ubiquity,*  2000

2. Ibid.

3. Ibid.

4. Chris Whalen, *Update: Are Countrywide Financial Bond Holders Bankruptcy remote?*, Institutional Risk Analyst, March 30 2008

5. Hank Paulson, *Statement by Secretary Henry M. Paulson, Jr. on Treasury and Federal Housing Finance Agency Action to Protect Financial Markets and Taxpayers Press Room of the US Dept of the Treasury,* September 7 2008

6. Carol Masser and Ellen Braitman, *Rogers Calls Fannie, Freddie Rescue 'Disaster,'* Bloomberg News, July 14 2008

7. Yves, Smith, *The Black Hole Gets Bigger AIG Back for Yet Another Bailout,* Naked Capitalism.com November 8 2008

8.  Greg Farell, *AIG to pay retention bonuses to executives*, financial Times, November 26 2008

9.  Yves Smith, *Yet more Retention Bonuses at AIG,* Naked Capitalism, December 13, 2008

10. Ben White, *On Wall Street, Bonuses, Not Profits,* Were Real, December 18 2008

11. Yves Smith, *Yet more Retention Bonuses at AIG,* Naked Capitalism.com, December 13, 2008

12. Ibid.

13. Christine Harper, *Bonuses for Wall Street Should Go to Zero Taxpayers Say,* Bloomberg News, November 11, 2008

14. Barry Ritholtz, *Big Bailouts, Bigger Bucks,* The Big Picture.com, November 25, 2008

15. Yves Smith, *Past Financial Crises Suggest Pain Far From Over,* Naked Capitalism.com, January 1, 2009

16. By Alison Fitzgerald and John Brinsley, *Treasury Seeks Asset-Buying Power Unchecked by Courts,* Bloomberg News, September 21, 2008

17. Chris Whalen, *Paulson Begins Gradual Wind-Down of GSE's within Conservatorship,* Institutional Risk Analyst, September 8, 2008

18. Caroline Salas, *Fannie, Freddie Takeover Diminishes Financing Options for Banks,* Bloomberg News, September 15, 2008

19. Jesse H. Jones, *Fifty Billion Dollars, My 13 Years with the RFC,* 1951

20. Ibid.

21. Ibid.

22. Ibid.

23. Ibid.

24. Amity Shlaes, *The Forgotten Man, A New History of the Great Depression,* 2007

25. Barney Frank, *Press Release, Frank Statement on TARP Provisions,* Votesmart.org, October 31, 2008

26. Ellen Brown, *A Radical Plan for Funding the New Deal, Yes Online Magazine,* December 14 2008

27. Yves Smith, *New IMF Study of Banking Crises Contradicts Bailout Bill Premise and Details,* Naked Capitalism.com, September 27, 2008

28. Ian Katz, Frank Says Bonuses, Acquisitions Violate Bailout Plan, Bloomberg News, October 31, 2008

29. Craig Torres, *Fed `Rogue Operation' Spurs Further Bailout Calls,* Bloomberg News, May 2 2008

30. Robert Hitt, AstroEcon.com, *Flash Update* September 3 2008

31. By James Rowley and Brian Faler, *Reid Says 'No One Knows What to Do' to Solve Crisis,* Bloomberg News, September 18 2008

32. Martin Hennecke, *Bailouts will Push US into Depression,* CNBC.com September 11 2008

33.  Bo Nielsen and Anchalee Worrachate, *Dollar May Get 'Crushed' as Traders Weigh Up Bailout*, Bloomberg News September 22 2008

34.  Ibid.

35.  Wikipedia, Hyperinflation: Inflation in the Weimar Republic

36.  Constantino Bresciani-Turroni, *"The Economy of Inflation — A Study of Currency Depreciation in Post War Germany,"* 1937

37.  Martin A. Armstrong, *A Brief History of World Credit and Interest Rates, - 3000 B.C. to the present,* Princeton Economic Institute, 1987

38.  Charles Kindleberger, *Manias, Panics, and Crashes,* 1978

39.  Nassim Taleb, *The Black Swan: The Impact of the Highly Improbable,* 2007

40.  Charles Kindleberger, *Manias, Panics, and Crashes,* 1978

41.  Ibid.

42.  Samuel Clemens, *The Gilded Age: A Tale of Today,* 1873

43.  Caroline Baum, *Feds Cast Scapegoat Net, Snag Cioffi and Tannin*, Bloomberg News, June 25 2008

44.  Darrell Hassler, *Commercial Paper Has Biggest Weekly Drop Since 2000,* Bloomberg News, August 23 2007

45.  George Soros, *The Worst Market Crisis in 60 Years*, January 23, 2008

46.  Richard Evans, *In Defense of History*, 2000

47.  Charles Kindleberger, *Manias, Panics, and Crashes,* 1978

48.  Richard Duncan, *The dollar Crisis: Causes, Consequences, Cures,* 2005

49.  Ibid.

50.  John Kenneth Galbraith, *The Great Crash* 1954

51.  Ibid.

52.  Larry Pesavento, The Trading Tutor.com

53.  Jack Zweig, *Market Wizards*, p127, 1990

## CHAPTER THREE

1.  Jack Zweig, 1989, Market Wizards: 134

2.  Mark Gilbert, *CDOs Lose Marbles; Credit `Kerplunks!* Bloomberg News, July 13, 2007

3.  Elliot Blair Smith, *Cioffi Fund Hoisted in Vodka With Tannin Began Bear's Endgame,* Bloomberg News, June 20 2008

4.  Ian Katz and David Scheer, *Two Sides to Story Define Wall Street in Cioffi's Tale at Bear,* Bloomberg News, June 20 2008

5.  Greg Church, Bloomberg News, July 2007

6.  Caroline Salas and Miles Weiss, *Goldman, JPMorgan Stuck With Debt They Can't Offload,* Bloomberg News, July 17, 2007

7.  Ibid.

8.  Ibid.

9.  Jim Caron, Morgan Stanley's Global Economic Forum, July 16 2007

10.  Richard Berner, Morgan Stanley's Global Economic Forum, August 2007

11.  Mark Zandi, Moody's Economy.com August 10 2007
12.  Shannon D. Harrington and Caroline Salas, *Corporate Bond Premiums Soar; Investors Shun Riskiest of Debt*, Bloomberg News, July 26, 2007
13.  Agnes Lovasz and David Yong, *Treasuries Gain as U.S. Subprime Crisis Spreads, ECB Adds Funds*, Bloomberg News, August 9, 2007
14.  Elizabeth Stanton, *Two-Year Treasury Yields Fall Most Since 2004 on Mortgage Woe*, Bloomberg News, August 9 2007
15.  Gavin Finch and Steve Rothwell, "*ECB Offers Unlimited Cash as Bank Lending Costs Soar*, Bloomberg News, August 9 2007
16.  Sebastian Boyd, *BNP Paribas Freezes Funds as Loan Losses Roil Markets*, Bloomberg Markets, August 9 2007
17.  Michael Patterson, *Slide in Europe prompts equities sell-off*, Bloomberg News, August 10, 2007
18.  Gavin Finch and Steve Rothwell, "*ECB Offers Unlimited Cash as Bank Lending Costs Soar*, Bloomberg News, August 9 2007
19.  Mark Zandi, Moody's Economy.com August 10 2007
20.  Yves Smith, *Carry Trade Unwinding*, Naked Capitalism.com, August 16 2007
21.  David Ader, Bloomberg News, August 2007
22.  Daniel Kruger, *Treasuries Rise on Concern About Ability to Trade Other Bonds*, Bloomberg News, August 16 2007
23.  Daniel Kruger, *Run on Treasury Bills Spurred by Subprime Contagion*, Bloomberg News, August 16 2007
24.  Matthew Brockett, *ECB May Scrap Plan to Raise Rates, Economists Say*, Bloomberg News, August 17 2007
25.  Caroline Baum, *Inflation Risks Vanish in Financial Market Haze:* Bloomberg News, August 20, 2007
26.  Mark Pittman, *Commercial Paper Market Roiled With $550 Billion Due*, Bloomberg News, August 21 2007
27.  John Kenneth Galbraith, *The Great Crash*, 1954
28.  Ibid.
29.  Charles Kindleberger, Manias, Panics, and Crashes 1978
30.  Ibid.
31.  Bernard Reis and John Flynn, False Security: The Betrayal of the American Investor, pp.134-135, 139, 58, 1937
32.  Jesse H. Jones, *Fifty Billion Dollars, My Thirteen years with the RFC*, pp 54, 62, 1951
33.  Ibid.
34.  Bernard Reis and John Flynn, *False Security: The Betrayal of the American Investor*, pp.134-135, 139, 58, 1937
35.  Ron Chernow, *House of Morgan*, p. 237 1990
36.  Ibid.
37.  David Wighton, *Citigroup faces the $700m music*, Financial Times, August 11 2007

38.  Michael Lewis, *"The Prince of Denial"* Bloomberg Markets January 2008
39.  Bernard Reis and John Flynn, *False Security: The Betrayal of the American Investor*, pp  24-25, 1937
40.  Ibid.
41.  Caroline Baum, *"Bernanke Sees Lesson in the Depression"* Bloomberg News, August 17 2007
42.  Caroline Baum *"It's Time to Meet Subprime Devil We Don't Know"* Bloomberg News, August 24 2007
43.  Bernard Reis and John Flynn, *False Security: The Betrayal of the American Investor*, p99 1937
44.  Caroline Baum *"It's Time to Meet Subprime Devil We Don't Know"* Bloomberg News, August 24 2007

## CHAPTER FOUR

1.   Steve Dickson, *Countrywide Says Market `Disruptions' May Hurt* Bloomberg News, August 9 2007
2.   Dimitris, *Mozilo's Perfect Storm,* Paper Economy – A US Real Estate Blog, July 25, 2007
3.   Chris Whalen, *Are Countrywide Financial Bond Holders Bankruptcy Remote?,* Institutional Risk Analyst, May 6 2008
4.   James Grant, *One of the Wildest Chapters in the History of Lending and Borrowing,* July 20 2008
5.   Andy Serwer, *Alan Greenspan: In his own words,* Fortune, September 17 2007
6.   Unknown, *Mozilo's Perfect Storm*, Paper Economy: A US Real Estate Bubble Blog, July 25 2007
7.   Bradley Keoun, *Countrywide Taps $11.5 Billion Credit Line From Banks,* Bloomberg News, August 16 2007
8.   Bradley Keoun, *Countrywide Taps $11.5 Billion Credit Line From Banks,* Bloomberg News, August 16 2007
9.   Ibid.
10.  Ibid.
11.  Jonathan Stempel, *Countrywide Says Lending, Borrowing Ability Sound,* Reuter's, November 28 2007
12.  *Bank of America to Buy Countrywide,* Financial Week, January 11 2008
13.  Jeff Kearns and Lynn Thomasson, *Countrywide Loses Most Since 1987 on Funding Concern,* Bloomberg News, January 8 2008
14.  John Poirier and Jonathan Stempel, *Bank of America in talks to buy Countrywide,* Reuters, Jan 10 2008
15.  Ruthie Ackerman, Countrywide, *BofA Could Team Up,* Forbes, January 10 2008
16.  David Mildenberg, *Bank of America to Acquire Countrywide for $4 Billion,* Bloomberg, January 11 2008
17.  Ibid.

18. Ibid.
19. Ibid.
20. Jesse H Jones, *Fifty Billion Dollars: My Thirteen Years at the RFC*, 1951
21. Chris Whalen, *An Involuntary Transaction: Why BAC + CFC May Never Close*, May 6 2008
22. Ibid.
23. Ibid.
24. Ibid.
25. David Mildenberg and Eric Martin, *Bank of America Should Skip Countrywide, Analyst Says*, Bloomberg News, May 5, 2008
26. Josh Fineman, *Bank of Americas Merrill Takeover May Be Tough*, Bloomberg News, December 5 2008
27. Yves Smith, *U.S. Negotiating to Backstop BofA Purchase of Merrill*, Naked Capitalism, January 14, 2009
28. David Scheer and Jesse Westbrook, Countrywide's Mozilo May Reap $83 Million in Takeover
29. David Scheer and Jesse Westbrook, Countrywide's Mozilo May Reap $83 Million in Takeover
30. Ron Chernow, *The House of Morgan*, p 114, 1990
31. Jonathan Weil, *Mark-to-Make-Believe Accounting Clams a Victim*, Bloomberg News, October 29 2007
32. Jonathan Weil, *Mark-to-Make-Believe Accounting Clams a Victim*, Bloomberg News, October 29 2007
33. Jonathan Weil, *Mark-to-Make-Believe Accounting Clams a Victim*, Bloomberg News, October 29 2007
34. FASB 157 http://www.fasb.org/st/summary/stsum157.shtml
35. Barry Ritholtz, *FASB 157 — Delayed, or Not?*, The Big Picture, November 15 2007
36. Barry Ritholtz, *Understanding the Significance of Mark- to- Market Accounting*, The Big Picture.com, Oct 1 2008
37. Barry Ritholtz, *Understanding the Significance of Mark- to- Market Accounting*, The Big Picture.com, Oct 1 2008
38. Stephen Taub, *FASB 157 Could Cause Huge Write-Offs*, CFO.com, November 7 2007
39. Barry Ritholtz, *Understanding the Significance of Mark- to- Market Accounting*, The Big Picture.com, Oct 1 2008
40. Bradley Keoun, *Wall Street Says -2 + -2 = 4 as Liabilities Get New Bond Math*, Bloomberg News, June 2 2008
41. Ibid.
42. Ibid.
43. Ibid.
44. Barry Ritholtz, *FASB 157 — Delayed, or Not?*, The Big Picture,November 15 2007

45.  Jody Shenn and Ian Katz, *FASB Postpones Off-Balance Sheet Rule for a Year,* Bloomberg News, July 30 2008

46.  Jody Shenn and Ian Katz, *FASB Postpones Off-Balance Sheet Rule for a Year,* Bloomberg News, July 30 2008

47.  Jody Shenn and Ian Katz, *FASB Postpones Off-Balance Sheet Rule for a Year,* Bloomberg News, July 30 2008

48.  Jody Shenn and Ian Katz, *FASB Postpones Off-Balance Sheet Rule for a Year,* Bloomberg News, July 30 2008

49.  Jody Shenn and Ian Katz, *FASB Postpones Off-Balance Sheet Rule for a Year,* Bloomberg News, July 30 2008

50.  Barry Ritholtz, FASB: *OK for USA to Turn Japanese,* The Big Picture.com, July 30 2008

51.  Charles Kindleberger, Manias, Panics, and Crashes, 1978

52.  Barry Ritholtz, FASB: *OK for USA to Turn Japanese,* The Big Picture.com, July 30 2008

53.  Yves Smith, *Is Another Emerging Markets Crisis in Motion,* NakedCapitalism.com, October 22, 2008

54.  Barry Ritholtz, *No Time to Waste,* TheBigPicture.com, Oct 13 2008

55.  Alan Abelson, *It Isn't Over,* Barron's Oct 20 2008

56.  Barry Ritholtz, *Gartman: The Reign of Thain Has Been Anything But Plain,* August 1 2008

57.  Christine Harper, *Lehman Hit by Biggest Rise in Debt Yields Since 2000,* July 2008

58.  Bradley Keoun, *Merrill Sells $8.55 Billion of Stock, Unloads CDO's,* July 29 2008

59.  Barry Ritholtz, *Actual Merrill CDO Sale: 5.47% on the Dollar*

60.  Christine Harper, *Lehman Hit by Biggest Rise in Debt Yields Since 2000,* July 2008

61.  Christine Harper, *Lehman Hit by Biggest Rise in Debt Yields Since 2000,* July 2008

62.  Bradley Keoun, *Merrill Sells $8.55 Billion of Stock, Unloads CDO's,* July 29 2008

63.  Ruel F. Pepa *Nurturing the Imagination of Resistance: Some important views from contemporary philosophers,* PhiloSophos.com

64.  Mark Gilbert, *CP fund Adds New Pyramid Scheme Layer,* Bloomberg News, Oct 18 2007

## CHAPTER FIVE

1.  E.J. Hobsbawm, *Industry and Empire,* 1968

2.  Tomlinson and Ben Livesey, *The Wreck on Northern Rock* - Bloomberg Markets p 73, May 2008

3.  Tomlinson and Ben Livesey, *The Wreck on Northern Rock* - Bloomberg Markets p 73, May 2008

4.   Ron Chernow, *The House of Morgan,* p123-124, 1990
5.   Ron Chernow, *The House of Morgan,* p123-124, 1990
6.   Ron Chernow, *The House of Morgan,* p123-124, 1990
7.   Tomlinson and Ben Livesey, *The Wreck on Northern Rock* - Bloomberg Markets p 73, May 2008
8.   Brian Swint and Jennifer Ryan, *BOE Reverses Policy, Lends Three-Month Emergency Cash,* Bloomberg News, Sept 19 2007
9.   Richard Tomlinson and Ben Livesey, *The Wreck on Northern Rock* - Bloomberg Markets p 73, May 2008
10.   Ibid.
11.   Ibid.
12.   Ibid.
13.   Ibid.
14.   Joe Mysak, *Goldman Draws Ire for Advising Default Swaps Against New Jersey,* Bloomberg News, December 10 2008
15.   Richard Tomlinson and Ben Livesey, *The Wreck on Northern Rock* - Bloomberg Markets May 2008
16.   T Stephanie Baker-Said, *The Risk Maverick: A Lesson for Wall Street,* Bloomberg Markets May 2008
17.   Alan Greenspan, *We Will Never Have a Perfect Model of Risk,* Financial Times March 16 08
18.   Wikipedia, Karl Popper
19.   Daniel Kruger, *Run on Treasury Bills Spurred by Subprime Contagion,* Bloomberg News, August 16 2008
20.   Murray Rothbard, *Making Economic Sense,* 1995
21.   Chris Whalen, *Are Countrywide Financial Bond Holders Bankruptcy Remote?* Institutional Risk Analyst, Whalen May 1st 2008

# CHAPTER SIX

1.   The House of Morgan, Ron Chernow p 154 1990
2.   Bernard Reis and John Flynn, False Security: Betrayal of the American Investor, 1937
3.   Ibid.
4.   Ibid.
5.   Ibid.
6.   Ibid.
7.   Ibid.
8.   Ibid.
9.   Ibid.
10.   Ibid.
11.   Ibid.
12.   Ibid.

13.  Ferdinand Pecora, *Wall Street Under Oath*, 1939
14.  Institutional Risk Analyst, Chris Whalen June 12 2008
15.  Richard Berner, Morgan Stanley's Global Economic Forum, September 2007
16.  Bill Gross, *Better Late Than Never*, Pimco.com, January 2008
17.  Paul McCulley, *Teton Reflections*, Pimco.com, September 2007
18.  Bill Gross, *Better Late Than Never*, Pimco.com, January 2008
19.  Bill Gross, *What do They Know*, Pimco.com, September 2007
20.  Angelo Mozilo, Bloomberg News, , August 25 2007
21.  Jim Grant, The New York Sun, June 19 2008
22.  George Soros, *New Paradigm for Financial Markets*, 2008
23.  George Soros, Wall Street Journal, June 2008
24.  Steve Matthews and Thomas R. Keene, *Harvard's Feldstein Says U.S. Dollar Has Further to Decline*, August 11 2008
25.  Paul McCulley, *The Paradox of Deleveraging*, July 2008
26.  Stephanie Baker-Said and Elena Logutenkova Bloomberg Markets, *The Mess at UBS*, July 2008
27.  Ibid.
28.  Ibid.
29.  Ibid.
30.  Ibid.
31.  Evan Kafka, *The Opportunist*, Bloomberg Markets, p 53 February 2008
32.  Yves Smith, *Fed Ponders Issuing Debt to Finance Its Mushrooming Balance Sheet*, December 10, 2008
33.  Yves Smith, *Fed Ponders Issuing Debt to Finance Its Mushrooming Balance Sheet*, Naked Capitalism *December 10 2008*
34.  Richard Tomlinson and David Evans, *CDO Boom Masks Subprime Losses, Abetted by S&P, Moody's, Fitch*, Bloomberg News, May 31, 2008
35.  BIS Jan 1990: *Japan's experience of financial deregulation since 1984 in an international perspective*
36.  Stephanie Baker-Said and Elena Logutenkova Bloomberg Markets, *The Mess at UBS*, July 2008
37.  Ibid.
38.  Ibid.
39.  Ibid.
40.  Ibid
41.  Evan Kafka, *The Opportunist*, Bloomberg Markets, p 53 February 2008
42.  Ronald Henkoff, *Uneasy Money* Bloomberg Markets, p 8 April 2008
43.  Lisa Kassenaar *The Reckoning*, Bloomberg Markets, p46 April 2008
44.  Richard Tomlinson and David Evans, *CDO Boom Masks Subprime Losses, Abetted by S&P, Moody's, Fitch*, Bloomberg News, May 31 2008
45.  Ibid.

46. Ibid.
47. Ibid.
48. Ibid.
49. Ibid
50. Ibid.
51. Ibid.
52. Wikipedia, Michael Milken.
53. Martin Z Braun and William Selway, *Schools Flunk Finance*, Bloomberg Markets, March 2008
54. Ibid.
55. Ibid.
56. Ibid.
57. Ibid.
58. Chris Whalen, *It's the Models Stupid: Interview with Josh Rosner*, The Institutional Risk Analyst, June 24 2008
59. David Evans, *Peddling Tainted Debt to Florida*, Bloomberg Markets February 2008
60. Ibid.
61. Ibid.
62. Ibid.
63. Ibid.
64. Ibid.
65. Ibid.
66. Ibid.
67. Ibid.
68. Chris Whalen, *It's the Models Stupid: Interview with Josh Rosner*, The Institutional Risk Analyst, June 24 2008
69. Bernard Reis and John Flynn, False Security: The Betrayal of the American Investor, 1937
70. Michael McDonald, *Auction Bond Failures Near 70%, No Sign of Abating*, Bloomberg News, March 5 2008
71. Michael Quint and Darrell Preston, *Auction Rate Collapse Costs Taxpayers, $1.65 Billion*, Bloomberg News, May 16 2008
72. Martin Braun and William Selway, *Insured Short-Term Muni Bonds Surge as High as 9%*, Bloomberg News, June 20 2008
73. Michael Quint and Darrell Preston, *Auction Rate Collapse Costs Taxpayers, $1.65 Billion*, Bloomberg News, May 16 2008
74. William Selway and Martin Braun, *Municipal Market Fire in the Disco Burns Borrowers*, Bloomberg News, July 3 2008
75. Martin Braun and William Selway, *Insured Short-Term Muni Bonds Surge as High as 9%*, Bloomberg News , June 20 2008

76. Michael McDonald, *UBS Emails Show Conflicts With Auction Rate Clients,* Bloomberg News, June 27, 2008

77. Darrell Preston and Michael McDonald, Wall Street Sold Auction Rate to Investors as It Warned Issuers, Bloomberg News, June 26 2008

78. Michael McDonald, *UBS Emails Show Conflicts With Auction Rate Clients,* Bloomberg News, June 27, 2008

## CHAPTER 7

1. Thomas Kuhn, *The Structure of Scientific Revolutions,* 1962

2. Richard Tomlinson and David Evans, *CDO Boom Masks Subprime Losses, Abetted by S&P, Moody's, Fitch,* May 31, 2007 last updated, October 3, 2008

3. Caroline Baum, *Volcker Stands Tall, Greenspan Keeps Shrinking,* Bloomberg News, April 9 2008

4. Investment postcards.com

5. Chris Whalen, *Is Risk Management Even Possible in an OTC Marketplace?,* June 16 2008

6. Marty Zweig, *Winning on Wall Street,* p3, 1997

7. Ibid, p 83

8. Ibid, p62

9. Ibid, p 93

10. Ibid p 183

11. Ibid p 79

12. Ibid, p 185

13. Joe Richter and Rich Miller, *Recession Risk Rises as Consumers Feel Credit Tighten,* Bloomberg News, September 4 2008

14. Caroline Salas and Jody Shenn, *Bush's Subprime Mortgage Freeze Stymies Bond Market,* December 7, 2007

15. John Robbins, Bloomberg News, December 2007

16. Bob Willis, *Jump in U.S. Jobless Rate Always Signaled Recessions* Bloomberg News, Jan 4, 2008

17. Judith Levy, *Inflation Fears May Curtail Fed's Rate-Cut Flexibility* – WSJ, January 4 2008

18. Christine Harper, *Goldman Gains in Worst Wall Street Quarter Since '01* Bloomberg News, December 18 2007

19. Fabio Alves, *Defaults to Quadruple as More Companies Cut to Junk,* December 18 2008

20. Unknown, *Ambac, MBIA Outlook Lowered by S&P, ACA Cut to CCC,* December 19, 2008

21. Shannon D. Harrington and Michael Shanahan, *Company Bond Risk Declines Second Day on Insurer Rescue Talks,* Bloomberg, January 24, 2008

22. Ben Bernanke, *The economic outlook, Before the Committee on the Budget, U.S. House of Representatives,* federareserve.gov, January 17 2008

23.  Elizabeth Stanton, *Bears Exceed Bulls by Most in 17 Years*, Poll Finds, Bloomberg, January 11, 2008

24.  Elizabeth Stanton, *Bears Exceed Bulls by Most in 17 Years*, Poll Finds, Bloomberg, January 11, 2008

25.  Kathleen M. Howley, *Wall Street Embraces Government to Avoid Recession*, Bloomberg, February 1 2008

26.  Ibid.

27.  Mike Shedlock, *No Underwriter Support For Failed Muni Auctions*, February 14 2008

28.  Unknown, *Dollar falls broadly on higher-than-expected U.S. jobless claims and weak GDP data* - Feb 28, 2008

29.  President George Bush, *Expanding Home Ownership*, whitehouse.gov, December 16 2003

30.  Alphonso Jackson, *BUSH ADMINISTRATION ANNOUNCES NEW HUD "ZERO DOWN PAYMENT" MORTGAGE*, hud.gov, January 14 2008

31.  Clive Crook, *Avoiding Foreclosures*, The Atlantic, November 21 2008

32.  Thomas Tucci, *Every Day Feels Like the 1987 Stock Market Crash*, IstockAnalyst, March 4 2008

33.  Abigail Moses, Hamish Risk and Neil Unmack, *Credit Swaps Thwart Fed's Ease as Debt Costs Surge*, March 6 2008

34.  Jody Shenn, *Fed's Loan Program Provide Little Aid to Agency Mortgage Bonds*, Bloomberg, March 11 2008

35.  Ibid.

36.  Kate Kelly, *Bear Stearns Neared Collapse Twice in Frenzied Last Days*, Wall Street Journal, May 29, 2008

37.  Ibid.

38.  Jeannine Aversa, *Federal Reserve Chairman Ben Bernanke warns of possible recession*, mlive.com, April 2 2008

39.  Unknown, *Bernanke Takes Bit In Teeth, Expands Fed Role In JP Morgan-Bear Stearns Deal*, The Resourceful Bear Blog, March 25 2008

40.  Craig Torres and James Tyson *Taxpayers May Be Liable From Bear, Mortgage Rescue* Bloomberg March 26 2008

41.  Ibid.

42.  Ibid.

43.  By Lisa Kassenaar and Elizabeth Hester, *The House of Dimon*, Bloomberg Markets, June 2008

44.  Unknown, Paulson's Plan: *Can Wall Street's Appetite For Leverage Stomach Regulation?*, Prince of Wall Street, April 9 2008

45.  Chris Whalen, *A Global House of Cards, Interview with Josh Rosner*, April 7 2008

46.  Ian Katz, *Congress May Force Securities Firms to Raise Capital*, Bloomberg News May 2 2008

47. Craig Torres, Fed `Rogue Operation' Spurs Further Bailout Calls, Bloomberg News  May 2 2008
48. Ibid.
49. Ron Chernow, *House of Morgan*, 1990
50. Yalman Onaran, *Lehman Chief Fuld Confident as Firm Slashes Mortgages*, Bloomberg News, June 16 2008
51. John Mauldin *The Road to Revulsion*, The MarketOracle.com, Jun 17 2008
52. Christine Harper and Yalman Onaran, *Danger Ahead: Fixing Wall Street Hazardous to Earnings Growth*, Bloomberg, Apr 28 2008
53. Christine Richard, Bill Ackman Was Right: *MBIA, Ambac on `Ratings Cliff'* Bloomberg, Jun 18
54. Ibid.
55. Ibid.
56. Brendan Murray and Dawn Kopecki, *Paulson Puts Treasury's Weight Behind Fannie, Freddie* Bloomberg News, July 14, 2008
57. Dawn Kopecki and Craig Torres, Lawmakers *Balk at Paulson's Fannie, Freddie Plan*, Bloomberg News July 15 2008
58. Ibid.
59. Brendan Murray and Dawn Kopecki, *Paulson Puts Treasury's Weight Behind Fannie, Freddie* Bloomberg News, July 14, 2008
60. Bradley Keoun, *Citigroup's $1.1 Trillion in Mysterious Assets,* Bloomberg News, July 14 2008
61. Ibid.
62. Ibid.
63. Josh Fineman, *Analysts Backtrack on Banking Stocks After Saying Worst Is Over,* Bloomberg News, June 25, 2008
64. Bill Gross, Dow *5,000 Redux*, Pimco.com December 2008
65. Simon Kennedy, Matthew Benjamin and Rich Miller, *Saving Capitalism No Sure Thing as Statism Undermines Economy,* Bloomberg News, December 22 2008
66. Ibid.
67. Paul McCulley, *All In,* Pimco.com, December 2008/January 2009
68. Yves Smith, *The Western financial System We Knew Has Collapsed*, Naked Capitalism.com, November 25, 2008
69. Yves Smith, *Groundwork for Trade Conflict Being Laid?,* Naked Capitalism.com, December 30, 2008
70. Bill Gross, *Andrew Mellon vs. Bailout Nation*, Pimco.com, January 2009
71. Chris Whalen, IndyMac, *FDICIA and the Mirrors of Wall Street*, Institutional Risk Analyst, January 6, 2009
72. Yves Smith, *The Western financial System We Knew Has Collapsed,* Naked Capitalism.com, November 25, 2008

# INDEX

Printed in the United States
137084LV00002B/1/P

9 780615 230924